A History of Central Europe

Robert C. Austin

A History of Central Europe

Nations and States Since 1848

Robert C. Austin
CERES, Munk School of Global Affairs & Public Policy
University of Toronto
Toronto, ON, Canada

ISBN 978-3-030-84542-1   ISBN 978-3-030-84543-8 (eBook)
https://doi.org/10.1007/978-3-030-84543-8

© The Editor(s) (if applicable) and The Author(s), under exclusive licence to Springer Nature Switzerland AG 2021
This work is subject to copyright. All rights are solely and exclusively licensed by the Publisher, whether the whole or part of the material is concerned, specifically the rights of translation, reprinting, reuse of illustrations, recitation, broadcasting, reproduction on microfilms or in any other physical way, and transmission or information storage and retrieval, electronic adaptation, computer software, or by similar or dissimilar methodology now known or hereafter developed.
The use of general descriptive names, registered names, trademarks, service marks, etc. in this publication does not imply, even in the absence of a specific statement, that such names are exempt from the relevant protective laws and regulations and therefore free for general use.
The publisher, the authors and the editors are safe to assume that the advice and information in this book are believed to be true and accurate at the date of publication. Neither the publisher nor the authors or the editors give a warranty, expressed or implied, with respect to the material contained herein or for any errors or omissions that may have been made. The publisher remains neutral with regard to jurisdictional claims in published maps and institutional affiliations.

Cover Franz Sedlacek, Winterliche Landschaft (1931). Photo: Wien Museum, https://www.wienmuseum.at/.

This Palgrave Macmillan imprint is published by the registered company Springer Nature Switzerland AG.
The registered company address is: Gewerbestrasse 11, 6330 Cham, Switzerland

Preface

Even before the Refugee Crisis of 2015–2016, many worried about the fate of democracy in Central Europe and the legacy of the events of 1989. The *annus mirabilis* seemed to have become somewhat jaded. Newspaper headlines spoke about democratic backsliding in Hungary and Poland. Hungary's governing Fidesz party shut down a US-accredited university in very dubious circumstances but started making plans for the opening of a massive Chinese university campus in Budapest largely paid for by Hungary. Poland says the communists must finally be dealt with even after 30 years since the end of communism in Central Europe. In Slovakia, an investigative journalist is murdered. In Austria, the far-right Freedom Party governed in a coalition until a sordid scandal ended things. Everyone looks to the European Union (EU) to restore the liberal order but nothing happens. The question is how did we get there and where does this all end? Are enough malign forces aligned to derail democracy and what until now has been the undeniably successful European integration project?

This book grew out of more than two decades of field research, including a two-year stint as a journalist in Slovakia in the early 1990s, teaching Central European history in the University of Toronto's European Studies Program and for 16 years as part of a University of Toronto Summer Program at Masaryk University in Brno, Czech Republic. I hope what lies ahead combines solid historical research and firsthand observations of the exit from communism to EU membership for Czechs, Hungarians, Poles and Slovaks in 2004, to renewed nationalism and confrontation with the EU's executive in Brussels.

Unlike other surveys, this book aims to give the reader not just a better understanding of political history but also a deeper understanding of the region's economic development, particularly as Central Europe moved from largely agrarian economies to Stalinist industrialism to the economic success that came with membership in the EU. By bringing the reader right to the present, with an emphasis on the extraordinary and unexpected impact of the 2015 migration crisis, the migration out of Central Europe, the weakening of democratic institutions, the re-emergence of the hastily buried "nation", the illiberal drift of Hungary and Poland, and the dramatic changes to Slovakia after the murder of an investigative journalist and his fiancé, a new Central Europe has emerged that shares some traits with the nationalizing states that followed the First World War. Some analysts point to dangerous parallels with the period between the two world wars with the rise of often intolerant nationalism and new narratives that reject the (neo)liberal consensus that came with the collapse of communism in 1989. Some even speak of re-opening border issues. Plus, Russia is back in the game through open links with the far-right parties, energy dependency, stoking ethnic rivalries and disseminating fake news. Russian President Vladimir Putin sees an opportunity to exploit a region that has always been at the mercy of outside players and where many big questions remain unanswered. Uncertainty is still the hallmark and the feeling of a crossroads hangs in the air.

After an introduction that defines Central Europe geographically along with its ethnic, linguistic and religious diversity by highlighting key flashpoints in the nation making process, the book takes as its starting point the 1848 revolutions, or the "Springtime of Nations" for much of Central Europe. It assumes that since then the region has been engaged in state and nation building of one kind or another with some often-unnoticed levels of continuity until now. This chapter provides a fresh examination of the nation building process by creating a useable past. It concludes with an examination of how nations within the Habsburg Empire willingly joined the fight on the Habsburg side in 1914 only to find themselves later fighting to establish independent states. While the book focuses on the states between Russia and Germany—the contemporary Czech Republic, Hungary, Poland, and Slovakia—Germany and Austria are also integral to the narrative. The Balkans, plus Estonia, Latvia, Lithuania, and Russia, are also present in so far as they impact the region or provide an important comparative aspect.

The First World War resulted in the creation of a wholly unexpected new Central European space that grew largely out of the defunct Habsburg Empire and a victory of Woodrow Wilson's vision of national self-determination plus ample doses of revenge. This chapter is based on considerable available new research from authors such as Pieter Judson's *The Habsburg Empire: A New History* which provides a fresh perspective on the ethnic dynamics of the Habsburg Empire and moves us away from the clichés or nationalist inspired histories that followed the end of the Empire in 1918. It also includes a discussion of various new and recast national narratives that appeared for the 100th anniversary of the end of the First World War. After all, Woodrow Wilson is a hero to Czechs, Poles and Slovaks, but a demon for Hungarians, who lost big at the 1919–1920 Paris Peace Conference.

The interwar period (1919–1939) that follows is one of failures on multiple levels in all of Europe—the promise of parliamentary democracy collapsed, minorities found themselves worse off than they had been under Habsburg rule and the interwar elite was incapable of dealing with the challenges of the times. Failures were the result of serious internal weaknesses, combined with often malign interference from neighbours and total indifference from bigger powers. Central Europe succumbed to dictatorship, intolerance and eventually varying forms of German domination. Indeed, Central Europe's fate sadly shaped the entire destiny of Europe. Central Europe's survival then (and now) was based on a world order that was not sustainable. The year 1938 in Vienna and Munich was emblematic of the abandonment of the region.

In the war's aftermath, one form of dictatorship was replaced by another with the Soviet takeover between 1945 and 1948. This chapter takes advantage of substantial new research on communist takeovers in hopes of capturing Stalin's sometimes focused or improvisational foreign policy towards occupied "Eastern Europe" from the coup in Czechoslovakia to "salami tactics" in Hungary. By injecting some nuance into the discussion, it hopes to better understand why many people, not all of them by default evil, may have embraced the communist system. In examining the communist period, the chapter emphasizes the collapse of regime legitimacy, everyday life under communist rule, the role of secret police services and the seminal moments of resistance—1956 in Hungary, 1968 and later Charter 77 in Czechoslovakia, and 1981 in Poland—and finally the Gorbachev factor. It seeks to give Central Europeans a degree of agency that has been denied to them by books that credit US Presidents Ronald Reagan and George Bush and Soviet leader Mikhail Gorbachev for the end of the Cold War while ignoring dramatic actions by local dissidents, opposition leaders and a nascent civil society.

The remaining chapters cover 1989 in all its variants, with winners and losers, from the popular uprisings in East Germany and Czechoslovakia to the negotiated transfers of power in Hungary and Poland, combined with the often less than helpful positions adopted by Western Europe and the United States in the early stages of communist collapse. It examines the myths of 1989 which for many left too many communists in power or even more simply too rich.

The region's relatively short and even easy road to NATO membership in 1999 and long road to European Union membership (1990–2004) are central to this narrative. The book provides the reader, in an accessible way, with an understanding of just what needed to be done so that Central Europe could re-join Europe. It concludes with Central Europe re-branding itself as something more than just a values and norms taker or imitator of the West but possibly a maker of new values and norms made clear by the region's rejection of migrant quotas and the liberal consensus more generally. This is best understood by the rise of what was deemed "illiberal democracy", new "us versus them" nation building campaigns in Poland and Hungary or other forms of populism. Adding to this, the region confronts a distracted European Union and an increasingly active China and Russia. In short, some of the big questions that brought so much instability to the region after the First World War have re-surfaced, leaving some to realize that big questions allegedly put to rest after 1989 are back.

In terms of audience, this is not an academic book. There are no citations, but I have provided a detailed section on sources for further study, including films and novels alongside the standard works of non-fiction. I think the book is useful not only as text but also for travellers who seek a bit more nuance in their understanding of what is a relatively complicated space.

Toronto, ON, Canada   Robert C. Austin

Acknowledgements

There are an enormous number of people to thank as this book is very much the product of more than three decades of field work and teaching in Central Europe plus multiple conferences held largely at the University of Toronto's Centre for European, Russian, and Eurasian Studies (CERES) at the Munk School of Global Affairs & Public Policy. I also benefited from several years of field trips with graduate students to Budapest before COVID-19 derailed things. The students always undertook interesting projects which enriched me too. The trip was always funded by Tom and Irene Mihalik. They are both not just exceptional people but exceptionally generous too.

In Europe, let me thank László Borhi, Ivan Chorvat, Martin and Jana Glogar, Sándor Hites, Jakub Janda, Lenka Kissová, Jan Klakurka, Ivan Krastev, Péter Krekó, Attila Marján, Sándor Orbán, Attila Pók, Don Sparling, Tamás Stark, Balázs Trencsényi, Richard Turcsányi and Márton Ugrósdy. A shout-out too to my friends at Budapest's Gerlóczy Hotel. There is something to be said about a hotel that knows what you need before you ask for it.

Closer to home, I received help from four stellar graduate students completing Master of Arts degrees at the Centre for European, Russian, and Eurasian Studies (CERES). Huge parts of this book were researched by Daniela (Dashi) Bouvier-Valenta, Alina Bykova, Catherine Lukits and Tess Megginson. I was very lucky in Toronto to have such creative and passionate students. Alina did the research especially for Chap. 3 Catherine was invaluable for contemporary Hungary, especially in cultural policy among other inputs and the impact of COVID-19. Dashi and Tess were indispensable for all things Czech, Polish and Slovak. Tess stayed on board to help with the final improvements and was always on hand for great suggestions. She worked on the suggested reading and viewing lists that follows the book. My dear friend Josef Čermák always made sure that Central Europe was part of my DNA.

At CERES, I am especially grateful to a really exceptional group of friends who are lucky enough to work in the same place. Thanks to Randall Hansen, Joseph Hawker, Larysa Iarovenko, Olga Kesarchuk, Katia Malyuzhinets,

Alexander Reisenbichler and Edward Schatz. Edward and Randall always provide great advice alongside incredible friendship, loyalty and huge laughs. My friends outside of the office are also a source of great inspiration and humour. Thanks to Ken and Maureen Campbell, Martin Hrobsky, David Kitai, Jordan and Barbara Oelbaum, Stefánia Szabó, and Thomas and Jodi Ungar.

I dedicate this book to my wife, Maureen, and my children, Andrew and Kate. We had some wonderful times in the region, especially in Brno, Budapest, Graz and Vienna. I hope this book encourages them to return to chart the rest of Central Europe's fascinating story.

Toronto, ON, Canada, 2021   Robert C. Austin

Contents

1	**Introduction: Flashpoints on the Road to 1918**	1
	Where to Start?	1
	Towards 1848	5
	1848: The Springtime of (Some) Nations	12
	German Unification and the Creation of Austria-Hungary	17
	A War to Save Everything	22
	Conclusion	25
	For Further Study	26
2	**The Interwar Failures, 1918–1939**	27
	Peace Treaties: St. Germain and Trianon	28
	From Democracy to Dictatorship to Subservience	34
	Abandoned by the West	40
	Conclusion	43
	For Further Study	44
3	**The Second World War in Central Europe**	45
	German and Soviet Rapprochement	46
	Life Under Nazi Rule	47
	Poland Under Soviet Occupation	53
	Operation Barbarossa	55
	The Holocaust in Central Europe	56
	Progression of Holocaust Measures	58
	Implementation of the Final Solution	59
	The Enforcement of Nazi Power and Jewish Resistance	60
	The Fate of Other Minorities Under Nazi Occupation	61
	Liberation	64
	Allied Crimes During the Liberation	68
	Conclusion	72
	For Further Study	73

4	**Making Most of Central Europe Communist**	75
	Wartime Conferences	77
	The Nuremberg Trials	82
	Postwar Refugees and Population Transfers	84
	The Marshall Plan to Rebuild Europe	88
	Communist Takeovers	88
	Conclusion	96
	For Further Study	99
5	**Communists in Power, 1948–1988**	101
	1956 in Hungary	105
	Czechoslovakia: 1968 and Normalization	109
	Poland: Permanent Opposition	115
	The Soviet Factor	120
	Conclusion	124
	For Further Study	125
6	**1989–2004: Roundtables, Street Protests, and the Long Journey Back to Europe**	127
	Lustration and Transitional Justice	138
	Joining Europe on Europe's Terms	141
	Conclusion	143
	For Further Study	145
7	**A New Central Europe or Past as Prologue?**	147
	Past as Prologue?	150
	External Players	163
	Conclusion	170
	For Further Study	172

Additional Reading	173
Index	177

About the Author

Robert C. Austin is Associate Director and Professor at the Centre for European, Russian, and Eurasian Studies, Munk School of Global Affairs & Public Policy, University of Toronto. His previous books include *Making and Remaking the Balkans: Nations and States since 1878* (2019) and *Founding a Balkan State – Albania's Experiment with Democracy, 1920–1925* (2012). He lives in Toronto.

CHAPTER 1

Introduction: Flashpoints on the Road to 1918

WHERE TO START?

A journey into the past and present of Central Europe can start in many places. It is a region with an immense amount of history in a very small space and there are as many differences as similarities. Unsurprisingly, history battles are still fought there, as events that are often long passed assume centre stage in contemporary national debates, particularly in Hungary and Poland. You could easily start a journey in Vienna, considered year after year as one of the best cities in the world to live in. Since the Habsburg family ruled over much of Central Europe since the 1500s, it makes some sense to start there. Maybe head to the Capuchin Crypt, where so many of the Habsburg rulers are entombed. The imperial sarcophagi are something to behold from the austere lead coffins of Anna and Matthias from the 1600s, to the baroque monstrosities of Empress Maria Theresa and her husband, Francis. Below and in front of them is their son, the reformer Joseph II, who opted for something far less showy—a simple lead coffin. The rest of the journey through the crypt is one of astonishing success and remarkable tragedies: Crown Prince Rudolf is there, who killed himself and his teenage mistress in 1889 in what remain mysterious circumstances. That strange story is best recounted in Frederick Morton's *A Nervous Splendor: Vienna, 1888–1889*. Franz Ferdinand, the heir to the Habsburg throne, who was assassinated along with his wife Sophie in Sarajevo in June 1914, is not to be found there. He married for love, not station in life, and waived his right to a space in the crypt. You need to go elsewhere to visit his tomb. The last emperor of the Habsburgs, Charles I, is not there either. His heart and that of his wife's, Zita, are in the Muri monastery in the canton of Aargau, Switzerland, not far from where the Habsburgs got their start in the eleventh century. Zita's body, however, did make it to the Capuchin Crypt. The Habsburgs, banished and even punished after the First World War, would be resurrected after the Second World War to meet the demands of modern tourism and identity sanitization.

Germany, which offers so much of what is now called "Dark Tourism"—travel to places associated with catastrophes—is not just a key Central European country, but often a shaper of the fate of Central Europe in both bad and good ways. German nationalism and militarism in the 1930s destroyed Central Europe but after 1989 German capital and industriousness helped re-build it. Berlin—the capital of Prussia, then the capital of the Second Reich between 1871 and 1918, then the capital of Hitler's Third Reich between 1933 and 1945, then a divided city during the Cold War, and now the capital of an entirely different Germany after the collapse of communism in 1989 and German re-unification in 1990—represents the gold standard of historical reckoning. Sure, controversies exist but the edgy and bohemian city lays it all out there for you. Start with The Topography of Terror, situated on the very grounds that housed the monster that was the Third Reich's security apparatus, and spend hours as you journey from the democratic Weimar Republic to Hitler's totalitarian state. The German presentation of the past is different than elsewhere in the region in that it acknowledges that Hitler mobilized on issues present after the First World War, and that many Germans voted willingly for Hitler and embraced his ideas. Victimhood nationalism—quite common in Austria, Hungary, and Poland—is not their thing and a strong sense of historical responsibility persists to this day. The jubilant faces, whether in the killing fields of the Second World War or Hitler's adoring crowds, say it all. One thing to keep in mind, though, is that the monuments to these crimes are not as old as you think, or even as old as they should be. That said, the fate of the Jews in Central Europe is more and more a subject of historical controversy, as many states conflate the horrors of communism with the fate of the Jews and seek to avoid recognition of their own roles in the Holocaust. Only the Germans fully accept their role and remain committed to the memory of the Holocaust.

Budapest, from 1867 until 1918, the joint capital of the Habsburg Empire, offers equally compelling starting points. Hungary is often at the front of the pack in creating new and divisive narratives of the past and, along with Poland, at the forefront of victimhood nationalism, building new monuments and removing old ones. The city's Freedom Square says a lot about Hungary's past and present. It is a carnival of mixed and even conflicting messages. But, at least since 1873, Budapest has often been used as a nationalizing project. Budapest's regularly changing political messages, told in the streets and squares, make it the most openly nationalistic city in Central Europe and indeed, based on its monuments, the saddest one. Indeed, Budapest is the archetype of the city as a nation building project. In a small space you find a monument to the liberation of Hungary by the Soviet Union in 1945 only metres away from the Embassy of the United States. Nearby, you find a larger than life statue of US President Ronald Reagan, erected in 2011 in recognition of his role in the collapse of communism, strolling happily towards the Soviet Liberation memorial and the US Embassy. The symbolism is hard to miss. Not too far away, near the

Margaret Bridge, is a reproduction of the actor Peter Falk as the famous TV detective Columbo and his dog. The show was a huge hit mostly in the 1970s, so the statue's appearance in 2014 is hard to explain. Falk was partly Hungarian.

At the southern end of the square, you come across the most controversial and indeed the ugliest monument in the entire city. Located strategically on the edge of the entry to an underground parking garage is the Memorial for the Victims of the German Occupation of 1944, erected in 2014, under the cover of darkness, unsurprisingly. It is the pinnacle of Hungary's quest for useable history in an otherwise bleak twentieth century. As we shall see later, the monument seems to suggest that Hungary is a victim, not a perpetrator. In front of the monument, its opponents established the Living Memorial, to encourage a more sophisticated and accurate representation of Hungary's role in the destruction of the European Jews in 1944. Compiled by a small and devoted team of activists, the memorial's stones, candles, suitcases, shoes, written stories, photographs, and multilingual explanations serve to keep the memory of Holocaust victims alive. It is a far more impactful monument to Hungary's catastrophes in 1944. Not far away, tucked away on private property belonging to a Calvinist church, is a bust of Miklós Horthy, a former admiral in the Habsburg navy and Hungary's key leader between the First and Second World Wars, who also oversaw the massive deportation of Hungary's Jewish population after 1944. For his supporters, he spared Hungary from the ravages of the extreme left and extreme right.

With thousands of statues and plaques, and more being added or moved given political demands, it could be confusing or even suffocating. Locals seem to pay scant attention to the cityscape. After all, clustered around Freedom Square are only tourists, most of whom are uninterested in the very real controversies over Hungary's often dark past. That said, it is never clear just how effective monuments are for shaping attitudes and just for whom they are put up for. As we shall see later on, the statue wars seem to be more diversionary in intent. Get everyone, especially outsiders, all focused on a controversial monument while the government does even worse things elsewhere. Like the Austrians, the Hungarians prove to be the masters of resurrection. Dead people, as we shall see, like László Rajk, Imre Nagy or Miklós Horthy, would come back from often unmarked graves to alter the course of history.

The fate of the Jews of Central Europe is also an extremely important starting point. In Warsaw, the POLIN Museum of the History of Polish Jews is a monumental achievement given that Poland's Jewish community was almost totally wiped out during the Second World War. Warsaw itself was totally wiped out by the Germans as they sought to destroy everything there that stood for Polish identity. The POLIN Museum offers a brilliant overview of ten centuries of Jewish life. But given how raw the issue remains in Poland, it does not enter into the role of non-Jewish Poles in the fate of Jewish Poles. Like in Hungary, Poland's quest for useable history often challenges accepted narratives and the role of local elites and ordinary people in the Holocaust. Holocaust memorials, many of which came far later than one might expect—Berlin's Memorial to the

Murdered Jews came in 2005, are an important aspect of Central Europe's memory landscape. Europe's first monuments came largely from the demands of survivors and were largely placed at former death and concentration camp sites. Only later did local and national governments get involved and thus these memorials became part of the cityscape. But more on this later.

Prague, for many the most beautiful city in Central Europe, is another gateway to an extraordinary past. The Castle, the 600-year-old Charles Bridge, and the Malá Strana give a sense of the long presence of the Czechs in this space. By comparison, cities like Budapest and even Berlin seem young. Plus, Prague was largely spared intensive bombing during the Second World War. Prague also offers other more recent perspectives on the past, and, like the Germans, they seem to get things better than what is on offer in Budapest or Warsaw. Museums to the communist experience are extremely sophisticated. Quite simply, the Czechs have far fewer skeletons in the closet and they, more than any post-communist country, seem to get where they belong and where they are headed.

Compared to their neighbours, the Czechs have managed to address the darker parts of their history without the same sense of perpetual victimhood. After 1989, the memory landscape changed. Soviet domination after 1948 and the occupation in 1968 were placed on the same plane as the Nazi occupation of Bohemia and Moravia from 1938 to 1945. Monuments to Roma victims, a group often intentionally ignored by their Central European counterparts, appeared in Brno. Since then, the stories that have come to dominate the memorial narrative seem to primarily focus on the home-grown resistance in Czechoslovakia and the heroism of Czechs, Slovaks, and others who worked in exile to fight against Nazi Germany. Prague is not as littered with imposing monuments, and even inaccurate monuments, to the Second World War, like Hungary. Perhaps the best-known and most general monument is one depicting the Czech flag, in colour, rising out of a round, grey pedestal in a small park in Klárov, at the foot of the Castle hill and by the river. Inscribed with "1938–1945" in gold lettering, it is dedicated to the resistance to the Nazi occupation of Bohemia and Moravia.

At the other end of the small park is another memorial honouring a group that fought against Nazi Germany. Erected by Prague's British community, it commemorates the Czechoslovak pilots who joined the Royal Air Force, many of whom returned to a Czechoslovakia where the new Communist regime imprisoned them for cooperation with the "fascist" West during the war. The centrepiece of the monument is a bronze double-tailed lion (borrowed from the Czechoslovak coat of arms) with wings, growling and crouched as if ready to take flight. The circular pedestal it stands on is inscribed with the names of the pilots. Unveiled in 2014 by the grandson of Winston Churchill, the monument was not without controversy. There are other small memorials scattered around Prague commemorating events or people who carried out acts of heroism during the war. The Main Railway Station houses a monument to Nicholas

Winton, who saved hundreds of Jewish children in the Kindertransports. It is tucked away in the hall that leads to the railway platforms. Throughout the city, one runs into plaques remembering people who were killed during the Prague Uprising in early May 1945, before the Soviets arrived and declared themselves liberators.

Primarily in the historically Jewish district, Josefov, one also comes across Stolpersteine—the gold metal paving stones found across Central European countries that mark the former homes of people who were targeted in the Nazi terror, many of whom were deported and killed in the camps. The Jewish district is also home to a large Jewish Museum, composed of a conglomeration of synagogues, a cemetery, and other historic buildings. The site of the former Terezín ghetto, the Germans' showcase camp during the war, is now also home to a museum. The country has been somewhat slower to face and remember the more uncomfortable parts of this period of history. Only recently has the site of the former camp of Lety, used as a concentration centre and launch pad for the deportation of the Roma and Sinti, been set on the path of becoming a memorial site as well, after many years of controversy. Other uncomfortable parts of this era of history, such as the death march of Germans from Brno immediately following the war and the expulsion of Germans from the Sudetenland, have also re-entered history books in recent years, though the topic remains sensitive, especially among older generations.

Towards 1848

Just what constitutes Central Europe is open to debate. For the purposes of this book, it means the often contested and vulnerable space that lies between Germany and Russia. This means the present republics of Austria, Czech Republic, Hungary, Poland, and Slovakia are the principal focus of the narrative. Russia, Germany, the Baltic States, and the Balkans will also be discussed. Central Europe has a shared history of past historical greatness both before and during Habsburg rule, periods of independence, subjugation, political instability and all the bad "isms" of the twentieth and twenty-first centuries: fascism, Nazism, nationalism, authoritarianism, communism, and populism.

While Eastern Europe was largely a Cold War and ultimately political term referring to the states that ended up in the Soviet sphere of influence after the Second World War, Central Europe, which existed as a term before the Second World War, came back to life after the end of communist rule in 1989. Eastern Europe joined Austria and a re-unified Germany, in a recreated Central Europe that sought, above all else, to be back where they were prior to 1939. After all, as the Czech/French writer Milan Kundera noted in a seminal essay in "The Tragedy of Central Europe" in *The New York Review of Books* in 1984, Central Europe was essentially kidnapped by the East, in that case the USSR, which was entirely alien to the historical context until then. Given the history of the region until then, particularly when one looks at the cultural impact of Central Europe on Europe as a whole, Kundera's point was a good one. After all, a political moment in time should not define Central Europe as Eastern Europe. The year 1989 was thus a return, in essence, to a lost homeland—Europe—and the abandonment of something that was imposed on them largely by force with a large dose of Western indifference. But by joining the European Union in 2004, Czechs, Poles, Hungarians, and Slovaks joined a kind of benign empire, thus ensuring that with such short and ultimately failed experiences with real independence, some Central Europeans would come to develop alternative viewpoints on the future European integration project.

Central Europe could be defined to a degree by the Danube River and its tributaries, and, as one of my colleagues in Brno noted, the presence of strudel and maybe schnitzel. Some parts of the region were integral to the Habsburg Empire until 1918 and Habsburg influence is undeniable, especially in some of the great cities and towns of the region and the legacy of German settlement and influence. The cities of Central Europe, which are visually very similar, were largely built by Germans. In the years prior to the mid-nineteenth century national awakenings to be urban was to be German. Central Europe also has a legacy of mixed populations which is harder to discern these days. Multiple religions: Catholics, Jews, Protestants, Orthodox, and Uniate. Multiple language groups: Germanic, Finno-Ugric, Romance, and Slavic. Existing on the margins, since their arrival in Europe, were the Roma too. Until the mid-nineteenth century, the region was essentially rural, feudal, and backward with some exceptions. The big transformative moments in European history arrived later here and eventually went through a different filter which gives the region a distinctiveness from Western Europe in some good and bad ways.

Before we examine Central Europe before, during, and after the revolutions of 1848, a few watersheds are necessary to explore. With the arrival of modern nationalism as the new religion of sorts, Central European nation builders needed a glorious past to make a glorious future. Some had that, some had to invent one. For the Hungarians, or Magyars more precisely, their arrival in the Carpathian basin sometime around 896 from somewhere in Central Asia, which was later known as the conquest, established a permanent Magyar presence in Central Europe with extraordinary implications. The Árpád dynasty established the largest and certainly most powerful of medieval dynasties ruling vast parts of Europe. Arriving as nomadic pagans on horses, the Hungarians later joined mainstream Europe under Stephen the First when they adopted Catholicism around the year 1000.

Hungarian predominance, and hence their golden era, ended slowly in the 1500s due to its defeats at the hands of the Ottoman Empire marched north through the Balkans and into Hungary and thus Central Europe. In 1526, in the Danube town of Mohács, the Hungarian king, Louis II, perished and so began the slow Ottomanization and Islamization of the once great Hungarian kingdom. After a protracted civil war, as Hungarians who had the right to elect their king, the Hungarian crown ended up with the Habsburgs and the Hungarian kingdom was partitioned. Bertalan Székely's 1860 painting "The Discovery of the Body of King Louis II" says it all. Hungary's pre-eminent national poet and hero of the 1848 revolution, Sándor Petőfi, would later note that Mohács was the "graveyard of Hungarian grandeur". This is an overstatement. Buda, the historic capital, fell to the Ottomans in 1541 and Hungary entered a period of Ottoman occupation that lasted until 1686 in Buda. It is worth noting, that Ottoman occupation, 300 plus years later became a siren call for nationalist governments seeking to resurrect Hungary's historic role as a bulwark against Islam as they "fought" a new wave of Muslim migrants in 2015 and after. In any case, one cannot underestimate the impact of the period of modern Hungarian nationalism. Ottoman occupation, which brought baths, mosques, and paprika, was otherwise a disaster for Hungary, leaving much of the country denuded along with massive population decline. The memories of a lost and vast territorial space would serve to shape the Hungarian world view from that point forward.

Historic Hungary, the medieval kingdom, was thus divided into three parts: Ottoman occupied, Habsburg controlled (or Royal Hungary with its administrative centre in *Pressburg*, in German, or *Poszony* in Hungarian; present-day Bratislava, the capital of Slovakia); and Transylvania, which was quasi-independent but in "vassal status" to the Ottoman Empire. In many ways, the growth of the Hungarian national idea, and the source of much of its independent spirit, would come from there in later years, and re-unification with Transylvania would become a key demand of Hungarian nationalists. The Hungarian crown, allegedly given to Hungary's first Christian king, Stephen, in 1000, is an object of extraordinary reverence in Hungary, symbolizing not just the continuity of the state, but Hungary's Christian entry into Europe and the importance of Christianity to Hungarian national identity. Previously housed in Budapest's National Museum, to mark 1000 years of Hungary as a Christian state, the crown was moved in an extraordinary ceremony by the first government of then Prime Minister Viktor Orbán in 2000 to sit in the domed hall of the Hungarian Parliament. Prior to arriving in the parliament, an elaborately decorated Danube boat took the crown to the seat to Esztergom, the seat of the Hungarian Catholic Church. But in 1526, the crown essentially passed to the Habsburgs in Vienna. Marriage was often the key to Habsburg success, and this was certainly the case then too. As the oft-repeated ditty goes, "May others go to war, you happy Austria, marry." By 1526, the Habsburgs in Vienna had grown their Empire substantially and their control over what ultimately became Czech, Hungarian, and Slovak lands was to last until the end of the First World War in 1918.

For the people who would become Czechs, they had also established themselves as a people with a revolutionary spirit too. Even before Martin Luther made his challenge to the Catholic Church in 1517, Jan Hus (1369–1415), a Bohemian priest, theologian, philosopher, and Rector of Charles University, was an essential precursor to the Reformation. Hus and his followers clashed with the Catholic Church in Bohemia, disagreeing with many of its practices, and their dissent unleashed a period of wars and strife. Hus himself was lured to a church council in Constance and asked to recant. He refused, was deemed a heretic, and was burned at the stake in 1415. His struggle, after the fact of course, became emblematic of the Czech struggle for independence.

If 1526 is watershed for the Hungarians, it is also for the Czechs. The lands of the Bohemian Crown, somewhat akin to the Czech lands today of Bohemia in the west and Moravia in the east, gradually came under Habsburg rule and its centralization tendencies. The Czech nobility resisted religious restrictions imposed by the Habsburg rulers and essentially dethroned them in 1618, even throwing some Habsburg officials out the window. In 1620, at the Battle of White Mountain, which holds the same importance for Czechs as 1526 does for Hungarians, the Czechs were horrendously defeated. The implications of the defeat were immense. The leaders were executed, a vicious campaign to restore Catholicism was implemented, and the Crown lands of Bohemia and Moravia were downgraded to a hereditary possession. This can be easily contrasted with the Hungarian kingdom, which although part of the Habsburg Empire after 1526, still enjoyed certain distinct and historical rights that were denied to the Czechs. Nevertheless, Czech resistance, in the Hussite tradition, was later employed as a vehicle for the creation of Czech national consciousness to great effect. In defeat, at least in nation building, the acts of heroes later become decisive victories in hindsight. Moreover, without a native nobility as existed in Hungary or Poland, Czech identity would develop along different lines, exhibiting a kind of pragmatism that will prove to missing elsewhere.

Lastly, in 1683 the Ottoman Empire, sitting comfortably in the city of Buda on the Danube River, decided time was right take Vienna, one of the centres of Western Christendom. They had tried once and failed in 1529. In 1683, with Grand Vizier, the Sultan's number two, Kara Mustafa at the head of a giant army, Vienna looked lost. Even the Emperor Leopold I fled. But the fortified city was saved by decisive help from the Polish King, Jan III Sobieski, and the military skills of Charles of Lorraine and Eugene of Savoy plus the poor decisions of Kara Mustafa who was later strangled in Belgrade and his head sent to the Sultan. A later nationalist Polish government after 2015 would use Sobieski's legacy to strengthen their own arguments for Poles again to stop a "Muslim invasion", that time in the form of Muslim migrants and refugees fleeing war and poverty. In any case, success followed success and Buda was liberated by Lorraine and Savoy in 1686, and a number of battles that followed pushed the Ottomans further and further south with great gains for Habsburgs. Historic Hungary was unified under Vienna's rule but at a price. Moreover, in the wake of their victories, more and more Germans settled in the region giving the urban centres a distinctly German look and atmosphere. The Hungarian nation builders of the late nineteenth century would give 1686 a decidedly Hungarian stamp later, best captured by Gyula Benczúr's 1896 painting *The Recapture of Buda Castle*. The Hungarian fighter, in national costume, is front and centre. The Habsburgs look rather unsullied, even powdered, and look on from the relative background. In any case, Savoy is not altogether forgotten. His equestrian statue sits in front of the Buda Castle, at least for now.

As in the rest of Europe, some would even say the world, the transformative moment was the French Revolution of 1789. But before that seminal moment, the fate of Poland deserves mention. With what is arguably a terrible geographic location, situated between three great powers, the great Polish Lithuanian Commonwealth was slowly removed from the map in a series of three partitions by the neighbouring powers of Austria, Prussia, and Russia. In the first partition of 1772, then Habsburg Empress Maria Theresa, allegedly wept but that did not stop her from grabbing 83,000 square kilometres of Central Europe. After all, in 1683, the Polish King Jan Sobieski had saved the Habsburg capital from the invading Ottoman Army. Poland was partitioned again in 1793 and 1795. The biggest winner was Russia, then Prussia, then Austria. Poland was re-created by Napoleon as the Duchy of Warsaw which appeared briefly in 1807 only to disappear again in 1815. Poland, which would not exist again until 1918, suffered immensely under three different administrations and the tragedy of the partitions cannot be minimized. There were also dramatic differences in the respective partition zones.

An understanding of the partitions, and their role in shaping Polish identity, can be understood by visiting the once German (Breslau) but now Polish city of Wrocław. The communist built rotunda, a great example of communist-brutalist architecture, was built in in the 1960s to house the famous Racławice Panorama which depicts, in an absolutely epic and even strange way, the famous Tadeusz Kościuszko Uprising of 1794 where the Poles defeated the Russians. Painted in Lviv, in what is now Ukraine, the painting is a remarkable 15 metres in height and 114 metres in length, and was given to communist Poland after the Second World War. Afraid to upset their then Russian masters in the ersatz world of communist brotherly love, the painting did not get displayed until the 1980s, complete with a recreated terrain in front. With remarkable detail, a whole world is presented complete with an extremely dated voice over in multiple languages. You can hardly move in the place with all the school kids, and the painting is clearly a site of pilgrimage given the line-ups. Thankfully, the youth do not seem to be buying the nationalism on sale, but instead cluster around the exit hoping to be first out.

But back to Central Europe of the eighteenth century. As noted, Poland disappeared and Poles were left under Habsburg, Prussian, or Russian rule. If a hierarchy of suffering is helpful, then the Poles in the Russian zone suffered the most, followed by the Prussian zone, and then the Habsburgs, who, as we shall see, often exhibited an admirable tolerance for regional particularisms. The ideas of 1789, and with it the arrival of modern nationalism in its wake, spread ever so slowly over the subject peoples of Central Europe. Until then, Europe was essentially a collection of feudal estates held together by the fear of God. For France, which was already a state, the French Revolution allowed them to begin making a nation. For Central Europeans, almost entirely stateless except for the Austrians who controlled the Habsburg Empire, the new nationalism meant that they would first have to build or re-build nations, then states. This difference would result in some really extraordinary outcomes.

The new vocabulary of the French Revolution and the Enlightenment that preceded it shaped the subsequent national awakenings that would set the peoples of the region on a path towards independence. The origins of the French Revolutionary Wars and the later Napoleonic Wars are numerous, but it is enough to say that the export of the revolution was central, especially since the new French state called for the end of feudalism which remained in Central Europe until 1848. By far the greatest impact came from Napoleon's relentless re-organization of the map of Europe between 1800 and 1815. Napoleon's armies, as both conquerors and liberators, left a new concept of the state and of the nation that was later adapted, in various ways, by a generation of nineteenth-century nation builders.

After multiple wars with multiple coalitions, Napoleon was defeated decisively not once, but twice, while the Great Powers (Austria, Prussia, Russia, and the United Kingdom) convened in Vienna in 1814 and 1815 to put Europe back together again after more than two decades of conflict. What this meant for the peoples of Central Europe was largely the return of the status quo as it existed in 1788 to a degree, although it was impossible to turn the clock back completely. Prior to the Congress of Vienna, some of Napoleon's changes were accepted. The Holy Roman Empire of the German Nation, in existence for 1000 years, was dissolved in 1806 and replaced by Napoleon's Confederation of the Rhine with much of contemporary Germany included. The Holy Roman Empire is not as difficult to understand as one may think. It was a loose organization of over 300 political units that owed fealty to its head, more often than not, the Habsburg Emperor. It was not a state, not even a confederation of states, and some liken it to the contemporary European Union. In any case, Napoleon reduced the number of states to just over 30 and the last ruler, Francis II, abdicated. Hitler later obsessed about the Holy Roman Empire, making it the First Reich, using its territorial vastness to justify German expansionism, and even having the famous crown moved from Vienna to Nuremburg where it was later picked up invading US troops in the Second World War. The Congress of Vienna replaced the loose collection of German states with the German Confederation with the Habsburg Emperor as its nominal head. Between 1815 and 1871, much of Central Europe's fate would be decided by the quarrels and wars that would later create a unified German state with the Prussian capital Berlin in the driver's seat, not Vienna.

The Great Powers that shaped the peace following decades of war re-created a neo-absolutist order that preserved as much of the pre-French revolutionary status quo as possible. In essence, they recognized it could not be 1788 as not everything the French put on the table in 1789 could simply be swept away. What this meant in practice was that Poland was gone again and they agreed to a balance of power that would prevent war between the powers, complete with regular meetings that would manage crises. The archetype of the post-1815 order was Klemens von Metternich, the Austrian chancellor who combined both reactionary and progressive tendencies as we shall later see. France was not completely destroyed but was more or less immediately re-integrated into the international system with the pre-revolutionary Bourbons back on the throne, at least until the February 1848 revolution in Paris. The Congress system as it was called, which later morphed into the Concert of Europe, has been lauded for its ability steer clear of large European conflagrations until the First World War broke out in 1914. There were plenty of wars though: the Crimean War, three wars of German unification, war between Russia and the Ottoman Empire, and the extremely bloody Balkan Wars of 1912–1913. By the standards of the Napoleonic and French Revolutionary Wars these conflicts were considered minor. The litmus test for conflict was determined by how many Great Powers were involved. But to see the period as one of peace misses the point, especially if you lived in the Balkans.

For Central Europeans, they were entirely back where they started—largely in the multi-national Habsburg Empire that had as its very core a hostility to nationalism. But the French Revolution and Napoleon had provided, in varying levels, the ideology of liberation and therefore nationalism. This means the period prior to 1848 is a period of nascent national awakenings based on some common themes for Czechs, Germans, Hungarians, Poles, and Slovaks. But there were important difference as varying levels of national consciousness existed within the peoples of the region. The nation building process, which came to its apogee with the establishment of independent states after the First World War, fell to groups of intellectuals who primarily prioritized language as being key to a new future.

If we think of flashpoints in the nineteenth century, then of course the revolutions of 1830 and 1848 need to be examined. The 1830 revolution matters for Central Europe only insofar as it tells us the challenges for the region and what separates these peoples from their neighbours in the West. By 1830, Greece was independent from the Ottoman Empire and the Greek Revolution provided the near perfect template for an independence movement in so far as it proved the importance of the role of the Great Powers in determining success or failure and the importance of mobilizing European popular opinion. The 1830 revolution, confined mostly to France, laid bare extreme social divisions, but also intensified political debate, boosted civil society, and populist nationalism, and increased the demands for peasant emancipation which was particularly important in the Habsburg Empire. One could also see the period as a struggle for national identity, constitutional government where there were no constitutions, and new constitutions where there were ones needing change and civil rights. Interestingly enough, the nationalism of nineteenth-century Central European nation builders was decidedly liberal in orientation. For Russian occupied Poland, 1830 brought a national uprising—the November uprising—which sought to overthrow Russian rule. The Poles would experience an on-and-off-again violent struggle with Russia.

Failures in Poland aside, the period between 1815 and 1848 did see some incremental changes. Despite the Habsburgs strict control over their subject peoples, national revivals did occur. Emblematic of these changes are the experiences of the Czechs and Hungarians. In the period prior to the 1848 revolutions, nation builders strove to convince people to read and write in the national language which they called linguistic revivals. In both the Czech and the Hungarian context, alongside the growth of civil society already mentioned was an explosive growth in published materials and a growing interest in national language and literature. The Hungarians, more so than the Czechs, feared that they could be assimilated by either Germans or Slavs. Similar ideas, albeit with less success, were finding their way into Slovak society.

Most telling of the period is the experience of the Hungarians and Count István Széchenyi. Széchenyi (and his father, Ferenc, too) is by far the most iconic example of a nineteenth-century nation builder. Deciding that the soul of nation was based on language, the Széchenyi family put their vast fortune to work for the Hungarian revival on two levels: culture and infrastructure. His father, Ferenc, had already helped lay the foundations for a Hungarian National Museum which later made its debut in 1846 in Budapest in a neo-classical building. István later put money down for the establishment of the Hungarian Academy of Sciences in 1825, situated in a renaissance revival building on the Pest side of the Danube embankment, as a repository of the nation's intellectual wealth and later a national theatre in the 1830s. Obsessed with infrastructure and Hungarian backwardness, Széchenyi's European travels, especially to the United Kingdom, suggested to him an evolutionary path was best, hand in hand with the Habsburgs, towards a modern Hungary. His most lasting legacy, especially to visitors to Budapest, is the Chain Bridge, which he partially paid for. Completed in 1849, it was the first permanent bridge between Buda and Pest.

For Széchenyi, the creation of a single capital city, a truly Hungarian national capital, that joined what were then the separate cities of Buda and Pest (and Óbuda too, which was the legacy of the early Roman settlement of Aquincum) was part of his vision for a renewed Hungary. Destroyed by retreating Germans in 1945 along with every other bridge in the city, the Chain Bridge ends on the Pest side at Széchenyi Square, in front of what is now the Art Nouveau Gresham Palace Four Seasons Hotel. Tellingly, that premier square in the city used to be Roosevelt Square named after the late US president in 1947. Later deemed less than heroic for his failure to save Central Europe from the Soviets, Roosevelt lost his square in 2011 in the never-ending process of naming and renaming streets in Budapest. But more on that later.

1848: The Springtime of (Some) Nations

The period between the Congress of Vienna and the Europe-wide revolutions of 1848 is a combination of reform and often conservative reaction. Most importantly, it was transformative for modern nationalism. The 1815 settlement, hailed for its ability to prevent really big wars until 1914, offered the people of Central Europe very little and 1848 would see similar failures. Prior to 1848, there were revolutions in 1830 which laid bare growing social tensions, emerging civil societies and the need for peasant emancipation. There was explosive growth in published materials too and an intensified political debate. The year 1848, which was the most revolutionary year in Europe's nineteenth century, was preceded by the usual stuff of revolutions: poor harvests, working class despair, and poverty. Things started out in Palermo, Italy, but it was events in France that once again set things in motion elsewhere, where the Orléans dynasty fell and events took even more dangerous turns elsewhere as news of King Louis-Phillipe's abdication spread. In Central Europe we see nationalism working hand in hand with liberals. The national builders of this period saw in the creation of national states serving at the same time the goals of liberalism. But rest assured, not all nations were considered equal—Germans, Hungarians, and Poles were above Czechs, Slovaks, or Croats, among others. What this meant in the German Confederation, the successor to Napoleon's Confederation of the Rhine, were calls for the creation of a unified German state.

In Vienna, under the almost iron rule of Klemens von Metternich, students, largely at the University of Vienna, took the streets to demand a unified German state, the end of censorship, serfdom, as well as freedom of the press, popular representation, and a constitution. The then Habsburg Emperor Ferdinand I, often maligned in history books as weak and not terribly bright, joined Metternich in hoping to crush the revolution by force and in Vienna's streets the barricades went up. In March, Austria found that the military could not restore order. Metternich, as the symbol of the old regime, fled for an exile in the United Kingdom which he had always admired anyway. The Vienna revolutionaries made some gains: the serfs were emancipated but other demands were rejected and, by the end of October, the revolution was completely suppressed. It would take the Hungarian Revolution to truly transform events in the Habsburg Empire.

Hungary, and indeed Hungarian identity, cannot be fully understood without reference to the events of 1848 and 1849. It was an inspirational moment for the Hungarians, and while a failure, its testimony to Hungary's capacity for revolutionary zeal stands out. In the years between 1815 and 1848 the lands of historic Hungary had changed dramatically. Despite the harsh rule from Vienna, Hungarians had engaged in a period of reform and nation building. The aforementioned Széchenyi family stand out here for their commitment to a new Hungary that was to remain an integral part of the Habsburg Empire, at least in the near future. Hungarian was headed towards becoming the language of state, and theatres and museums were appearing. The Hungarian Diet, or parliament, was increasingly active.

The period is best approached by understanding three essential figures: Lajos Kossuth, Sándor Petőfi and Istvan Széchenyi. Indeed, a visit to Hungary under any government, confirms that these three are the most important national figures. Kossuth, a lawyer, ardent opponent of serfdom, was also a firebrand of a journalist. His paper *Pesti Hírlap* (Pest Gazette) would come to seek radical solutions, and he waged a war on feudal institutions. He had spent some time in jail for his agitation. Petőfi was a young poet who would give voice to the demands of people for an end to foreign rule, and Széchenyi was an infrastructure person who saw in England a model for Hungary's modernization. Age can tell you a bit—at the time of the revolution, Petőfi was 25, Kossuth was 46, and Széchenyi was 57. Kossuth and Széchenyi differed too on nationalism but agreed on the notion that Hungary was essentially Hungarian, Széchenyi hoped that the other emerging nations in historic Hungary would drift towards assimilation because of Hungary's general progress over time. Kossuth was more inclined to think that a Hungarian government and a Hungarian democracy would turn people, and he was more afraid of allowing too much leeway to Slavs and Romanians.

In 1848, Petőfi's *National Song*, which asked Hungarians if they wanted to be slaves forever, was the call to arms and together the Hungarian revolutionaries drew up a list of demands for the leadership in Vienna. The March Laws, as they were called, essentially gave Hungary home rule within the Habsburg Empire. Kossuth was hailed as a hero in Vienna too by the students. The Laws were an extraordinary liberal triumph ensuring a Hungarian government, the abolition of serfdom, the unification of Buda and Pest as a single city, universal suffrage, unification administratively with Transylvania, and a free press. They were accepted in full by the Habsburg Emperor, leading contemporary historian István Deák to call what happened in 1848 a "Lawful Revolution". The Hungarians got their own cabinet of notables including Kossuth as Minister of Finance and Széchenyi as Transport Minister. For a moment, the Hungarians appeared to be the only winners in 1848.

Hungary's temporary victory in the spring of 1848 turned sour for a number of reasons. Most importantly, they got the national question wrong and this would not be the last time that the Hungarians would misread the situation. The Hungarian first policy of Kossuth prevailed but as hostility to the Hungarian exception grew among nationalities and in Vienna, the Hungarians started to listen to minority demands, but never rejected the vision of a unitary state dominated by the Hungarians. Unlike the exclusive nationalisms of the twentieth and twenty-first centuries, the Hungarians basically asserted that while everyone was equal, some were more equal than others. Hence, if you were willing to assimilate, there was room. There is no better example of this than Petőfi. Everyone was aware of his background—mixed Serb and Slovak—he was easily welcomed as Hungary's national poet.

Hungary's push for more and more, especially a move towards the establishment of a Hungarian national army, put them on a path to conflict with Vienna by the summer of 1848. Having put down the revolution in Vienna and in Italy too, the Habsburgs turned on the Hungarians and the war that started by September 1848 pitted the Hungarians against Vienna and the Croats, Serbs, and Slovaks too. The Hungarian Revolution morphed into an independence war. By December, Ferdinand I stepped down in favour of his nephew, who became Franz Joseph I. Only 18 years old, he was far less inclined to curry favour with the Hungarian revolutionary leadership. In response to the changing situation, Franz Joseph introduced a new constitution of sorts that answered a few of the 1848 demands. Importantly, all nationalities were declared equal. The Hungarian exception was over. Franz Joseph would shape the Habsburg Empire until his death in 1916.

In April 1849, on Kossuth's initiative, the House of Habsburg was dethroned and Kossuth became the head of state. Just what type of state Hungary was to become was to be decided at a later date. Confronted initially with a string of Hungarian victories, Franz Joseph called on the Russian Tsar Nicholas I to invade Hungary from the east in June. By August, the Hungarians surrendered and Kossuth fled into a life of activism and exile. Feted everywhere he went, the United States was especially enthralled with Kossuth when he arrived there in 1851. Kossuth has several memorials in the United States, including a bust in the capitol rotunda. Austrian repression, under the leadership of Julius Jacob von Haynau, was swift. Thirteen generals were executed at Arad. János Thorma's epic painting made for the millennium celebration of the Hungarian arrival to Europe, *The Martyrs of Arad* (1896), captures this moment as the leaders, surrounded by priests, prepare to be shot. Hungary's Prime Minister, Lajos Batthyány, after trying to kill himself by stabbing himself in the neck, was executed just the same in October 1849 in the same place that would become Freedom Square with its weird collection of monuments and politicized messages. The legacy of 1848 and 1849 in Hungary was a decade of neo-absolutism, but 1848 became a valuable symbol later as the deal made then would be resurrected in the 1867 compromise with Austria.

Unlike in Hungary, the Czechs to their eventual credit had no native nobility, which to me at least, always goes a long way to explain the resilience of Czech democracy. The nobility in Bohemia and Moravia was essentially Germanized, with the dominant urban classes communicating primarily in German and often speaking no Czech. Like elsewhere in Central Europe, the redevelopment of the Czech language began in the late eighteenth century in literary salons. One of the most important nation builders in the early nineteenth century was František Palacký, a son of a schoolteacher. He became the official historian of the Bohemian Diet, publishing the first volume of a history of the Czech people in 1836. Throughout these early decades of the nineteenth century, a sense of Czech identity spread primarily in towns, and by the 1840s, there was a large Czech reading public, though this movement was still primarily cultural, rather than political.

By March, Bohemians were petitioning for civil liberties and creating a National Committee. With the Bohemian Diet lacking a strong leader or the backing of a Czech gentry, the radical intellectuals of Prague, inexperienced in political matters, took charge of the movement. On March 11, they assembled a meeting and articulated calls for a variety of freedoms, including freedom of expression, the end of censorship, educational, and administrative equality for Czechs and Germans, the unification of Bohemia, Moravia, and Silesia under their own chancellery, and the abolition of *robot*, a system of compulsory labour.

After the fall of Metternich later that month, Czech demands radicalized, calling for unity and full autonomy of the three regions alongside

Czech-German equality. In June 1848, the Pan-Slav Congress opened in Prague, attended by groups based on linguistic affiliation. The attendees drafted a manifesto to the peoples of Europe, which called to stop the conquests of peoples and nations and originated the idea of self-determination. It was disrupted on June 12 by fighting between radical students, both Czech and German, and imperial soldiers led by the militaristic Prince Alfred zu Windisch-Grätz, whom the students wanted removed. As the students marched against the Prince on Wenceslas Square, Windisch-Grätz retaliated by firing into the crowd, putting the city under martial law, dissolving the National Assembly, and shutting down the Pan-Slav Congress. These riots effectively ended Bohemian radicalism, and the movement was left to the Czech moderates, who were now more eager to cooperate with Vienna than before.

In July, the new Constituent Assembly opened in Vienna, with most peoples of the Empire represented. Approximately half of the representatives were Slavs, and work was slow to begin and progress, as there was no common language that all spoke. The Czechs, under the leadership of Palacký, called for a transition to federalism with a parliament in Prague that would be equal to one in Pest, but they refused to support Lajos Kossuth because of his oppression of the Slovaks, the Croats, and the Serbs. Their demands, which have come to be knows as a programme of Austroslavism, were rather moderate and insisted on preserving Austria at all costs. They feared the German National Assembly in Frankfurt and the prospect of a united Greater Germany more. In fact, Palacký had received an invitation to attend this Assembly as one of six Austrian representatives, but he had refused on the grounds that he was a Bohemian Slav and thus ineligible to participate in a German National Assembly. His letter of refusal marks a pivotal assertion of the Czech nation's right to existence.

As unrest developed in Vienna in the fall, the Court fled to Olomouc and the Assembly to Kroměříž, both in Moravia. On 2 March 1849, the Assembly, increasingly moderated over the preceding months of unrest, finalized and unanimously passed a new Constitution. It called for a constitutional and hereditary monarchy, the creation of new provinces based on historic territories, provincial governors answering only to the provincial diets, self-administration for municipalities, restrictions of the absolute power of the Emperor and the requirement that the Imperial ministers answer to a new, two-chamber Parliament, and a Bill of Rights modelled on the Constitution of Texas. The new chancellor, Felix zu Schwarzenberg, decided, however, to dissolve the assembly, most of its members fled, and their efforts came to naught. The Empire returned to centralization, with a new Constitution modelled on that of Prussia.

The year 1848 was not the hopeful turning point its protagonists had hoped for. The brief marriage of liberalism and nationalism was unprecedented and was never to occur again. A decade of neo-absolutism followed in the Habsburg Empire. The plans to make the Germanic Confederation into a liberal constitutional state failed. The German question was to become central as both Vienna and Berlin struggled to be the pre-eminent German power. Otto von

Bismarck, then a young politician in the Prussian legislature but destined to become the key figure in German unification, had come out against the liberals in the German confederation and held a pretty dim view of parliaments in general. His views would come to prevail in the 1860s. However, the failed revolutions of 1848 made possible the events of 1918.

German Unification and the Creation of Austria-Hungary

Franz Joseph I assumed the Habsburg throne when he was only 18 and he stayed there until he was 86. Franz Joseph was known for his military discipline, his attention to detail and his hatred of beards. As we shall see, he would re-make the city of Vienna and the entire Habsburg Empire by bringing the Hungarians, the real demons of 1848–1849, as equal partners in what would become Austria-Hungary in 1867. But that story begins in Berlin, the Prussian capital.

The fate of Central Europe was, as will be the case again in the twentieth century, decided by Germany. The creation of a single German state, ruled by Berlin and not Vienna, was the most important diplomatic achievement of the nineteenth century, making Otto von Bismarck the most successful politician of the period. For Germany, Bismarck engineered three wars to achieve his goals: one with Denmark, one with Austria, and one with France. Habsburg defeats in their territories in Italy during the wars of Italian unification, and later humiliating defeats against Prussia, ensured the success of the "little German" solution: that is, the unification of the German confederation and the complete exclusion of Austria.

Bismarck's Prussia had a number of advantages over not just Austria but the other German states as well. It controlled the key industrial part of Europe, it had a strong economy, and a paramount position in the Customs Union or *Zollverein*. Unlike Austria, Prussia was more homogenous, did not have to worry about Hungarians, and possessed a very strong ruling family and an extremely well-developed public administration.

After settling things in Prussia's favour in Denmark, Bismarck turned on the Habsburgs. After the humiliating defeat of Austria and some of its smaller German confederation allies by a far better prepared Prussian army, the Peace of Prague in August 1866 took Austria out of German affairs. Bismarck temporarily created the North German Confederation but he successfully unified Germany by January 1871 in a war with France. The new German empire was proclaimed in the French palace of Versailles, with Emperor Wilhelm 1 of Prussia as the new German Emperor. It took three wars and none of them Bismarck actually started. Bismarck could not have been happier with his vision of a united Germany, built by "iron and blood", just as he had predicted. Bismarck's Germany was a far cry from the one envisioned by the 1848ers chanting *"Deutschland uber alles"*.

A unified, authoritarian, illiberal, and Prussian-dominated Germany spelt doom in the long run for Central Europe. However, in the short run, Bismarck seemed magnanimous. He eschewed Wilhelm's call to march onwards to Vienna. Instead he helped the Habsburg Empire re-define itself for a new era when Vienna had to look east and south, not west and north. Bismarck understood that the survival of the Habsburg Empire was essential for European stability and he did not see any gains to adding Catholic Austrians into his protestant dominated state.

In 1867, Austria officially became Austria-Hungary, or the Dual Monarchy. While changes in the monarchy were in the air before, it was the defeats in 1859 in Italy and in 1866 that hastened change, which started out as a small and ended up big. There was, after all, growing nationalism, mostly top-down stuff of the Széchenyi or Palacký variety that we witnessed in 1848 that sought a kind of federalism. Franz Joseph started his rejuvenation project with the Hungarians in 1865 but was forced to speed things up. Plus, Franz Joseph's wife, Empress Elizabeth, or Sisi, was a known promoter of a new programme for the Hungarians. Sisi would learn Hungarian and spend much her time in her residence at Gödöllő east of Budapest.

Rumours abounded about Sisi and her affairs. It is enough to say she was extremely unhappy, in an equally unhappy marriage, and was murdered by an anarchist in Geneva in 1898 who happened be there to kill someone else. The Sisi cult persists in Austria, and the 1865 painting of the 28-year old Elizabeth in a satin dress covered in stars by Franz Winterhalter is everywhere. Sisi was reinvented as a marketing strategy in the 1990s around the centenary of her death to serve the needs of modern tourism, re-branding, and Austria's quest for useable history. She joined the Mozart Kugeln as the face of Austria. Even though Habsburg memories and symbols were banished from Austria after the First World War, they came back after the Second World War as a national brand designed to appeal to largely foreign tourists. Sisi proved to be very lucrative. Worth watching is Romy Schneider, whose life was as tragic as Sisi's, in the three films where she portrayed Empress Elizabeth.

In the spring of 1867, after negotiations with Hungarian liberals led by Ferenc Deák and Gyula Andrássy, the April Laws were back in the form of the Compromise or *Ausgleich*. Hungary was fully independent in its domestic affairs which would later spell another kind of doom for its minorities. Franz Joseph arrived in Budapest in June to formally accept the crown of Saint Stephen. The settlement acknowledged that the Hungarians were different after all, and that their historic independence was simply more historic than anyone else. Not everyone, especially the Czechs, agreed.

The new state was unique. The Austrian half was called Cisleithania because the Leith River separated the two halves. The new country solved a couple of problems. It gave the Hungarians something special and the Hungarians in turn offered the Croatians a mini-compromise, or *Nagodba*, in 1868 which gave them a degree of autonomy but still under Budapest's rule. The new state had three shared ministries: finance, foreign affairs, and defence. The foreign ministry position alternated between the two halves of the monarchy. The Emperor of Austria/King of Hungary wielded enormous power. In terms of territory, the agreement resurrected historic Hungary as it existed prior to the Ottoman invasion in the 1500s. Hungary was tied to Western Europe in a way that had never happened before.

While the Austrian half would stress its multi-national a character, the Hungarians, as if foreshadowing things to come, would briefly embrace a liberal approach to the nationalities that was never really implemented and later abandoned it for harsh "Hungarianization" campaigns and intolerance. In essence, between 1867 and 1914, Hungarian politics was defined by the issues related to the many national groups that lived there: Germans, Romanians, Serbs, Slovaks, Jews, Roma, and Ruthenians, for example. It would be fair to say that initial policies, to a degree, were mindful of the 1848 failure. The 1868 Nationalities Law, the work of a true liberal, Baron József Eötvös, offered broad rights to the nationalities by confirming linguistic rights. However, the challenge was that while it promised much and was indeed liberal in spirit, it fell short on implementation. There was always an important asterisk to the law that said everything was more or less within the limits of what is possible. Plus, there were no sanctions for transgressions.

In the end, the law was essentially abandoned by Hungary's rulers. It needs to be clear that the Hungarians rulers, who were drawn almost exclusively from the gentry, resisted reform at every step including substantial land reform. Most importantly, unlike the Austria government, the voting franchise was hardly touched making Hungary rather uniquely outdated. To be sure, the gentry class wanted to hold its dominant position, but they feared that any change to the voting franchise would also empower the minorities. In terms of voting rights, while much of Europe went one way, Hungary went another by actually reducing the franchise.

For example, by the 1870s there were massive changes in the national education curriculum that took Hungary further away from tolerance. Slovak language schools were shut in 1874 and the Slovak Cultural Center was closed in 1875. With growing hostility to minorities came also a rise in anti-Semitism in what was an otherwise tolerant Hungary. After all, Europe's largest synagogue designed by Austria's Ludwig Forster and finished in 1859 is the breath-taking Dohány Street synagogue in the heart of Pest. Hungary's Jewish community, which numbered roughly 5 percent but was heavily urbanized: in 1910 nearly half of Budapest's doctors, lawyers, and journalists were Jewish. The Budapest Jews were on the one hand a showcase of successful assimilation. But for many others they were potentially hostile to the traditional Hungary its gentry was trying to preserve, with its big estates semi-feudal atmosphere, Christianity, and national costumes. Jews, some argued, brought capitalism and secularism, which amounted to a huge threat. Readers familiar with Hungary in the twenty-first century should find a bit of *déjà vu* in this.

On the plus side, the years preceding the First World War were notable for scientific, cultural, and artistic achievements. Indeed, Vienna became the epicentre of that making the city a kind of birthplace of modernity. The period gives us the Secession movement of Gustav Klimt, Koloman Moser, Joseph Maria Olbrich, Carl Moll, and later Klimt's protégé Egon Schiele and others, the architecture and design of Adolf Loos and Otto Wagner, the new approach to the mind by Sigmund Freud and countless others. Franz Joseph also transformed Vienna making it the Vienna one visits today. In 1857, the medieval walls, which had saved Vienna twice from Ottoman invasion but proved useless against Napoleon's armies, were torn down making room for the magnificent Ringstrasse. It showcased Austria's great achievements through a new parliament, city hall, opera, university, theatre, public parks, gardens, and museums. Different architectural styles appeared: renaissance for the university, gothic for the city hall, and Greek revival for the Parliament. The symbols of the new Vienna embodied civic pride, progress, parliamentary government, education, and culture.

However, darker things were there too. The anti-Semitism of Vienna's Mayor Karl Lueger, who is credited also with making Vienna a modern city, is indicative of the dark forces behind the façade of fin de siècle Vienna. Austria's Jewish community had been more or less freed from restrictions by Joseph II 1792 Edict of Toleration. As in Budapest, while Jews were less than 10 percent of the city's population, they were the majority of the city's doctors, journalists, and lawyers. Moreover, the Jews of Vienna were integral to the financing of Vienna's cultural flowering. The story of Gustav Klimt's *Portrait of Adele Bloch Bauer*, painted between 1903 and 1907, tells multiple stories. It tells us of the role of Jews in Vienna's creative milieu but also of the new anti-Semitism that came after the First World War and Austria's complicated relationship with fascism, anti-Semitism, and memory after the Second World War. The painting was subsequently nationalized in a way by Austria after the war and displayed in the Belvedere Gallery until after a lengthy legal battle, it was returned to the heir of the original owner. As well, while Lueger ran the town, Adolf Hitler was eking out an existence in flophouses there trying to sell his watercolours. Hitler learned his anti-Semitism from Vienna and Lueger. Josef Stalin was also surviving there too around the same time. Stalin, however, still has a plaque outside the Schönbrunn guest house where he stayed briefly in 1913. Complete with a profile of an older Stalin, the plaque was placed there in 1949 by Austria's communists. As we shall see later, little did they know then that Stalin would in fact save Austria from communism after the Second World War.

The biggest change to a city was Budapest. Its transformation is the most comprehensive in the nineteenth century. If you imagine Budapest in 1848 it was a hardly a metropolis but a city of roughly 120,000 mostly German-speaking people, dreary, dirty, and depressing. To recall, the 1848 revolution saw Buda and Pest (and Óbuda or Old Buda, too) united as a single city. This was Széchenyi's dream to have a single city to make a great European capital that, if things went according to plan, could rival Vienna. It never did but the Hungarian tried. The Habsburgs had annulled the 1848 decision, but the 1867 compromise opened up the possibility to unite once again which was completed in 1873 by joining Buda, Pest, and Óbuda. Budapest's new planners, complete with a powerful board of public works, had ambitious goals: create a world class city that was also an exercise in nation building. In 1892, Budapest officially joined Vienna with the title "Capital and Residence".

As an incentive, the Hungarians were also planning a celebration of their millennium in Central Europe in 1896 so the pressure was on. They borrowed some ideas (and money) from Franz Joseph's Vienna, Haussmann's re-do of Paris and London, but they injected their own eclecticism into things. The millennium celebration was also designed to sever the Hungarians from its "eastern" past and wed the future to the West. Rumour had it they scholars had decided the Hungarians arrived in 894 but was changed to 896 in order to get things completed. The number 96 became the lucky one. Leaving aside Széchenyi's Chain Bridge, completed in 1849, and cultural buildings already mentioned, the rush to the millennium and the fair that accompanied it delivered remarkable things. A new bridge was built to honour Franz Joseph in 1896—Franz Joseph I Bridge is now Liberty Bridge. Franz Joseph also helped pay for the Budapest Opera house on the new Champs Elysees-esque boulevard that ran from the heart of Pest to a city and Heroes' Square. The boulevard, with its grand apartments, neo-renaissance mansions and shops, started out as Sugar street and changed its names as regime types came and went. In 1885 it became Andrássy Street, after Gyula Andrássy, the key figure in the 1867 compromise and later foreign minister of Austria-Hungary. In the period after 1920 it had squares named after Hitler and Mussolini. During the communist period (1948–1990) it changed its name three times—from Stalin Street to Avenue of Hungarian Youth during the 1956 revolution to People's Republic Street. In 1990, it was back to Andrássy Street.

Two new train stations, *Keleti* (Eastern) and *Nyugati* (Western), were constructed, rings roads on the Pest side, art galleries, a renovated and refurbished castle district and continental Europe's first underground line that ran below Andrássy Street. Epic art was also the order of the day on a massive scale. Benczúr's aforementioned *Liberation of Buda Castle* among others is typical of the era for encapsulating the Hungarian struggle for survival. Mihály Munkácsy's 16 × 5 metre fresco titled "Hungarian Conquest of the Carpathian Basin" depicts Árpád's and the Hungarian tribes' arrival in the Danube basin in 896. Originally painted for the new Parliament's Chamber of Representatives, it was deemed too big and now decorates the wall in the Speaker's Audience Chamber. Munkácsy's other great fresco decorates the roof of the foyer of Vienna's Kunsthistorisches Museum.

More things came after 1896 like Saint Stephen's Basilica in downtown Pest, 96 metres tall, of course, Heroes' Square with its Millennium Monument, the art-nouveau Academy of Music and Gresham Palace. The Millennium Monument in Heroes' Square deserves a bit more detail. Built as a kind of Valhalla to Habsburg and Hungarian greats, it was never really completed until 1929, which allowed the Hungarians to sweep away the Habsburg statues and have someone like the anti-Habsburg hero Kossuth to appear. Like almost every project of the era, the nationalities did not even appear as an afterthought. As in 1848, Hungarian nationalism remained inclusive, in that you could easily become Hungarian as long as you learned Hungarian.

But by far the most spectacular accomplishment is the Parliament. It was intended to be finished for 1896 but completed in only in 1902. Nothing captures better the essence of how the Hungarians saw themselves and their future in Europe. If anything, the twentieth century was the Hungarian century. It turned out as anything but that. Neo-gothic, modelled to a degree after parliament in London, the architect Imre Steindl achieved the unachievable but sadly died only weeks before it opened. It is one of the world's largest public buildings at 265 metres long, 123 metres wide and, of course, 96 metres in height. With its two massive chambers it has always been an anomaly of sorts for a country that has such a bad and limited experience with parliamentary democracy.

By 1900 it was a metropolis and one of the best examples of a city as nation building tool especially given that the whole project served as a warning to the nationalities. German speakers started speaking Hungarian and assimilation was the order of the day. Budapest, due to both assimilation and growth, became a truly Hungarian city. Indeed, for Hungary the period between 1867 and 1914 amounts to a kind of golden era with 1900 the zenith. The ambience is best captured by John Lukacs's *Budapest 1900*. Lukacs highlight the enormous changes—huge growth in population becoming Europe's seventh largest city by 1900, banks, schools, newspapers, and railways lines. Like Vienna, Budapest's Jews played an outsized role in all this and would pay a price later. In hindsight, Budapest was a city built for a greatness that never really happened as the Hungarians headed for a catastrophe largely of their own making. If Hungary's official narrative, at least the one on display in the National Museum, suggests that they were simply prisoners of dualism, nothing could be further from the truth.

A War to Save Everything

An extraordinary number of books have been written examining the origins of the war, its implementation, and the multiple peace agreements that ended it. For the purposes of this book, it is enough to say that much of Central Europe started the war on wrong side of history but ended up on the right side. Historians can largely agree on what factors caused the war but often disagree on which ones to emphasize. In any case, it is important to note that the war that came in the summer of 1914 served, at least at the beginning, multiple interests. The alliance structure, that locked Austria-Hungary and Germany together on the one hand and the United Kingdom, France and Russia on the other, was a key determining factor. Plus, an arms race had been heating up and more and more we saw states largely beholden to the influence of war hungry military leaders. Austria's Chief of the General Staff Conrad von Hötzendorf was emblematic of this tendency. He had long argued for war as a way to go back to the good old days before democracy. Plus, there was a real problem with elements in Serbia doing their best to de-stabilize the Habsburg Empire. The nationalists wanted war because it would advance their cause. Many socialists argued the same. Conservatives sought a war to hold back social change. The Hungarians, who end up as the war's biggest losers, were also on side and given their role in blocking every reform of the Empire, it is fair to say that they are instigators too hoping that by dealing with the Serbs Vienna would also help put to rest the simmering nationalist tendencies in their space too.

By assassinating Franz Ferdinand and his wife Sophie in Sarajevo on 28 June 1914, the assassin Gavrilo Princip went on to become the most successful terrorist in history. He set out to destroy the Habsburg Empire and create conditions for all Serbs to live in one state. By the end of the war, that was all achieved. Princip, who was only 19 then, and arrested immediately after the shooting, first tried to kill himself with cyanide but failed. He spent the next four years in jail in Theresienstadt where he died of tuberculosis in April 1918 just months before the war ended. He knew full well that his acts would haunt the world forever. Theresienstadt, named by Joseph II for his mother, Empress Maria Theresa, was a Habsburg fortress town. It is now in the Czech Republic. It would become even more notorious during the Second World War when the German occupiers would make it the location for their showcase concentration camp for Jews as a way of convincing the world that their intentions really were noble after all. This was of course a lie. But more on that later.

Princip's act did start the war and instead of letting Austria deal with the Serbs, who had really invited the catastrophe, all of Europe jumped in to save everything possible or create a new reality—socialism, conservatism, liberalism, nationalism, the old order, the good ole days, the new order, the old regimes, and the new regimes. The Italians, wary of missing out, joined the Entente side in 1915 in exchange for parts of the Balkans. They too could not allow Europe to go somewhere without them. Because they had no choice, Central Europe's subject nationalities were on side too—they had yet to become the forces of disintegration they would become as the war evolved. Readers interested in a distinctly Czech take on the First World War Jaroslav Hašek's *The Good Soldier Švejk*, written shortly after the war and inspired by the author's own experiences, providing a comical and telling look into Austro-Hungarian soldiers during the First World War, focusing on the character of Josef Švejk, an enthusiastic soldier whose incompetence exposes the many faults of the Austro-Hungarian military.

It is important to avoid reading history backwards. The Habsburg Empire was not destined to collapse. As others have noted, the Vienna half of the monarchy worked quite well. The weak link was the Hungarian half which had consistently pursued short-sighted policies.

The Central Powers mobilized some 23 million people, of which 8 million came from the Habsburg Empire. The Entente mobilized 42 million men. For Austria-Hungary it needs to be stressed that the nationalities were not fifth columns. They would become that as events during the war, especially the

Bolshevik Revolution and Russia's exit from the war, would hasten the collapse of Austria-Hungary. To be sure, at least at the start of the war the "subject" peoples hoped the war could get them a better deal in a new empire. But the facts on the ground changed. Lenin's success in October and his decree on peace was not entirely meant for the Russian audience. Lenin expected a new international order, and the notion of self-determination and new states was on the table. The new state's first foreign minister, Leon Trotsky, who also spent time hanging around the cafés of pre-war Vienna, particularly the Café Central, published the secret treaties that laid bare the cynicism of the war. It was a brilliant move. The disintegration of the old empires was on the table in what was a foreign policy masterstroke.

But things were changing elsewhere. The US entry into the war in April 1917 emboldened the champions of national self-determination and democracy. Strong diaspora communities of Central Europeans in the United States lobbied the US Department of State. Governments-in-exile were set up. The interwar Czechoslovak leader Tomáš G. Masaryk, who during the war was an exile politician, comes to mind as the archetype of this period, as he had been calling for the break-up of the Empire throughout the war. Ignacy Paderewski, a key spokesperson for renewed Polish independence also developed a friendship with Wilson. There were others. The future of Central Europe was in some ways made in the United States, and President Woodrow Wilson emerged as the spokesperson of this vision and he played an outsized in shaping Central Europe even though he never travelled there. As such, Wilson memorials were in some places in Central Europe, but not in others. As we shall see, it makes sense that we find him in the Czech Republic, Poland, Albania, Serbia, and Slovakia. Ask any Albanian about who saved Albania from disappearing after the First World War and they will say Woodrow Wilson. Slovakia even entertained a proposal to name Bratislava "Wilson City" after the war. For reasons specific to Germany and Hungary as we shall see, he is almost nowhere to be found in any of those countries. Only Austria is the exception, as Wilson gets a small memorial in Klagenfurt for his role in keeping the Austrian part of Carinthia in Austria after the war. In essence, he gets a monument because on that occasion, Wilson's concept of self-determination worked for the Austrians. A recent exhibit to the legacy of 1918 100 years later in Hungary vilified him and blamed him, and French Prime Minister Georges Clémenceau, for the calamities that followed the war.

Wilson's response to the changing world was the Fourteen Points of January 1918 that set in motion the disintegration of the Habsburg Empire. For Central Europe, points 10, 13, and 14 matter most. Point 10, in a somewhat ambiguous way, pointed to self-determination for the peoples of the Habsburg Empire. What Wilson actually said was that "the people of Austria-Hungary, whose place among the nations we wish to see safeguarded and assured, should be accorded the freest opportunity to autonomous development". What this came to mean, especially as the facts on the ground changed, was that independence for some nations was assured. Point 13, drafted with Paderewski's help, was more explicit. It called for the re-creation of a Polish state with access to the sea. Point 14 called for the creation of an association of nations to safeguard peace, independence, and territorial integrity. The subsequent League of Nations that was formed and its minority rights treaties would have a very specific impact on Central Europe as we shall see.

Conclusion

In March 1918 the Bolsheviks negotiated a disastrous peace treaty with Germany at Brest-Litovsk that took Russia out of the war. Germany acquired immense territory to its east foreshadowing something similar from Hitler. For Lenin and Trotsky, the peace treaty was, at least for them, a temporary setback that would not matter in the long when proletarian world revolution triumphed. The treaty revealed an even nastier side of Germany ambitions in its east which would re-appear in 1939. Lenin and Trotsky were proven wrong in the long run but in the short run they still had to fight to keep Russia together in a prolonged civil war that would last until 1921. Russia, which would become Soviet Russia, would prove to be the only multi-ethnic empire to survive after the war.

The year 1918 also proved to be the undoing of the Habsburg, German and Ottoman empires too. The former had performed very badly in the war, especially in the Balkans in early battles with Serbia. Franz Joseph, in power since 1848, died in 1916 and was succeeded by his nephew who became Charles I, destined to rule for only two years where he tried, without success, to get Austria out of the war and to reconstruct the Empire by federalization. Labour unrest, food shortages, and implacable nationalities helped to scuttle all his plans. Croats, Czechs, Poles, Serbs, Slovaks, and Slovenes were finished with Vienna's rule. Circumstances at the war's end forced him to renounce participation in Austrian affairs, but he refused to abdicate. After two failed attempts to reclaim the Hungarian crown in 1921, he died in exile in 1922 in Portugal. Austria's destiny was to be a small, bitter, and poor nation beset by the same political violence that defined much of Europe in the 1920s and 1930s.

The year 1918 was a particularly bad one for other reasons. As noted, at the turn of the century, Vienna was the centre of a cultural and artistic explosion. In 1918, the war ended but a flu pandemic—erroneously called the Spanish flu even though it started in the United States and spread to Europe by US soldiers—in the same year wiped away some of the Empire's greatest artists and designers: Gustav Klimt, Koloman Moser, Egon Schiele, and Otto Wagner. Gavrilo Princip also died in 1918.

Germany, while never occupied, surrendered in November 1918 after four fruitless years of trench warfare. The Kaiser fled in November and spent his life in exile in the Netherlands. A republic was declared, and the new Germany entered into a prolonged period of instability and low-level civil war as left and right fought it out. The Weimar Republic, named after the city where it was proclaimed, would face enormous challenges from within and without, leaving it an easy victim to the machinations of extremists who would be the principal architects of instability. The same extremists would also tout themselves as the only guarantors of stability.

The year 1918 in the Hungarian half of the monarchy did not fare much better. Lacking a government in exile like the Czechs or Poles, or even likeable leaders, it fell to the aristocracy to find a way out. By October 1918 they had a new council that promised a totally different future. With Count Mihály Károlyi, one of Hungary's largest landowners and from a very famous family, the new government immediately cancelled the 1867 compromise. Like Charles in Vienna, Hungary promised voting reform, federalization, and democratization. But the facts on the ground told another story as we shall see. Moreover, Károlyi's plans would go awry, spelling even more disasters for Hungary in 1919 and 1920. On 28 October 1918, the Czechs declared independence setting off an unstoppable chain reaction of disintegration. National self-determination of a kind would determine the fate of Central Europe when the peacemakers gathered in Paris in 1919 to re-make much of the world.

For Further Study

Books (Fiction and Non-fiction)

Graml, Gundolf. "History, 'The Sound of Music,' and Us." *American Music* 22, no. 1 (2004): 133–144.
Hašek, Jaroslav. *The Good Soldier Švejk and his Fortunes in the World War*. London: Penguin, 2000.
Judson, Pieter. *The Habsburg Empire: A New History*. Cambridge, MA: Harvard University Press, 2016.
Lukacs, John. *Budapest 1900: A Historical Portrait of a City and its Culture*. New York: Grove Press, 1990.
Rady, Martyn C. *The Habsburgs: To Rule the World*. New York, NY: Basic Books, 2020.
Roth, Joseph. *The Radetzky March*. London: Granta Books, 2002.
Stach, Reiner. *Kafka: The Early Years*. Princeton, NJ: Princeton University Press, 2016.
Storch, Ursula. *Klimt: The Collection of the Wien Museum*. Ostfildern: Hatje Cantz, 2012.
Taylor, A.J.P. *The Habsburg Monarchy, 1809–1918*. London: H. Hamilton, 1948.
Winder, Simon. *Danubia: A Personal History of Habsburg Europe*. London: Picador, 2013.

Films

Amadeus (1984). Directed by Miloš Forman. United States.
Der Untertan [*The Kaiser's Lackey*] (1951). Directed by Wolfgang Staudte. East Germany.
Sissi (1955). Directed by Ernst Marischka. Austria.

CHAPTER 2

The Interwar Failures, 1918–1939

As we have seen, one cannot view the Habsburg Empire as on some inexorable drift towards collapse. New national, and what were also dangerously nationalizing and nationally defined, states were by no means inevitable, although the war made them possible. However, as the facts on the ground changed and self-determination appeared irreversible, it really did not matter how much reform either Budapest or Vienna promised, as the fate of the region was decided by the victorious Great Powers. But, at the same time, we cannot see the period after the war as just an inevitable march towards authoritarianism, intolerance, rampant ethnic cleansing, and genocide. Bad forces needed to align. That aside, the Central Europe that emerged after the war was extremely vulnerable and also a power vacuum. Into that vacuum went the worst elements of the twentieth century.

As the peacemakers gathered in Paris in 1919–1920, the task was enormous. Trotsky's publication of the secret treaties had exposed the brazenness of war aims while Wilson's Fourteen Points had introduced some worthy and even lofty goals. Wilson, although he never travelled to Central Europe, would end up shaping its destiny in multiple ways, which, as noted earlier, made him either a hero or a villain. He holds a special place in Hungary's official history, where he is maligned as an ill intellectual who let his second wife make all the decisions. The key problem for peacemakers was Germany with multiple ideas circulating. In the end, the Versailles Treaty assigned Germany with war guilt, occupation, reparations, and territorial losses to the East and West . Too much has been made of the harshness of the treaty as worse was done elsewhere. Moreover, while the Bolsheviks were considered too savage and not invited to the salons of Paris to make a new world, they were there in spirit, as halting the spread of their radical ideas was a key aspect of the peace settlement and after. The world needed to be "safe for democracy", as Wilson said, but also safe from the Bolsheviks too. As we shall see,

© The Author(s), under exclusive license to Springer Nature
Switzerland AG 2021
R. C. Austin, *A History of Central Europe*,
https://doi.org/10.1007/978-3-030-84543-8_2

with only tiny exceptions, the left almost disappeared in Central Europe and the Balkans after the war, as politics was largely the domain of the right and extreme right with ruinous implications.

Peace Treaties: St. Germain and Trianon

Alongside the Versailles Treaty, two additional treaties shaped the future of Central Europe. Indeed, the maps of 1919–1920 still shape the region from Poland to Albania with only a few exceptions. Republic-style government with a commitment to parliamentary democracy became the norm and new states appeared and some states re-appeared: a tiny Austria and tiny Hungary, Albania re-emerged, Czechoslovakia, Estonia, Finland, Latvia, Lithuania, and Poland. There were some monarchies too: a smaller Bulgaria emerged and an enlarged Romania came to be as well. One of the biggest victors of the Peace Conference was the creation of the Kingdom of Serbs, Croats, and Slovenes, better known as Yugoslavia.

With the Habsburg Empire defunct in 1918, Austria started its experience with republican style of government as the first Austrian republic (1918–1938). Unlike the Hungarians, who would spend much of the twentieth century lamenting massive territorial losses, Austria would accept its lot but try to unify with neighbouring Germany. *Anschluss*, as it became known, was for most Austrians after the war the best solution. Already in November 1918 a German, Austria emerged out of the Empire claiming territory in the Czech lands, Poland, and Tyrol, which also sought unification with Germany. This was not to be, as the victorious allies banned the unification idea and gave Austrian territory to the new Czechoslovakia and Italy too. Hitler would successfully put *Anschluss* back on the table in 1938.

The Treaty of Saint Germain-en-Laye of 10 September 1919 confirmed Austria's miserable future. Austria was left with little more than its historic crown lands. It handed over territory to Italy and Romania in addition to its territorial losses that helped create Czechoslovakia, Poland, and Yugoslavia. The loss to Italy would hurt the most with the new border between South and North Tyrol at the Brenner Pass, leaving a majority German-speaking population in Italy. Hence, self-determination did not work there, and Sud-Tirol became heavily mourned and memorialized in Austria since then. Austria, with its questionable national identity between the wars, was an unstable collection of right and left militants, an often progressive and over-populated Vienna countering a Catholic and conservative countryside. Add to this its own brand of Austro-fascism, the meddling of Italy's fascist dictator Benito Mussolini (and later Hitler), interwar Austria was volatile and a hotbed for political extremism. The Vienna of 1900 was a distant memory and Vienna of 1919 drifted to obscurity and was on the verge of starvation saved only by US relief.

Hungary was a trickier story. Count Károlyi's new republic of 1918 collapsed, and he fled to a life in exile, sometimes vilified, sometimes not, depending on who was in power. Hungary's new neighbours grabbed as much land as they could with the encouragement of the Allies. Károlyi's government fell to a communist/terrorist government led by Béla Kun in March 1919 which did enormous harm to Hungary's prospects at the Peace Conference. Kun, a journalist from a middle class family had fought in the war for Austria-Hungary and was captured by Russia. He was smart enough to join the Bolsheviks and even impressed Vladimir Lenin. He returned from Russian captivity in 1918 and seized power more by coup than anything else. The fact that Hungary went communist for the next 133 days would do more harm than anything else in shaping the terms of the final peace treaty. Kun and his commissars did a lot in their brief time in power, even setting up a film studio and attempting a redo of Heroes' Square in Budapest to reflect the new beginning. He was more memorable for the Red Terror where hundreds of their opponents were killed. They fought as well to keep territory and get some back but were beaten by the Romanians. Like Trotsky, Kun countered on a world revolution that never came Kun fled to an exile in Soviet Russia only to be shot on Stalin's orders for "counter-revolutionary" activities in August 1938. Kun, of course, confessed to his crimes after years of imprisonment and torture. His story, and countless others from devoted communists, is best captured in the Budapest-born Arthur Koestler's novel *Darkness at Noon* (1940). Besides further destroying Hungary's prospects when borders were decided, Kun's other legacy was to poison things for Hungary's Jews. Since Kun and the leadership were largely secular Jews, they Jews became the new scapegoat when the Hungarians could no longer blame state breaking minorities like the Slovaks. Plus, by entering politics, the Jews had crossed the invisible line that Hungary's aristocratic leaders had set. Jews could be many things in the imagined world of Hungary's rulers—bankers, doctors, journalists—but not politicians.

In this chaos of 1919 came Admiral Miklós Horthy, a former adjutant to Emperor Franz Joseph and the last commander-in-chief of the Navy of Austria-Hungary. He arrived in "red" Budapest on a white horse, conjuring up images of Árpád in the Munkácsy painting. He restored the Hungarian feudal aristocracy to power and brought his strict Calvinist Christianity to the country. Kun's *Red Terror* gave rise to Horthy's *White Terror* which killed even more people. Both terrors targeted the Jews. In the White Terror alone some 20–30 percent of the victims were Jews. Horthy was never a fascist but for certain he was an anti-Semite, just maybe not one of the murderous types. In 1934, Horthy erected a monument to the victims of the Red Terror not far from the Parliament. It was destroyed in 1945 but it came back in 2018 in the same location. Unveiled by Orbán's government as a pure political message, there was never a memorial to victims of the *White Terror*.

Horthy's Hungary was conservative, with some democratic trappings (looking very similar to the style of government to emerge under Viktor Orbán after 2010), Christian, and feudal in essence, as the pre-war land arrangements were left largely untouched with a very restrictive voter franchise. His National Unity Party was the only one that mattered. Horthy ruled over a real anachronism. The cosmopolitan Budapest built in 1867 was gone. The city was built for a greatness that never happened. Horthy called the shots entirely dismissing Prime Ministers regularly, but he tolerated a faux opposition. To his credit, he did keep Hungary's home-grown fascists at bay until he was ousted by Hitler in 1944. Like Mihály Károlyi, he went in and out of favour in Hungary's ever changing historical narrative. The communists after the Second World War loathed him and would have liked him hanged rather than enjoying his life in exile in Portugal. After 2010, Horthy was back in the pantheon of national heroes.

Horthy stayed in power as regent in the Hungarian kingdom until 1944 when the Germans removed him for his failure to deliver on the elimination of Hungary's Jews. Horthy's ambitions for Hungary were tempered with the Treaty of Trianon in June 1920, the last of the Paris treaties for Europe. Too much has been written on Trianon to say much more. On the one hand, the Hungarians got what they deserved given the legacy of minority policy and their general enthusiasm for the war, even if they took a bit longer than Germany or Austria to get onside. Hungary's official narrative downplays their role in the war by arguing that they were dragged into the conflict, but they also pay scant attention to the harshness of their nationality policy. Nevertheless, they did come out worse than any other country, including Germany. Count Pál Teleki, a key interwar politician but a better geographer, delivered his famous *carte rouge* which showed, based on 1910 census data, where Hungarians lived in blazing red in historic Hungary in the hope that self-determination would be applied to them as well. For dramatic effect, he left areas with sparser populations white. It was not to be, and the treaty often used the ethnic principle largely against them. The implications were stark: Romania was handsomely rewarded with Transylvania, upper Hungary with its agriculture and Carpatho-Ukraine went to Czechoslovakia, Serbia got territory, and even Austria got a chunk of territory, Burgenland. The western Hungarian town of Sopron got a plebiscite and decided to stay in Hungary.

If one looks at just the facts it is without parallel far worse than Versailles. Historic Hungary was reduced by two-thirds territorially and lost half its population. An integrated trading and economic unit was broken. The army was reduced to 35,000. The Hungarians blamed Wilson because they thought he hated them although research shows that Wilson never had it in for the Hungarians. Hungary entered a period of mourning with flags at half-mast and the politics of symbolism, always important in Hungary, took off as the imagery of a partitioned nation took over along with the slogan "No, No, Never" (*Nem! Nem! Soha!*). Hungarian politics and its flawed democracy would be shaped by the quest for treaty revision at all costs. Horthy, like Hitler, hated Bolshevism and the Jews but both had a special loathing of Czechoslovakia. In 1936, Horthy apparently challenged 86-year-old Czechoslovak President to a duel. Horthy was 20 years his junior. Horthy's enthusiasm for treaty revision meant that he also encouraged Austria and Poland to make deals with Germany. Hitler would help Hungary put things "right" again in 1938 and after. In any case, as we shall see later, the Treaty of Trianon enjoyed a longer shelf life than any other treaty. A Pew research poll among NATO members in 2019 found that 67 percent of Hungarians still think the territory of neighbouring countries belongs to them. The Greeks were a close second. Trianon still shapes Hungarian policy in lots of peculiar ways. Chapter 6 explains its resilience as a mobilizational tool long after both the St. Germain and Versailles Treaties faded in public consciousness.

Most significantly, as Hungary found itself on the losing side with Austria and Germany, more than three million Hungarians found themselves under foreign rule. Some, estimated at 300,000, saw the writing on the wall and fled to Hungary which added its own problems that the government tried to solve with racist policies. Since minority rights were perceived as a zero-sum game by host governments, the Hungarians, like most minorities in Central Europe, fared badly in their new host states. Plus, it made regional cooperation, at least with Hungary, a near impossibility as the interwar Central European alliance structure, embodied in the Little Entente of 1921, brought together Czechoslovakia, Romania, and Yugoslavia, and was decidedly anti-Hungarian. Finally, multi-ethnic Hungary emerged as a largely homogenous state with only significant minorities of Jews and Germans. There were large numbers of Roma too, and not just in Hungary, but nobody was counting them yet.

Trianon spelled disaster for the Jews who were widely being blamed for Kun and the treaty. They found themselves no longer needed as Hungarians looked for jobs they were not qualified for. Numbering roughly 500,000, which before the war was largely a patriotic and assimilated community, they found themselves in trouble. The new government used the statistics against them—they were 5 percent of the population, but 20 percent of Budapest's population. Jews dominated certain sectors—law, medicine, mining, banking, and journalism. The Jews became the new scapegoat now that the Slovaks and others had their own states. In the political chaos of the time many fled—like inventors of the hydrogen bomb Leo Szilard and Edward Teller, filmmaker, director, and producer Alexander Korda, or the painter and designer László Moholy-Nagy among others. What the new laws meant in practice was that Hungary had Europe's first anti-Jewish laws in 1920 with the introduction of *numerus clausus* restrictions that were embraced in one way or another by Hungary's entire elite. The laws were easily sold to the Hungarian population who already bought the line that the Jews had destroyed Hungary and that the laws would allow Hungarians to "take back control" of their economy and cultural life. The law stipulated that Jews, as six percent of Hungary's population, should be only six percent of university spots. At that moment, Jews were roughly 30 percent of university enrolments. The law was repealed in 1928 but remained in spirit and came back even worse in 1938, 1939, and 1941.

Czechoslovakia—formed as an agreement between Czechs and Slovaks, bringing together the crown lands of St. Wenceslaus and Slovakia, along with Ruthenia—appeared even before the end of the war. Czechoslovakia had never existed, and because of that, was a country made up of territory from the Habsburg Empire. The historical boundaries of Bohemia, Moravia, and Silesia included a large group of Germans living in the borderlands, who would soon become known as "Sudeten Germans" and the territory known as the "Sudetenland". Right on the new borders of Austria and Germany, the majority German-speaking territory, which also housed a large amount of the country's industrial power, would continue to cause problems for Czechoslovak democracy throughout the interwar period.

Given its legacy of industrial development within the Habsburg Empire, it was in a strong economic position with the inclusion of the Sudetenland. In 1918, the bigger the better dictated the thinking keeping in mind that in 1989, when communism collapsed, that would no longer be the case. The new state was a tiny Habsburg Empire, in a way, with large minority groups—the Germans even outnumbered the Slovaks. Also, there were substantial Hungarians and the Ruthenians in the country's east. The Roma were there too, but not counted in the census (yet). Promising the new state would be like Switzerland, Czechoslovakia did extremely well out of the Paris treaties, which helps to explain why Hitler hated the country so much. They were likely the best liked in Paris possessing a sophisticated and cosmopolitan leadership around the Czech leaders Masaryk and Edvard Beneš and the Slovak Milan Štefánik, who regrettably died in a plane crash in May 1919. Masaryk was not the typical figure of interwar Central Europe. He was a professor of philosophy and sociology and has a background that underlined a genuine commitment to democratic norms. In a rarity, given the times, he was even nominated for a Nobel Peace Prize twice. Beneš was the foreign minister and, like Masaryk, had completed a PhD and taught Sociology. Both abhorred war. Štefánik, the dreamer, adventurer, and astronomer, remains one of the most important figures of twentieth-century Slovakia. Rumours always persisted that he was murdered. The Czech's big struggle was with Poland over control of Teschen, in what had been Habsburg Silesia, and possessed a mixed population of Czechs, Germans, and Poles. The new states even fought a brief war for it in early 1919. The conflict was later solved by Great Power intervention, but it would come back again in 1938.

The new state was imperfect, but its track record between the wars was exceptional especially in its management of democracy and minority rights. One telling example was the richness of Czechoslovak democracy—only there could one find a legitimate Left and even a legal communist party. Its key fault was Czecho-centrism: for example, Czech was the language of state, which limited the role of non-Czechs. But again, with the standards in that period, it was ahead of its time despite its periodic bullying of the Slovaks and Germans and the marginalization of others. The Czechs, who felt their national awakening had gone the furthest by 1918, believed they were obligated to "educate" the Slovaks. This patriarchal attitude pushed the Slovaks to demand more from Prague. On the plus side, given the horrible fate of Jews in Central Europe even before the war, Czechoslovakia was well and above the most tolerant country. While democracy in the region was largely destroyed elsewhere by a combination of external and internal forces, Czechoslovak democracy would die entirely from external forces.

An independent Poland of a sort had emerged during the war under the Central Powers in 1916, but a real independent Poland, based largely on Wilson's 13th point, appeared in 1918. The new state faced even more challenges than the others. It had to contend with the legacies of the partitions which set all three regions apart from each other on every level. Plus, as a buffer state between Russia and Germany, Poland would have to grapple with rapacious neighbours. While the past weighs heavily everywhere in Central Europe, it was heaviest in Poland. In this context, various versions of just what the Polish state should look like emerged and like everywhere except Hungary, the battle between left and right played out and, like everywhere else, ended in dictatorship.

To start though, Poland offered an extremely dynamic political space with multiple Polish and ethnic-based parties. Much of the period was shaped by two key figures: Roman Dmowski and Józef Piłsudski. In addition to a perilous geographic position, Poland, like Czechoslovakia, was an extremely mixed country. While Catholic Poles were 70 percent, 30 percent were Ukrainians and Belarussians in the east, and Germans in the west. Poland also included a large and mostly urbanized Jewish population which was confronted the anti-Semitism inherent in Poland's nationalism. Dmowski's National Democrats, in many ways the precursors to Poland's contemporary Law and Justice Party, sought a truly Polish state by offering exclusive nationalism and was largely hostile to Poland's minorities. For many Poles, their attitudes towards Ukrainians and Belarussians was largely based on the alleged superiority of the Polish nation. Assimilation was the only option. Piłsudski's Socialists, who ended up shaping the period, rejected the extreme nationalism of the right and offered a much more inclusive policy to the minorities.

Territorially, Poland was a net victor in Paris, but all observers noted that the Poles by far gave the longest history lessons and sought the most territory. In any case, they did win relatively big and with wars fought between 1918 and 1921, did even better. Of particular concern, at least for Germany, was the establishment of the Polish Corridor. The Corridor, majority German but only just, was roughly 10,000 square kilometres, and separated Germany from East Prussia. It was established as part of Wilson's points which guaranteed Poland's access to the sea. If you think of all the Hungarians left outside Trianon Hungary, think of the Germans, too, left outside Germany. The Free City of Danzig (Polish: *Gdańsk*, later to become famous as the birthplace of the communist opposition movement Solidarity in 1980) was also created as a result of the Treaty of Versailles. The League of Nations administered the city, as the treaty stated it was not to join either Germany or Poland. The overwhelming majority of the city's citizens were German, but the city's free status gave Poland its access to the Baltic Sea. By the mid-1930s the city's German citizens had largely bought into Hitler's vision for them.

From Democracy to Dictatorship to Subservience

Central Europe, and Europe in general, faced a number of challenges, but there were some bright spots in what emerged as an otherwise dark interlude from one war to the next. Wilson's envisioned League of Nations did emerge as a potential defender of the new treaties and a form of a rules based international order. In 1928, the Kellogg-Briand Pact abolished war, unless in self-defence, as an instrument of national policy. It sounds silly now, but it meant something then. What seemed most promising then was that the pact included the United States which had avoided tying themselves to Europe.

German war reparations were revisited not once but twice, with American intervention in the form of the Dawes (1924) and Young (1930) Plans that stabilized Germany financially. Germany gradually re-joined the world, first in a weird treaty with Soviet Russia in 1922 at Rapallo that allowed the two pariahs to get things they needed: Germany a chance to circumvent military restrictions imposed by Versailles and the Russians got access to German technology. The Locarno Treaties of 1925 brought Germany back by encouraging Franco-German rapprochement. Germany even recognized its Western borders but not those in the East. The Locarno Treaties were a disaster for Poland as they were not even part of the discussion. Peace, at least a temporary one, came to Western Europe. As a reward, in 1926, Germany even joined the League of Nations, although they left seven years later.

Keep in mind that the borders decided at the Peace Conference created an enormous number of national minorities—ethnically mixed states were the order of the day. Germans, largely urbanized, were everywhere in Central Europe. Poland was only 68 percent Polish, Romania only 72 percent Romanian—only Austria and Hungary had homogeneity. The Balkans was no different. Leaving aside multi-ethnic Yugoslavia with its Albanians, Croats, Macedonians, Montenegrins, Serbs, and Slovenes, Bulgaria had its large Turkish minority, Albania its Greeks, Greece its Turks and Macedonians. Plus, the Roma were everywhere in Central Europe, just hopelessly ignored and oppressed. The Second World War, would, to a degree, end what was a failed experiment in minority rights management. The European Union would emerge as the only viable source of enforcement of these rights.

The League of Nations introduced, for the first time, the notion of collective rights for minorities and the new states of Central Europe we obligated to sign on. Minority rights were not merely altruistic as there were genuine fears that without them disintegrative trends would gain the upper hand. Thus, the League became the arbiter of these countless disputes as minority groups brought countless challenges. Poland struggled particularly with its Ukrainian minority. The aforementioned anti-Jewish legislation in Hungary is also another example where on two occasions the League challenged Hungary on the law claiming that they violated Hungary's commitments under the Minority Rights Treaties.

However, as minority challenges may have been one of Central Europe's biggest stumbling blocks, it is worth examining an alternative scenario that took place between Greece and Turkey in the early 1920s. The defeated Ottoman Empire was handed the Treaty of Sèvres, the last of the five Paris Peace treaties. Sèvres was far worse than even Trianon—it envisioned the complete partition of the Ottoman Empire. Sèvres's betrayal of Western attitudes still resonates in Turkey today. Turkish nationalists rejected the treaty and in a war with Greece fought the Turkish War of Independence which created the modern republic of Turkey.

Greece, hoping to fulfil expansionist national aims to create a Greece of five seas, lost badly. Instead of signing on to minority rights, Greece and Turkey engaged in population exchanges. As opposed to an international legal based order to protect minorities, this was an alternative solution. Turkey's ethnic Greek citizens moved to Greece and Greece's Turkish citizens moved to Turkey. The Turkish Independence War became known to Greeks as the Asia-Minor Catastrophe. Both states were relatively homogenous. A total of 1.7 million people were moved—1.2 million Greeks from Turkey and half-a-million Turks/Muslims from Greece. Only the Greek Orthodox Church leadership remained in Istanbul and a small minority of Turks in Thrace in Greece. Population exchanges, as a form of serious policy, would haunt Europe for the entire century. The fate of minorities, especially Germans living in Austria, Czechoslovakia, and Poland, along with Hungarians living in Czechoslovakia, Romania, and Yugoslavia, would create enormous challenges to regional stability in the years preceding the Second World War. The nation builders in new states made no room for outsiders in their national narratives. These horrible outcomes were not lost on policymakers during the Second World War or after the end of the war or even at the end of communism in Central Europe. Homogeneity, for many decision makers, meant stability.

A weak and vulnerable region was saddled with being a bulwark against a resurgent Germany and stopping the spread of communism from the USSR. The region's best bet lay in keeping Germany weak and Soviet Russia excluded. But that was not to be. Being a bulwark against anything meant Central Europe had to work together. Faux cooperation only came with Soviet domination at the end of the Second World War.

Horthy was a strong anti-communist—he experienced the Red Terror—and a strong anti-Semite who blamed the Jews for the Kun interregnum. He still argued that Jews needed to find a proper place in society, which was not politics, and Horthy strongly supported the anti-Semitic legislation of the time. Horthy, at least according to his supporters then and now, emerged as the protector of Hungary from the extreme left and the extreme right. He was the "Saviour of the Nation". One poster of the era showed strong arms on a ship's wheel navigating rough seas of huge red waves. Below the scene the only word was "HORTHY!" Horthy became the country's regent/governor guided by his Calvinist commitment to "Christian morality" and the "nation".

Hungary turned out to be low-hanging fruit for Hitler. The polyglot and allegedly genteel Horthy was for sure an Anglophile but the United Kingdom could not provide treaty revision. Horthy's ersatz democracy drifted closer and closer to Germany to the point where Horthy and Hungary willingly cooperated to destroy the post-Paris European order. In 1932, Horthy appointed Gyula Gömbös, a near-fascist who likely wanted to be a fascist, to the post of Prime Minister and he moved quickly to embrace first Mussolini and then Hitler. But Horthy was able to restrain Gömbös's more sinister instincts. Gömbös stayed in power until he died in 1936 but by then Hungary was firmly in German camp. As we saw in the First World War, while Hungary's bellicose nationalism may not start wars, they will willingly follow others into one, especially Germans. Hungary's options did change dramatically with Hitler in power. Horthy likely even thought he could advise and even guide Hitler. After all, Horthy was an admiral and Hitler a mere corporal. Hitler proved to be the key to Hungary's territorial revision.

To be sure, Hungary had its own real fascists that were not mere copycats of Hitler's. Like Romania, which had the Iron Guard, Hungary had its Arrow Cross led by the notorious lightweight Ferenc Szálasi, who, despite his utter lack of talent for speaking or writing, was beyond inspirational for his followers. Twice sentenced to prison for subversive activity and anti-Semitic agitation, he served only one sentence between 1938 and 1940. Despite constant harassment from Horthy's government which loathed the extremists, the Arrow Cross would do surprisingly well in elections getting 750,000 votes of 2,000,000 in Hungary's very restrictive voting franchise. Power would come to them through the German army in 1944 with horrible results. That story is told in the next chapter.

Masaryk did not have to deal too much with home-grown fascists or subversives and he had nothing in common with Horthy's aristocratic approach. In keeping with trends in Czech identity, to a degree he linked himself to the martyr Jan Hus which worked as a great role model for Czechs but hardly worked for either Catholic Slovaks or Germans for that matter. Plus, it was a real stretch to create something verging on a shared history for the Czechoslovak state. To his credit, he did reject the link to the great and medieval past as unhelpful in the nation and state building process. Plus, he argued that Czechoslovakia's links with the West had to prevail.

The Czechoslovak state did provide a more humanistic approach to the issues of the day. For the Slovaks, the key issue was the full implementation of the Pittsburgh Agreement of May 1918. The agreement, to be fair, promised the Slovaks something that they did not get. This was partly because of the different levels of developments that existed between the Czech lands and Slovakia. What the American Slovaks hoped for was a true joint state of sorts with Slovaks largely running their own administration. This was not the case. The Czech position, and the Czech-centric nature of the state, was partly because the Czechs felt they were better qualified to run the country but also because of the state's incredible vulnerability. Fear of border revision was paramount everywhere, but it was especially present in Czechoslovakia which engendered a kind of existential crisis. It was not just a fear of Germany and Austria joining but also of a Habsburg restoration. In this situation, it meant the Slovaks gravitated to a more Catholic-oriented party, the Hlinka Slovak People's Party, which pushed for a stricter adherence to the terms agreed in Pittsburgh. This is not to say that the Slovaks were a disintegrative force, only that their vision for the state had real federal aspects.

The impact of the economic collapses in the US in 1929 changed the fate of Europe in horrendous ways. For Central Europe, it certainly emboldened the authoritarian models but also ramped up the disintegrative trends among the minorities. Czechoslovakia was particularly hard hit by this as the Sudeten Germans living in the north and west of Czechoslovakia were hard hit by the collapse of export markets.

Poland's trajectory was equally grim. In the left-right struggle, Piłsudski won out. Plus, things on the foreign policy front were hardly encouraging. Recall that the Locarno Treaties of 1925 had left the question of Germany's eastern borders open and that the Soviets and the Germans had been cooperating since the Rapallo Treaty of 1922. In 1926, amidst the usual problems—poverty, financial crisis—Poland slipped into dictatorship with Piłsudski's coup that was embraced by the majority of the population as a way to ensure stability. The depression of the 1930s made everything even worse. The Germans of Poland, just like their brethren, in Czechoslovakia, drifted to Hitler's Nazis. Indeed, the Polish Corridor would surface later as one of the many German justifications for war. In April 1935, Poland had a new constitution that created a highly centralized presidential system designed for Piłsudski. But unfortunately, Piłsudski died in May 1935.

Since Central Europe was desperately trying to fulfil its role as bulwark against Bolshevism, the question of the USSR remained paramount. As noted, the Germans and Soviets had agreed to cooperate in 1922. The power struggle to replace Lenin ensued which place Joseph Stalin at the helm by 1928. Of the massive changes introduced by Stalin, the standouts were collectivization of agriculture, five-year economic planning, and the idea of *Socialism in One Country* within the context of the fact that the USSR confronted a capitalist encirclement. The latter reflected in its most basic form, meant that world revolution was on hold and the USSR's success would be the best way to ensure the general success of communism globally. In terms of Central Europe, Stalin saw the region as simply as ring of essentially right-wing anti-Bolshevik governments which was largely true. As noted, only Czechoslovakia presented a relatively different political spectrum. Germany was also an exception and there Stalin did have some influence as through the Moscow-run Communist International, Stalin could direct the activities of Germany's influential communists. In the ongoing low level civil war of the Weimar Republic, Stalin originally based his policy on the flawed notion that for communists their main enemy was on the left, the Social Democrats, and not on the right. This prevented, at least to a degree, left wing cooperation that did open up possibilities for Germany's right and far-right.

The Soviet and Comintern line would alter in the 1930s when Stalin began a far more sincere rapprochement with Europe and the United States. The meant the US finally recognized the USSR in 1933 and in 1934 the Soviets entered the League of Nations. Stalin's Foreign Minister, Maxim Litvinov, who served as Foreign Minister from 1930 to May 1939 brought both a cosmopolitan veneer to Soviet diplomacy and a push for collective security. Stalin's foreign policy was predicated on the notion that some kind of war was inevitable with the capitalist world and that the USSR needed defined spheres of influence in Central Europe, especially the Baltic States.

If 1933 witnessed a long-awaited normalization between the US and the USSR, it also saw Hitler achieve power in January. Hitler and the National Socialist German Workers' Party (Nazis) made short work of Germany's fragile democracy and achieved a totalitarian state in what was record time making him the envy of Mussolini who had been in power since 1922 and Stalin who had full control by 1928. Put in power by the old guard and the business elite in hopes or returning to an imaginary past, Hitler made German democracy irrelevant within 12 months of achieving power legitimately. His vision, partially outlined in *Mein Kampf*, spoke of the twin dangers of Jews and Bolshevism—two sides of the same coin. Hitler's model, and its perceived economic success, did offer a compelling model for all the aspiring autocrats and totalitarians in Central Europe. Hitler was determined to overthrow the order set down in Paris in 1919–1920. That meant that the two countries facing the biggest immediate challenge were Austria and Czechoslovakia, given Hitler's pre-occupation with Germans living outside Germany's borders.

In the Czechoslovak case, Hitler had the three million plus Germans living there to manipulate, especially since the majority of them gravitated towards his National Socialists. The Czechoslovak government had already reacted to the changes in Germany by banning parties that endangered the "unity" of the Republic. With local fascists and others banned, the Germans largely chose a home-grown fascist-type party, the Homeland Front, led by the Konrad Henlein, a First World War veteran, a gymnastics instructor, and the leader of the ethnic German gymnastic society. Henlein's party narrowly missed being banned as well, but Masaryk stepped in and allowed the party to remain as long as they changed their name to the Sudeten German Party. Henlein's party, like Hitler's, were experts at creating chaos in order to claim that only they could end the chaos.

Czechoslovakia's May 1935 elections confirmed incredible support for Henlein, the largest of any party, along with other disturbing dis-integrationist trends, plus a big vote in favour of the communists. Henlein would later go on to become Hitler's appointee in the Sudetenland after Czechoslovakia was occupied in March 1939. He was captured by US forces at the end of the war and to avoid hanging, committed suicide in captivity in May 1945. The Slovaks were just as strident as the Germans demanding real autonomy in a newly configured state. But May 1935 also saw brought some faint hope. A treaty of mutual assistance was signed with the USSR that ensured Soviet assistance but only if France got involved first. Czechoslovakia's strengthened ties with the USSR did not win any regional allies, especially in Germany and Hungary where anti-Bolshevism was non-negotiable.

Austria's experience was equally disturbing. In the first decade after the war, Austria was unstable, extremely weak and reduced to near total insignificance. Austria's two major parties—Christian Socials and Social Democrats—formed hardened blocs and even developed their own paramilitary armies creating a highly polarized society. Into this mix, was Mussolini's meddling, plus home-grown Austro-fascism and Germany's National Socialism.

In 1932, when Engelbert Dollfuss of the Christian Social party became chancellor he determined to end the chaos by establishing and authoritarian state like Italy. Dollfuss was no Hitler as he was not attempting to completely remake Austrian society. His was a more classic authoritarian dictatorship and his rule was essentially Austro-Fascist by merging his party with the array of far-right groups in Austria. He disliked the Austrian Nazis but determined the best thing for Austria's future was the destruction of the Social Democrats and thereby assuring Mussolini (and Hitler) that Austria would not be Bolshevized. Violence, among other factors, helped him destroy the Social Democrats. But dealing with Nazis would not be easy, especially since their ranks in Austria swelled after Hitler became Chancellor. The independence of Austria, at least for a while, depended on the capricious and wholly unreliable Mussolini. Despite Mussolini's defence of Austrian independence, Hitler had made clear already in 1926 that Austria should become part of Germany.

Following the general trends practically everywhere else in Europe, Austria slipped into authoritarianism starting in March 1933. With the Parliament unable to function, Dollfuss gradually took control and Dollfuss essentially destroyed the Austrian constitution by destroying Austrian institutions. The lessons of 1933 would not be lost on Austrians after they regained their independence in 1955. Dollfuss's coup likely had the support of the majority of the population and brought the beginning of Austro-fascist rule, beholden to Mussolini, which lasted until Germany invaded Austria in March 1938.

But Dollfuss did not last long in power as little did he know that maybe the Social Democrats were not his number one enemies. Instead, it was the Austrian Nazis who went after him especially after he banned them in June 1933. Hitler responded to the ban by imposing an unmanageable tourist tax for Germans entering Austria which destroyed the tourism sector. Dollfuss did work towards the creation of a totalitarian state and had the support of the Catholic Church, the army, the police, and the bureaucracy. Within Austro-fascism was a very visible strain of anti-Semitism that had been deepening since the end of the war. The Austrian Nazis played the usual card: make as much chaos as possible to show that Dollfuss could not maintain control and herald themselves as the sole guarantors of stability. In February 1934, the Social Democrats were banned too, and in May 1934 Austria had a new constitution. In July 1934,

Dollfuss was assassinated in his office by Nazis. Dollfuss's assassins first denied him a doctor and then a priest as he bled to death. Hitler had encouraged the coup.

Mussolini smelled trouble and thought about his own intervention to save Austria from a German-takeover, which was dangerous for Italy given its control over South Tyrol. Hitler, already well-known for seeing how far he could go, pulled backed and reined in the Austrian Nazis, but only for a time. Dollfuss's successor, Kurt Schuschnigg, would govern with the same repression that his predecessor had. But Hitler's only retreated temporarily, and he continued to beat up on Austria. In July 1936, Austria and Germany reached an agreement whereby Germany recognized Austrian independence and promised to stop interfering in Austria, as long as Austria was pro-German, stopped anti-Nazi propaganda, and released all its Nazis in jail. Germany lifted the tourist tax. Another tactical retreat by Hitler as it was becoming increasingly clear that Austria had few supporters outside of Italy. But Italy was already in too deep with Germany to make any real difference.

Abandoned by the West

In 1938, Central Europe was cut loose and abandoned to the Germans and later the Soviets too. It also began a time of profound border changes that left a lasting impact on the region and its peoples. As we shall see, with limited to no international reaction, between March 1938 and August 1939, Austria disappeared, the Sudetenland went to Germany, Hungary grabbed southern Slovakia and Ruthenia, Czechoslovakia disappeared, Albania disappeared, the Poles grabbed contested Teschen, an "independent" Nazi puppet state of Slovakia appeared, and the most cynical of all agreements, the Nazi-Soviet Pact of August 1939, concluded the pre-Second World War remaking of the map of Central Europe. Worse things lay ahead.

If we start in February 1938, Hitler gave a three-hour speech where his vow to protect the German minority outside Germany's borders was made even more explicit. There was even a conciliatory tone to the speech—reminding everyone of Wilson's Fourteen Points, the denial of rights to Germans and the fate of "Nazi sympathizers" in Austria. Austria's Schuschnigg gave a speech too. In it, he appealed to his fellow Austrians to save Austrian independence and in reference to Austria's red and white national colours, declared, in German, "red and white until we are dead". To get another perspective on the Austrian drift into Germany's embrace, watch the *Sound of Music* (1965) which empathizes a certain side of Austrians that was not always obvious in the 1930s. The film played an outsized role in shaping Western attitudes towards Austria and Austrians to their immense benefit. What seems most obvious, given the attraction of German nationalism and anti-Semitism, is that the majority of Austrians were waiting to be saved by Hitler's Reich.

For Austria, things were dire. Schuschnigg travelled in February to meet Hitler at his Eagle's Nest, in Berchtesgaden, just across the Austrian border.

This meeting is extremely well-documented. If Admiral Horthy could expect respect from Hitler, the same did not apply to Schuschnigg, who was simply berated by Hitler who characterized Austrian attitudes towards Germany as a prolonged act of "high treason". Schuschnigg got his marching orders from Hitler and his henchmen, Foreign Minister von Ribbentrop, Franz von Papen, German Ambassador to Austria and Wilhelm Keitel, head of the German Armed Forces. Sometimes novels tell the stories of the 1930s (and after) better than the historians. The fate of Austria and the Hitler/Schuschnigg meeting is made more real in Eric Vuillard's novel *The Order of the Day* (2018).

Austria's new relationship, essentially a satellite of German, was the outcome. Most importantly, key Nazis joined the government, including Arthur Seyss-Inquart as Security Minister. Schuschnigg tried to buy time with a referendum on 13 March to decide Austria's future—to be free and independent or join Germany. It was hardly a free vote—only *yes* ballots were distributed. Hitler was enraged and ordered the cancellation of the vote. The Germans invaded Austria on 12 March 1938 to enthusiastic crowds. Schuschnigg appealed for no bloodshed in his final "May God Bless Austria" speech. Seyss-Inquart became Austria's new chancellor, legalized Austria's disappearance as a state and saw it integrated as a mere province in the Third Reich called *Ostmark*. Austrians were over-represented in the upper echelons of the Nazi party and Seyss-Inquart would later rise in the Nazi ranks after his stint in Austria going on to be a high functionary in German-occupied southern Poland and later *Reichskommissar* to German-occupied Netherlands. He was arrested after the war, charged with conspiracy, war crimes, and crimes against humanity in executed after his trial in the Nuremburg International Military Tribunal.

We will never know precisely how many Austrians supported the *Anschluss*. It is likely a majority of them. Hitler ran his own manipulated plebiscite in April that saw more than 99 percent in favour. The German takeover harkened back to 1918 when Austria tried to join Germany after the war and it also promised to end the two decades of economic failure and political instability. Most importantly, for many, the Germans would solve the Jewish question. Scenes of Jews cleaning Vienna's streets define the moment as Jews faced "Aryanization" campaigns, expulsion, property theft, and violence with worse to come. Lots of Austrians were made rich by this state-sponsored looting.

Mussolini was easily bought off and did not protest Austria's disappearance. He was looking ahead to an invasion of Albania by then, so he did not feel too left out. Hitler was grateful. Not much else was said as Mussolini had Albania on his mind anyway. Wilsonian self-determination took a nasty and unexpected turn. Next up was the Germans of Czechoslovakia who were sold-out by the British, French, Italians, and Germans in September 1938 in Munich. But prior to that, Hitler met Horthy and received him like a king. The goal: soften him up and get his help in the destruction of Czechoslovakia. The story of Munich and the dismemberment of Czechoslovakia has been well-told. Indeed, the Munich refrain has come to define betrayal and is the go-to alibi for all kinds of leaders trying to justify a war to prevent a war. The Czechoslovak delegation got its deal even though there was no Czech version of the agreement. The Czechs lost more than the German minority as Czechoslovakia was destroyed economically and became more or less defenceless. Only the USSR seemed willing to help but getting troops there would take too long.

Chamberlain famously referred to the German desire to remove Czechoslovak territories as "a quarrel in a faraway country between people of whom we know nothing". Chamberlain also called the country insignificant. That comment still resonates in Czech society. Upon his return to London after signing the Munich Agreement, the British prime minister experienced a surge of popularity, as British citizens commended him for preserving peace on the continent. However, Chamberlain's political opponent, Winston Churchill, accused the prime minister of being dishonourable, and predicted that Hitler would start a war anyway. Czechoslovakia's fragility and seeming artificiality were laid bare. The Slovaks (and the Ruthenians) turned a crisis into a cynical opportunity, saw an opening, and pushed for more autonomy, which they got. For the Slovaks, their Wilsonian moment of self-determination had arrived with Hitler's help. Slovakia drifted into one party rule by the Hlinka Slovak People's Party, which meant anti-Semitism, extreme nationalism and fascism of the copycat kind, complete with its own version of the Hitler Youth alongside fascist uniforms and salutes. The Czech lands did not fare much better, becoming an authoritarian state run by rule by decree fighting, real and perceived enemies everywhere, complete with its own waves of anti-Semitism.

In October 1938, Poland occupied the Czechoslovak region of Teschen with the approval of Nazi Germany. The annexation resulted in the expulsion of thousands of Czechs from the region and the *Polonization* of the territory. Poland had Germany's model to emulate as their takeover of the region looked just like the Nazi annexation of the Sudetenland, arguing that Poles deserved the same rights as Sudeten Germans. All Czech and German language education ended, and all Czech organizations were banned. In September 1939, less than a year after the Polish annexation, the city would come under the control of the Nazi Germany.

Hitler's victory in September 1938 was followed by more territorial revisions that had been alluded to in Munich regarding Hungarian (and Polish) minorities. Gathering in Vienna's Belvedere Palace, Hitler helped Horthy to what became known as the First Vienna Award in November 1938. The award allowed Hungary to occupy a chunk of Slovak territory with over 80 percent Hungarian population. Horthy arrived on his trademark white horse in what was, until Trianon, the Hungarian-named town of Kassa that became Slovak Košice to be Kassa again and to become Košice after Hungary lost the war. The Slovaks blamed their loss of territory on the Czechs and, of course, the Jews.

In less than a year, Churchill's prediction came true when Germany annexed the rest of the Czech lands, which consisted of what was left of the territories of Bohemia and Moravia in March 1939. The country ceased to exist for the better part of six years. A governmental crisis fought over the Czech-Slovak relationship played into Hitler's hands who decided he would recognize

Slovakia as independent. The German army invaded on 15 March 1939 and justified their actions in light of "Czech mistreatment" of its minorities. There was almost no resistance as the Czech lands—Bohemia and Moravia—became the Protectorate of Bohemia and Moravia. Hitler also allowed Hungary to reintegrate Subcarpathia with 500,000 people (only 5–10 percent Hungarian) and 4600 square miles. Slovakia was permitted to retain a quasi-independence in Hitler's new European order—as long as they towed the line.

Conclusion

The period between 1919 and 1939, known in hindsight as the interwar period, was primarily a dark one. Eleven new states emerged in Europe: new borders, new currencies, new nationalist narratives, and new democracies. The states of Central Europe seemed to buy in to the idea of parliamentary democracy. But democracy did not fare well. In Hungary, it is likely the Treaty of Trianon made it impossible for Hungary to be even a low-quality democracy. The Czechoslovak exception did work to a degree, only to be destroyed by Germany colluding with indifferent Great Powers. Poland was a dictatorship by 1926, Germany in 1933 and Austria in 1934. Outside of Central Europe, the story was no better. In the Balkans, Albania was a dictatorship by 1925, Yugoslavia 1929, Bulgaria and Romania in the mid-1930s. Greek democracy collapsed in the 1930s too. The Turkish Republic was never a democracy. It was indeed a combination of external and internal factors that led to such a continent-wide catastrophe. Into the mix, we see some extremely mediocre people in power trapped in narrow nationalist visions and looking for scapegoats. Keep in mind that outside of the Czech lands, one could not even speak of a middle class. In most cases, we see peasants and a conservative nobility trying to hold on to an imagined past.

The Paris peace treaties were not as bad as many later made them out to be. The challenges were immense. In the end, and this was not the fault of the peacemakers, a series of nationalist and nationalizing states appeared in Central Europe. States like Poland, Czechoslovakia, Romania, Yugoslavia, the Baltic States of Estonia, Latvia, and Lithuania, and even tiny Albania were determined to maintain the territorial status quo laid down in Paris. Bulgaria, Hungary, Germany, and Greece sought to overturn the status quo and national minorities were often the vehicle for territorial revision. Formal security arrangements for the region were lacking: there was only the Little Entente and vague commitments to Czechoslovakia and Poland. By the mid-1930s an alternative political model had taken hold everywhere. It was either fascist or authoritarian, always intolerant and determined to change the order of things. The year 1938 turned out to be the watershed year in that it was clear that Central Europe was in fact lost to the Germans and their Hungarian allies. All bets were off, then, as the region's vulnerability transformed it into a killing field. A region that in the late nineteenth and twentieth centuries punched above its weight in science, music, and literature shaped the fate of Europe again, in only tragic ways.

For Further Study

Books (Fiction and Non-Fiction)

Boschwitz, Ulrich Alexander, and Philip Boehm. *The Passenger: A Novel.* New York, New York: Metropolitan Books, Henry Holt & Company, 2021.
Heiman, Mary. *Czechoslovakia: The State that Failed.* New Haven: Yale University Press, 2009.
Illyés, Gyula. *People of the Puszta.* Budapest: Corvina Press, 1967.
Orzoff, Andrea. *Battle for the Castle: The Myth of Czechoslavakia in Europe 1914–1948.* New York: Oxford University Press, 2009.
Seegel, Steven. *Map Men: Transnational Lives and Deaths of Geographers in the Making of East Central Europe.* Chicago: University of Chicago Press, 2018.
Wiskemann, Elizabeth. *Czechs & Germans: A Study of the Struggle in the Historic Provinces of Bohemia and Moravia.* London: Macmillan, 1967.
Wolff, Larry. *Woodrow Wilson and the Reimagining of Eastern Europe.* Stanford: Stanford University Press, 2020.
Zweig, Stefan. *The World of Yesterday.* London: Pushkin Press, 2011.

Films

Babylon Berlin (2017). Directed by Henk Handloegten, Achim von Borries, and Tom Tykwer. German.
Budapest Noir (2017). Directed by Éva Gárdos. Hungary.
Talks with TGM (2018). Directed by Jakub Cervenka. Czech Republic.
Woman in Gold (2015). Directed by Simon Curtis. United Kingdom.

CHAPTER 3

The Second World War in Central Europe

The Second World War in Central Europe was characterized first by betrayal from Western powers that still resonates today and occupation by Germany and later the Soviet Union. Both these factors help explain the region's persistent sense of vulnerability. For many people, a double, even triple, occupation that amounted to unspeakable horrors characterized their wartime experience. The region, which has historically been stuck between two major empires, found itself literally divided between the Germans and the Soviets between 1938 and 1945. The beginning of the war, which started a year after the Munich Conference in September 1938, is remembered as a time when Western Europe turned its backs on the small nations of Central Europe in the hope of prolonged peace. The end of the war, which came just months after the Yalta Conference in February 1945, is again regarded with betrayal and resentment by some Central Europeans, as Western leaders once again appeased a dictator, this time Joseph Stalin, and allowed him to retain what he received in 1939 and gain control over the entirety of the region.

The war in Central Europe was particularly brutal, starting from mass repression against Jews in Austria and Germany, spanning German-occupied Poland, where the major killing camps were established, and culminating in Berlin in the spring of 1945. In many ways the fate of Central Europe shaped the fate of Europe as it faced mass murder and destruction on a level that Western Europe never saw. This was where two totalitarian leaders faced off, leaving absolute ruin in their wake. Cities like Berlin, Budapest, Dresden, and Warsaw were almost entirely reduced to rubble, and Poland lost about 21 percent of its population—six million people—one of the highest death tolls in the conflict. The notion of victim, and indeed who was the biggest victim, is very much part of Central European identity.

While German allies like Hungary or puppet states like Croatia or Slovakia were largely untouched by Nazi soldiers for the majority of the war, Poland was

© The Author(s), under exclusive license to Springer Nature Switzerland AG 2021
R. C. Austin, *A History of Central Europe*,
https://doi.org/10.1007/978-3-030-84543-8_3

especially targeted. Hitler's theory of the world, motivated by eugenics and Social Darwinism, which had nothing to connect it to Darwin's *Origin of the Species*, perceived most Slavs were a lesser race of humans, and that they needed to be subjugated and put to work by German masters, or eradicated entirely. Motivated by a desire to colonize Eastern Europe for the benefit of the German people, Hitler deemed that Slavs were not deserving of the bountiful natural resources of their lands. His drive for Lebensraum, or living space for the German people, was put to the test in Poland and much of Eastern Europe. Hitler aimed to entirely rid Central and Eastern Europe of Slavs and Jews through extermination or by resettling them in Siberia. Because Hitler targeted not only Jews, but also the "lesser" Slavic people, there is a sense of collective victimhood in this region, and the plight of the Jews had largely gone ignored until recent years.

Upon his successful takeover of Bohemia and Moravia in March 1939, and Slovakia made irrelevant, Hitler finally turned his attention to Poland. Although Hitler had signed a peace agreement with Poland in 1934, he did this only to prevent Poland from creating an alliance with France before Germany had a chance to prepare its army, and he now considered this agreement null and void. Hitler created another strategic peace agreement, the Nazi-Soviet Pact, with the Soviet Union to avoid a two-front war, knowing that his incursion into Poland would likely trigger a conflict with the Western powers. Despite the agreement, Hitler only wanted to use the deal to stall a war with the Soviet Union while he defeated or made peace with Western opponents, and ultimately intended to invade the country anyway, which he deemed necessary to defeat the Jews and Communists and achieve Lebensraum in the East.

German and Soviet Rapprochement

The Molotov-Ribbentrop Agreement was made between German and Soviet foreign ministers, Joachim von Ribbentrop and Vyacheslav Molotov, and signed on 23 August 1939. It was a precursor to the invasion of Poland, which Germany occupied on 1 September 1939. The Pact consisted of two parts: first, it outlined a peace agreement between the German and Soviet governments, pledging that neither party would attack each other for ten years, and to divide East and Central Europe amongst them, including splitting Poland in half. It also stipulated that neither party would side with the Allies. Ukraine fell under the German sphere of influence, as Hitler was interested in acquiring its agricultural resources, with Ukrainians as slaves, to feed the German people while the Baltics were given to the Soviet Union. The Nazi-Soviet Pact remains to this day a source of great controversy. In the current Russian narrative, fearing a war with Germany with no allies, the pact was a necessity for the USSR and largely in keeping with the trends of the time when borders became meaningless. For everyone else, it was a cynical agreement that started the Second World War. Russian President Vladimir Putin dismissed a European Union resolution in 2019 that stated that the pact laid the groundwork for the Second

World War which he argued was akin to blaming the USSR, alongside Germany, for the war. What is clear is that Soviet negotiations with the West on a security agreement collapsed largely because of the Soviet insistence on a sphere of influence—something the West had been unwilling to give.

Secondly, the Pact involved an elaborate trade agreement in 1940, which fortified German forces in the face of conflict with the West. The Soviets sent the Germans tons of food, such as grain, and natural resources, such as oil. In return, they received various manufactured goods, weapons, and machinery, such as trains, tanks, and explosives. The Pact was kept secret until the end of the war, when a copy of it was found in the Nazi archives. However, the Soviet Union denied the existence of the document until the fall of the USSR in 1989, when it was condemned by the last Soviet General Secretary, Mikhail Gorbachev.

Hitler justified the invasion of Poland by falsely claiming that the country had been working with the French and British to encircle the German forces and declare war. Just a week after the Molotov-Ribbentrop Agreement had been signed, German forces invaded the country. Two days later, on 3 September, France and Britain declared war on Germany. The Soviet Union occupied its part of Poland on 17 September 1939. Poles and others living there would experience a brutal Soviet occupation, followed later by a brutal German occupation to be followed by another brutal Soviet occupation.

The Allies had assumed that Poland would be able to defend itself for at least a few months, and Poland had said it would be able to fight for at least six months. However, Polish forces mobilized late, and the country fell within weeks, on 27 September. The last Polish unit surrendered on 6 October.

LIFE UNDER NAZI RULE

As we have seen in 1938, Austria was simply absorbed into Germany before the war, and any evidence of Austrian independence was suppressed and erased. Austrians fought in the German army and participated in organizations such as the SS and the Nazi Party. Indeed, given Austria's much smaller population vis-à-vis Germany, Austria provided an outsized contribution to the upper echelons of the Nazi power structure. By the end of the war, about 250,000 Austrian soldiers were dead or missing in action. Even more Austrian soldiers were held by Soviet forces as prisoners of war, and many of them served time in Soviet forced labour camps. 20,000 Austrian civilians had been killed in Allied bombing raids by the end of the war. While most Austrians supported Nazi policies, there was a small but significant resistance movement, which caused more than 10,000 Austrians to be arrested, and about 2700 to be executed. Austria was also the destination of many foreign workers during the war, who were made to take the places of Austrian civilians who had gone to the front in factories to keep the country's industrial production going.

While the pre-war Austrian regime had elements of Anti-Semitism, Jews were still allowed to participate in public life, and Austria housed many prominent Jews who had fled repression in Germany. However, this quickly ended after the annexation, and Jews were immediately targeted by Austrian and German forces. Aryanization policy meant that Jews were shunned from public life and forced to perform humiliating chores like scrubbing sidewalks. Sigmund Freud and his family left in June 1938 only after considerable international pressure. Roma were also targeted by German forces. They were forced to register with the government and were rounded up by the thousands to be sent to concentration camps in Germany. On 9–10 November 1938, Austria and the rest of Germany experienced *Kristallnacht*, when thousands of pogroms against Jewish businesses and homes were carried out. The police participated in these attacks, meaning that the Jews had nowhere to turn for safety or assistance.

In the 1943 Moscow Declaration, the Allies declared the *Anschluss* null and void, affirmed Austria to be the "first country to fall to Hitlerite aggression", and the myth that Austria was Hitler's first victim took root with long-term implications largely to Austria's benefit. The Allies pledged to reinstate the country as an independent state at the end of the war. Unlike Germany, Austria was also exempt from paying reparations to the Allies after the war. However, major Austrian cities and infrastructure were severely damaged, and it became one of Europe's poorest countries after the war. The state struggled to get by for several years after the end of the conflict, until money from the American-led Marshall Plan improved the situation after 1948.

While Czechoslovakia did not exist as an independent state during the war, with the traditional Czech lands of Bohemia and Moravia occupied and Slovakia a puppet state, the Germans regarded Czechs as a civilized people with German ancestry, so they were not as mistreated as the Poles, Ukrainians, and Russians. Czechs were to be "Germanized" and those who refused would be deported east. By the very cruel standards of German occupation, the Germans also treated the Czechs relatively well because the country was responsible for a large proportion of wartime manufacturing so it was deemed best not to harass the population in the interest of efficiency.

Despite early occupation by the Germans, the Czechs had a healthy resistance movement for the majority of the war and collaborated with the British during this time. Czech resistance during the Second World War remains a fundamental aspect of contemporary identity. Thousands of Czechs were arrested and killed in reprisals for resisting German occupation, including instances where entire villages were destroyed, especially after Operation Anthropoid successfully assassinated Reinhard Heydrich, a senior SS officer and Hitler's "Viceroy" in the protectorate since September 1941. Heydrich was killed by Czech and Slovak partisans parachuted into Bohemia in May 1942. Heydrich, who was also the chief architect of the destruction of the European Jews, was adored by Hitler. Hitler reacted to the assassination with incredible violence against the Czechs by ordering the arrest and execution of 10,000 Czechs. On the day of Heydrich's funeral, the village of Lidice near Prague, which allegedly aided the Czech agents involved in the assassination, was burned to the ground. The Czech government, headed by Edvard Beneš, had already escaped to London and remained there in exile, often coordinating with rebels back in the Czech lands. Czech partisan groups were also organized. On 4 May 1945, a national uprising started in Prague, quickly becoming 30,000 strong, who fought against 40,000 German troops for several days. On 8 May, the German troops gave up, and on 9 May the Red Army entered the city.

However, tens of thousands of Czech Jews fell victim to the Nazi machine and were deported to death camps. About 86,000 Jews were deported from the occupied Czech lands of Bohemia and Moravia, and about 71,000 of them died. Jews were initially deported to Czech transit camp Theresienstadt, where they were mixed with transports of Jews arriving from Austria, Germany, Slovakia, Hungary, and other European countries. Theresienstadt, or Terezín in Czech, served as the model camp where visiting delegations could see the "humanity" of German policy. Most Jews were sent onwards to eastern ghettos or death camps such as Auschwitz and Treblinka in occupied Poland.

After the dismantling of Czechoslovakia, the newly independent Slovak Republic became an ally of Germany, and a puppet state of the Third Reich. It was used as a strategic base for operations in Eastern Europe, and it participated in the attack against the Soviet Union in June 1941. It also declared war on the United Kingdom and the United States in December 1941.

Unlike Hungary, Slovakia consented to the removal of its approximately 88,000 Jews, and many of them were deported in 1942. The Slovak fascist group, called the Hlinka Guard, was also responsible for killing thousands of Jews during this time. About 57,000 were deported and systemically murdered in the Nazi camps before the Slovak government heard what had happened to them and refused to give up any more Jews of the 24,000 left. Several thousand managed to escape to Hungary at this time. The deportations stopped for over a year between 1942 and 1944, but after the Slovak National Uprising, Germany officially occupied the country, and they resumed again. In total, about 70,000 Slovak Jews were sent to death camps, where 60,000 of them were killed. In total, about 263,000 Jews who lived in Czechoslovakia before the war were murdered.

The Slovak National Uprising, which started in the provincial town of Banská Bystrica in Central Slovakia, lasted between August and October 1944. The uprising began with a rebel force of just under 20,000 soldiers, but this figure grew to over 60,000 after September, and was supplemented by 20,000 partisans. The uprising was supported by soldiers from 32 nations, including the United States, the United Kingdom, France, the Soviet Union, Poland, the Czech lands, and others. The rebellion was eventually squashed by the German Wehrmacht troops, and members of the rebellion were sent to concentration camps. Some escaped and joined partisan divisions. After that, Slovakia lost all of its independence, and an official German government was installed there for the remainder of the war. However, the German success was short lived, as the

Red Army arrived in the country in January 1945. After the war, Slovakia lost its independence and re-joined the Czech lands.

Hungary was another willing ally of Germany although it often pretends to be a reluctant one, or at least one that never really had a choice. As we have seen, the Hungarians saw collaboration with the Nazi regime as a way to get back vast territories which they had lost under the Treaty of Trianon, specifically Transylvania. By pledging to work with the Germans, and joining the Axis alliance in late 1940, the Hungarian state remained intact, and they had a large degree of freedom compared to other European countries for the majority of the war. The two "Vienna" Awards, one already mentioned in 1938 where the Hungarians took part in the partition of Czechoslovakia as a result of the Munich Agreement and the second in August 1940, which gave them a substantial part of Transylvania. Hungary had regained much of its "lost" "territory and the nation was jubilant. Horthy was likely at the height of his popularity. He doubled Hungary's size, bringing over two million ethnic Hungarians "home". In 1941, Horthy broke a friendship treaty with neighbouring Yugoslavia and, taking advantage of the German invasion of the country, invaded too and seized more pre-Trianon territory. Horthy's prime minister, the geographer Pál Teleki whom we first saw with his map at the Paris Peace Conference, decided it was better to kill himself than to violate a friendship treaty. His suicide noted, among other things, that Hungary had "allied itself with villains". In keeping with the dependency on Germany, Hungary took part in the German invasion of the USSR and sent the very ill-prepared Hungarian army there in late June 1941 with catastrophic results during and after the war.

While Hungary was generally in lockstep with Germany, in policy towards the Jews it was anything but. In fact, in 1944, Hungary was an enclave with the largest remaining Jewish population in Europe—approximately 800,000 people. Although the country had a large anti-Semitic movement, and was home to the Arrow Cross fascist party, there had been no concerted effort to kill Jews in the country. (Although nearly 20,000 were deported to Ukraine in 1941, where they were shot by the Einsatzgruppen.) In fact, when Hitler started to pressure Hungarian leader Miklós Horthy to deport the Jews in 1942, his prime minister, Miklós Kállay, personally protested, and they were spared. Nonetheless, the Hungarian regime was still quite repressive towards Jews, Hungary had already imposed anti-Semitic legislation in 1920 and followed German policy as early as the 1930s, restricting their ability to participate in public life and preventing them from marrying ethnic Hungarians. In April 1943, Horthy met Hitler again, this time near Salzburg. Hitler blamed the influence of the Jews on Hungary's poor war performance and demanded that steps be taken. Horthy would meet Hitler one more time in the same place in March 1944 to be told he was finished, more or less.

After Germany and the Axis powers faced a staggering defeat at Stalingrad in February 1943, the Hungarian leadership began to suspect that Germany would lose the war and tried to negotiate a peace agreement with the Allies.

When Germany caught wind of this plan, as the Allies leaked Hungary's intentions, they occupied the country on 19 March 1944. Horthy kept his job but was effectively turned into a puppet of the Nazi regime, while Kallay was sacked and replaced by a pro-Nazi prime minister, Döme Sztójay, who immediately set about deporting Hungary's large Jewish population, although at that point it was already clear that Germany would likely fall to the Red Army. Given the small size of the German occupying force, the Germans relied on extensive assistance from the local authorities. Arriving with the German soldiers was Adolf Eichmann, the deportation expert of the Nazi regime. His team was less than 200 people. Rural Hungarian Jews were rounded up and crammed into crowded and unsanitary ghettos, where they awaited deportation. In Budapest in June, the mayor decreed that the city's 220,000 Jews were forcibly expelled from their homes and put into about 2000 apartment buildings, or Yellow Star Houses, as a first step towards deportation. In just 56 days, about 440,000 Jews were deported by the middle of summer 1944, mostly to Auschwitz, though some were sent to the front to dig trenches. Of the 426,000 Jews who were sent to Auschwitz, about 320,000 of them perished in the gas chambers. The only Jewish community left in Hungary remained in Budapest.

Horthy, afraid of being subjected to war crimes trials after the impending end of the war, forced the German-backed leadership in Hungary to stop the deportations, and attempted to negotiate with Soviet forces, who stood at the Hungarian border in fall 1944. At this time, the Germans arrested Horthy, and installed the leader of the Arrow Cross party, Ferenc Szálasi, in his place. Under Szálasi, the Arrow Cross party terrorized the Jews of Budapest, subjected them to forced labour, and brutally murdered hundreds of them. In November 1944, the survivors were rounded up and put into a ghetto, which held approximately 70,000 people. Up to 20,000 ghetto inhabitants were told to remove their shoes and shot by the Arrow Cross on the banks of the Danube River. The powerful memorial, "Shoes on the Danube" installed in 2005, memorializes the Jews shot there and left to die. Thousands were also marched to the Austrian border that winter, and many died along the way in the freezing temperatures. Of the 825,000 Jews who lived in Hungary before the war, only 255,000 survived. Nonetheless, the survival rate in Hungary was much higher than in most other occupied Eastern and Central European countries. The fate of the Jews in Hungary remains, to this day, extremely controversial. Hungarians can often downplay their role in implementing the Final Solution, hence the memorial to German occupation in Budapest. Most historians acknowledge that the Hungarian state was not a mere bystander in the deportations. Plus, even before the Germans arrived, the infrastructure and conditions for the policy had already been set up. The Germans simply sent everyone into action.

In January 1945, the Red Army arrived in Budapest, and they liberated the country by April. But the liberation was not without sacrifice—the siege of Budapest is remembered as one of the most destructive urban battles of the war and has been compared to the battle of Stalingrad. Hitler was particularly interested in keeping Budapest under Nazi control, as the last Axis crude oil plant was located in the country. While the Soviet and Romanian troops arrived in central Hungary in early November 1944, it took them over six weeks to make it to Budapest because they were tired, poorly supplied, and facing a very determined Axis force. The city was shelled extensively in the new year as the Red Army tried to take it, and the majority of buildings were damaged or destroyed, along with all its bridges across the Danube that were destroyed by the Germans fleeing to the western side of the city. Just after Christmas, supply lines broke down, so city residents went hungry. Many were killed as they were foraging for food in the streets. The city fell on 14 February 1945. The Soviets were not particularly kind to the Hungarian people. They looted homes, raped women, and rounded up many innocent Hungarians to inflate the numbers of captured soldiers.

Poland was arguably the centre of the war in the east and an understanding of the war is essential to an understanding of Polish national identity. The country was used as a testing ground for Hitler's racial ideology. Ultimately, it ended up literally divided between Germany and the Soviet Union. The dividing line was along the Bug River. A central part of Poland became known as the General Government, and included major cities such as Warsaw, Lublin, and Kraków. It was managed by the Germans from the historic city of Kraków and led by a sadistic lawyer and Nazi Party member named Hans Frank. The majority of the land that the Soviet Union took during its 1939 invasion of Poland was later transferred to Ukraine and Belarus after the war.

As soon as Germany took over Poland, Nazi troops started expelling Polish residents from the region, starving them, and putting them in concentration camps within occupied central Poland. This process slowed considerably after the German invasion of the Soviet Union, as resources were diverted to the front. Nonetheless, by 1942, two million Germans had been resettled into eastern Poland. Millions of Poles lost property and money during forced resettlements. Agricultural products were confiscated, so large portions of the population starved. The living standards in Poland were far worse than other European countries as a result, and a large proportion of the population perished. In total, 2.3 million Poles were deported to work in Germany. There, they were kept in camps surrounded by barbed wire, prohibited from going into public spaces or taking public transit, and treated poorly, especially as the war effort began to result in shortages in 1942/43. While much of Western Europe, and even parts of Central Europe experienced decent conditions in the first half of the war, the situation in Poland was markedly worse from the very onset of the conflict.

Until 1941 Poland was doubly occupied by German and Soviet forces, both of whom were focused on eradicating the nation of Poland as a whole and collaborated on this until the start of Operation Barbarossa in June 1941 with the German invasion of the USSR. In the German section, under a strict policy of Germanization, it was forbidden to teach Polish. The Germans were keen to eliminate Polish culture, and to this end they closed or destroyed public institutions such as schools, universities, museums, and theatres, and arrested or killed Polish intellectuals. After a battle at Ciepielów, 300 Polish soldiers were undressed from their army uniforms and killed under the guise of being partisans. The army leadership was aware of the excessive repression and violence against the Poles but did nothing to stop it. Anyone who resisted the Germans was indiscriminately killed. This category included those who "resisted" through education, so those who were well educated were particularly targeted. More than 61,000 Polish elites were identified as threats to the Nazi regime. Those who were not arrested or sent to labour camps were killed, sometimes in mass executions, especially in reprisals for the Polish resistance movement. The Nazis especially cracked down on the Polish Catholic Church and killed or deported the vast majority of nuns and priests, especially in areas close to the German border. Hundreds of Polish POWs were also murdered in cold blood, which violated the Geneva Convention on the rules of war.

The Polish people suffered a great deal under Nazi occupation. Polish land and property were ruthlessly plundered by the German army, and the riches were sent back to Germany on trains. Millions of Poles who were deported from their home regions or forced into labour camps lost money and homes, and they never got them back after the war. Children who appeared Nordic were taken from their parents and subjected to various racial, physical, and psychological tests, and those who passed were made to partake in the Germanization programme. Nearly 5000 Polish children were given German names and re-educated in Germany. Those children who "failed" to pass the tests were sent to orphanages or concentration camps, where many of them died from starvation or got murdered. Most children who were taken away were never reunited with their families. Concentration camps were opened for Polish labourers, including the infamous Auschwitz, where Polish workers were literally worked to death. Poles who refused to work during the harvest season were subjected to the death penalty. The Germans also started to experiment with death by gas and starvation in the camps. In 1939, the Germans started gassing disabled people in hospitals in mobile vans to make room for Germans, which was one of the early attempts at testing the mass extermination that would later turn into the mass killings of the Holocaust.

Poland Under Soviet Occupation

While most of the population in German-occupied Poland was ethnically Polish, the situation was more mixed in the portion that the Soviet Union claimed, with large numbers of ethnic Ukrainians and Belarussians there. Initially, many residents of the Soviet-occupied territories welcomed Soviet rule, but they were soon discouraged, as Soviet repression grew, and the administration called on the deportation of hundreds of thousands of "enemies of the people". Tens of thousands of Polish soldiers were also executed by the Red Army, most notably in the Katyn Forest massacre in the spring of 1940, where 22,000 people were executed near the Russian city of Smolensk. When it was uncovered in 1943 by German troops, they blamed the Soviets, and the Soviets blamed the Germans. The Allies did not question the Soviet version of events. The fall of communism re-opened the question of what actually occurred and it is now clear that Stalin ordered the murder of a huge part of the Polish intelligentsia including doctors, lawyers, military officers and teachers. As we shall see in Chap. 6, in 2010 Katyn would again create enormous trauma for Polish society in 2010.

The Soviets proved to be just as cruel as the Nazis, and they too wanted to eradicate Polish culture. Soon after the partition of Poland, Soviet forces began looting homes and stores, and confiscating goods. They did this with impunity. The Soviets went about a policy of Sovietization which was quite similar to the German policy, but instead of permanently closing down Polish institutions, they expelled those who worked there, and re-opened them with Soviet figureheads, to spread propaganda, and teach the Russian language. Polish currency was replaced by the ruble, which meant that millions of people lost their savings. All Polish organizations were banned, unless they were associated with the Communist Party, and religious groups were persecuted. Like the Germans, the Soviets repressed the Polish intelligentsia by arresting them and deporting them with the justification that they were enemies of the state. More than one million Poles were deported under Soviet rule. Over half of the deportees perished, either during transport or at their new locations. Many of the dead were children. The Soviet Union refused to follow wartime conventions, and murdered hundreds of thousands of prisoners of war. They excused this by saying that they did not view Polish soldiers as prisoners of war, but as rebel forces who were a threat to the regime. Thousands of Polish soldiers were also sent to the Gulag.

Despite the brutal dual occupation of their country, the Polish government never surrendered, and instead went into exile in London. There, they established a variety of underground institutions, such as a parliament and a judiciary, and they worked hard to support the resistance movement at home. The Polish resistance movement was one of the largest in Europe and started almost immediately after the country was occupied. The Polish Home Army was supported by the government-in-exile, and the People's Army was supported by the Soviet Union. The resistance groups' numbers swelled to nearly half a million near the end of the war, and they were responsible for staging the Warsaw Uprising in the summer of 1944, which is known as the largest military effort made by any European resistance group during the war. In Warsaw, the Polish Home Army fought for 63 days, starting from August 1. About 16,000 members of the Polish resistance were killed, as well as 150,000 to 200,000 Polish civilians, the majority of whom were executed. Between 2000 and 17,000 German soldiers were reported dead or missing after the uprising. The uprising was eventually squashed near the end of September 1944. The Poles were convinced to lay down their arms in the fear that more civilians would die. Hitler stated that Warsaw needed to be razed to the ground in order to be pacified. The entire population of Warsaw was expelled, and the city was deliberately demolished by the Germans. Eighty-five percent of the buildings were destroyed, and the Nazi leadership discussed the possibility of turning the city into an artificial lake. Many members of the Polish Home Army were arrested by the Soviets after the war on the accusation that they were fascists and enemies of the state.

Some Poles resisted by housing Jewish children and falsifying documents to keep them safe. However, many Poles were also aggressive towards the Jews, and even went about killing them before the Nazis arrived. As a result of the brutal treatment by Germans and Soviets, the Poles were not sympathetic towards Jews after the war. The sense of collective suffering was too great to acknowledge that Jews as a distinct group had suffered the most. The idea of Jewish suffering was ignored further due to the Soviet influence in Poland after the war, which similarly did not acknowledge the Jewish loss, largely due to Anti-Semitism, and because the state had lost over 23 million people of its own, by far the largest death toll of the Second World War.

Operation Barbarossa

The Soviet-German pact lasted less than two years. After easily defeating France in 1940, Hitler decided it was time to engage in the war of annihilation on the eastern front, which he had been planning for years. The invasion of the USSR, which brought seemingly early and easy victories, was a turning point in Nazi policy, especially towards the Jews. Stalin was entirely unprepared for the German offensive. He dismissed reports from his spies in the German government who warned him that Germany was planning an attack as Western lies meant to mislead him and trick him into waging an exhaustive war with Hitler. Terrified of provoking Hitler, Stalin refused to mobilize his army, despite warnings from the highest-ranking members of his leadership team, and the supreme Marshal Georgy Zhukov of the Red Army, who had received firsthand reports of the German army amassed near the border the night before the offensive. He thought that Germany would not want to attack the Soviet Union, given that it needed raw materials to supply its army during its military drive in Western Europe. Stalin assumed that given Germany's defeat on two fronts in the First World War, the state would be unlikely to repeat the same mistakes and would want to deal with the West first.

Aside from the fact that the invasion of the USSR fulfilled Hitler's most critical long-term foreign policy, the attack was also a pragmatic move. His *Blitzkrieg* on the United Kingdom was not achieving the necessary results and, lacking the naval capabilities he required to take on Europe's greatest seafaring nation, he decided to work on a more tangible goal—the overland defeat of the Soviet Union. Hitler amassed an army of three million soldiers, and along with half-a-million soldiers from his Axis allies, including Hungary and Slovakia. The massive force stood ready to attack the Red Army. The Wehrmacht issued a number of rules that involved waging a war on the civilian population, something that is entirely prohibited by the Geneva Convention on the laws of war. Collective action against entire populations of civilians was also sanctioned, especially in areas where there was partisan activity. But Hitler was not perturbed by this, as he said he was planning a war of annihilation against his sworn enemies: Jews, Slavs, and Communists, which he believed were in league together. The Germans also believed that because the Soviet Union had not ratified the Geneva Convention, it meant that the rules did not apply to their soldiers and civilians, but that was wrong given that Germany had ratified the Convention, and its forces were therefore beheld to its rules. High-ranking German officials were committed to winning a lasting victory against the Russians by murdering and repressing their intellectual and political elite, a tactic that had already been tried in Poland.

Operation Barbarossa was the largest German offensive of the war. The troops attacked the Soviet army along a 2000-mile border spanning all of Europe, from the Baltics to the Black Sea. The Red Army, which was woefully unprepared, was driven back deep into Soviet territory, as German forces easily broke through the front lines, and millions of soldiers were encircled and captured. In total, more than five million Soviet troops were captured, and 3.3 million of these were strategically starved to death or killed in other ways by German forces throughout the duration of the war.

As the Germans pushed into the heart of the Soviet Union, they raped, plundered, and burned thousands of villages along the way. Mass rape was a serious issue on the Eastern Front, and in contrast to German conduct in the Western countries, it was rarely punished when the victims were Jews, Poles, or Soviet civilians. Often, Eastern European women were raped by German soldiers and then murdered. When Jews were raped, the perpetrators were sometimes punished, but not for raping—they faced disciplinary measures for violating Germany's racial purity laws. This systemic torture of the Slavic people no doubt contributed to the scale of Red Army violence and retribution that occurred when the Soviets took Berlin.

In the span of less than six months, the Germans stood at the gates of Moscow. But the Soviet Union did not fall as quickly as anticipated, and the Germans were unprepared to fight a winter war. They were pushed back considerably in the following months, and never fully regained the momentum they had in the beginning of the war.

The Holocaust in Central Europe

Jews in Germany had already faced repression for several years by the time Hitler invaded Poland. As we have seen, Hitler's incremental approach to what was called the Final Solution took Germany through legalization by the Nuremburg Laws (the Reich Citizenship Law and the Law for the Protection of German Blood and German Honor) of September 1935 which essentially removed citizenship for Germany's more than 500,000 Jews, state-sponsored violence, forced emigration under bad terms, musings about moving the Jews to Madagascar to ghettoization. However, in the Soviet invasion he saw the invasion as a catalyst for realizing his master plan—exterminating Europe's

Jews and expanding control over a purified Europe, which would be ruled by the master class of Germans.

Hitler was particularly harsh towards Eastern European countries because of his hatred for Slavs and his interpretation of the Judeo-Bolshevik myth, which proposed that the Soviet Union was run by Jews, and that Bolshevism was a Jewish construct. Hitler wrote that Jews were the cause of the world's problems and would ultimately bring about an apocalypse. In his mind, conflict and the fight for resources was a natural aspect of the human condition, and the Jews, who allegedly advocated for reason, democracy, and civic institutions, were a serious threat to the natural world order. In his mind, the spread of Jewish influence would lead to a rise of bastardized races who would overrun and destroy the Germans.

Hitler was inspired by the history of the United States, including the genocide of Indigenous populations in North America. He believed that what had occurred there had been the natural way, and that it proved the supremacy of the European race. Indeed, when it came to dealing with the European Jews, he borrowed North America's colonial language verbatim, calling it the "Jewish Question", after the "Indian Question" of centuries past. He believed that once the weaker, more dangerous race was removed, he would have room to expand across the continent and help Germany become a great nation, as the Europeans had done in the Americas.

Hitler wrote that the Slavic race was a weak group of Asiatic sub-humans who needed someone to manage them. In his *Generalplan Ost* or Master Plan for the East, he outlined that the fertile ground of Ukraine and Russia was to be the source of plentiful resources for the German people through colonization and enslavement. He attributed the relative success of the Russian empire (and of the Soviet Union) to German influence and input in that region. Most importantly, he saw the removal of Jews as the key to toppling the mighty Soviet power, which he presumed was being governed by Jews. Without the Soviet Union standing in the way, Hitler would have almost unlimited space and resources for his empire of supreme Germans. In his mind, the Soviet Union would fall to the Germans quickly, given that it was governed by a lesser people, and if it did not fall fast enough, drastic measures would have to be taken to deal with the Jews, especially those behind German lines, who would no doubt try to sabotage the military effort. If the Soviet Union did not capitulate fast enough, Hitler would undertake a policy of total annihilation against the Jews of Eastern Europe. Scholars speculate that this is why German forces were so cruel towards Jews in the region—they were seen as enemy agents working with the Red Army, who were set on stalling the Nazi war effort.

Although Jews were the primary victims of Nazi occupation in Eastern Europe, Hitler's ideological approach to Slavs as sub-humans resulted in great cruelty towards Eastern European civilians. Millions of Soviet citizens were starved to death or randomly killed. The Reich's official policy of economically exploiting the Soviet region showed that German policymakers were well aware that their actions would lead to millions of deaths. German soldiers were allowed to participate in all sorts of violence with impunity, as long as it was deemed ideologically motivated. During the occupation, thousands of villages were raided and burned, especially in retaliation for partisan activity.

In the occupied territories, the feared German Einsatzgruppen followed the advancing army, killing anyone that was deemed an enemy. The Einsatzgruppen numbered only 3000 so their work required willing collaborators and Germans found them. Most firing squads were composed of locals, not Germans. Long before the arrival of mechanized murder Jews and others faced the "Holocaust of the bullets". Although Czech, Hungarian, and Slovak Jews faced great repression and eventual deportation, the worst measures were taken in occupied Poland, where Jews were killed in villages, burned in barns and houses, and executed in mass graves in the forest.

Progression of Holocaust Measures

As Hitler progressively took over more of Europe, Jews were forced into thousands of ghettos set up across occupied cities. The ghettos were inspired by the practices of centuries past when Jewish residents of European cities were made to live in segregation from the rest of the population. Make no mistake, ghettoes were meant to kill people. Conditions in ghettos were abysmal—they were overcrowded, plagued by diseases, and suffered from chronic shortages of food and medicine. In the Warsaw ghetto, which was the largest among all ghettos, 30 percent of the city's population was crowded into 2 percent of its area. Ghetto life was unsustainable. The Jews were crammed into tiny apartments and made to work, but they were barely paid and could not afford basic supplies. Eastern European ghettos were often the most crowded because they received trainloads of deportees from Western Europe.

Jews in the ghetto were forced to identify themselves by sewing a yellow star onto their clothing and wearing an armband that identified them as Jewish. The Nazis selected Jews to participate in the *Judenrat*, or the Jewish Council, which was responsible for overseeing the daily functioning of the ghettos. The Nazis also selected Jews to act as policemen in the ghettos, and enforce Nazi orders, such as organizing deportations to concentration camps and killing centres. Jews who became policemen often did so thinking that they would be spared from Nazi violence if they collaborated.

The ghettos were meant to be a temporary measure until the Reich could decide what to do with the European Jews. In the late 1930s, Hitler was still considering the idea of sending the Jews to Madagascar, where they could live in perpetual segregation in a punishing environment, which would teach them a lesson for attempting to change the natural world order. However, as Hitler proposed this idea to officials in other countries, such as Poland, he was met with confusion, and the plan eventually fell apart. As the war with the Soviet Union dragged on, Hitler began to realize that more drastic measures would have to be taken and began planning a "Final Solution to the Jewish Problem".

Implementation of the Final Solution

In the beginning of the war in the East, Jews were largely killed in their own villages behind the German front line. While the Einsatzgruppen, German forces that followed the invading Germany army, is the most infamous group that targeted the Jews, many of the soldiers who murdered them had been ordinary civilians before the war, including police officers serving in reserve army battalions. Typically, a group of about 100 soldiers would arrive in a village and murder over 1000 Jews over the course of one or two days. Executing Jews by firing squad was a gory and gruesome business. At the beginning of the effort, the soldiers were usually unprepared for the task, and a lot of alcohol and drug cocktails were sometime necessary to encourage them. Concerned about the mental well-being of their troops, the Nazis eventually switched to faster and more "painless" and expedient methods of extermination, meant to kill more people faster, including gas vans and finally, death camps located in occupied Poland.

It was not always the Germans who killed Jews. Sometimes Poles killed them before the Germans arrived, or helped the Germans to curry favour. The Polish role in these events is extremely controversial in Poland. For Poles, their suffering outweighs any collaboration with the Germans. The Germans motivated the Poles to carry out their own violence against the Jews by equating them with the upholders of the Communist system, which was hated across the region. Polish complicity, like Hungarian, is very controversial in Poland, especially as the post-communist governments have often tried to relativize and conflate the fate of Jews with the fate of ordinary Poles during the war and the communist period.

While occupied Poland housed the majority of German killing camps, and the Warsaw ghetto was the largest of all wartime ghettos, most Jews in the country never set foot there. Instead, they were killed in their villages, and thrown in mass graves in the forest. By late 1941, the ghettos started to be destroyed, as Jews were either deported to concentration camps or shot by the thousands in rural areas. Prior to 1941, the camps had largely been used for mass labour, but after the German defeat at Moscow, the Nazi leadership came to the realization that the war would last longer than they initially anticipated. By 1942, the German leadership agreed that the Jews would have to be exterminated, and three camps were set up for that purpose: Treblinka, Belzec, and Sobibor. Later that year, Auschwitz-Birkenau was also designated a killing camp, and more than a million Jews eventually perished there, including almost 500,000 Jews from Hungary deported in 1944.

Aside from hunger, endless work in terrible conditions, and abuse by guards and German soldiers alike, Jews in concentration camps were often subjected to terrible medical experiments. The Germans conducted absurd tests to find out how people might fare without air, or in freezing water, and they tested Jewish twins in an effort to understand how to create conditions for German women to have twins and increase the birth rate. The experiments were usually cruel and deadly, and were hardly based in any established science. Oftentimes, what the Nazis called experiments was just torture.

The largest and most infamous camp of the Nazi era was no doubt Auschwitz-Birkenau, which started as a labour camp for Polish workers, and later turned into a death camp. Auschwitz was the only place where prisoners were tattooed with ID numbers. Nearly 1.5 million people passed through Auschwitz, and the vast majority were killed there, including 960,000 Jews out of the one million who were sent there. Instead of using carbon monoxide in the gas chambers, like it had been done in previous operations, the gas chambers at Auschwitz were equipped with Zyklon B, an insecticide typically used on rats and other vermin, which turned into lethal gas when it was pumped into the air. The gas was initially tested on Polish prisoners and Soviet POWs in 1941 before it was administered to the Jews, who arrived in spring 1942.

Auschwitz started out with two gas chambers, but they were too small to accommodate the large number of prisoners brought there. Four more were soon built and put into operation in summer 1943. The gas chambers worked until late 1944, when Heinrich Himmler himself ordered them to be taken apart and destroyed, so the evidence would be hidden before the Red Army liberated the region. In total, 2.7 million Jews died in the concentration camps, and the other half were exterminated in the countryside, died of poor living conditions in ghettos, or were arbitrarily shot at some other juncture of the Final Solution. In 1942 about three-fourths of Europe's Jews were still alive, but in the span of year, the vast majority had perished, and less than 25 percent remained by winter 1943.

The Enforcement of Nazi Power and Jewish Resistance

It is astounding to consider the facts: sometimes, only ten officers would be in charge of more than 8000 Jews, particularly during transports in trains. In ghettos and concentration camps, there was only a handful of German guards who were responsible for managing thousands of Jews. The victims largely outnumbered the perpetrators, but they were afraid to rebel due to the fear that the German troops would punish them with increased violence and death. While there are scattered cases of individual Jews who escaped Nazi captivity, either by running away from ghettos, or by jumping off trains, or by joining partisan forces, the majority of Jews complied with Germans orders, or attempted to hide. Jews sometimes participated in a more covert version of resistance, such as smuggling materials in and out of ghettos, and collaborating with rural populations. Nonetheless, such instances were relatively rare, as the Nazi perpetrators enacted a regime of terror which discouraged subjugated populations from resisting and wrought extremely harsh punishment on those who did.

A notable exception is the Warsaw ghetto uprising of April 1943. The ghetto housed more than 70,000 people, and earlier that year the order was given to empty the ghetto and send its occupants to concentration camps. At this point, about 300,000 Jews in the ghetto had already been murdered or deported, and most Jews had already heard about the infamous death camps and what occurred there. However, they were slow to act due to fear of retribution and general disorganization, and more than half of the ghetto's inhabitants were deported. Once Himmler ordered the ghetto to be destroyed entirely, the Jews started organizing to take a stand. By the middle of April, the Warsaw Jews had mobilized a force, bought weapons (largely from Poles outside the ghetto), and were prepared to fight against the Germans. They were outnumbered approximately 750 to 2000 or 3000, but they beat back the Germans and their collaborators in the first days of the rebellion. Twelve Germans were killed or wounded, and they broke the resistance in just a few days, but small groups hid throughout the ghetto and attacked German forces for weeks afterwards. Seven thousand Jews were killed, and the ghetto was eventually entirely destroyed. About 20,000 Jews were thought to be in hiding at the time, and as the ghetto was burned to the ground, they were killed in their hideaways and crawl spaces. The remaining 42,000 Jews were sent to concentration camps, where the majority of them died. Nonetheless, the Warsaw ghetto uprising is remembered as the largest rebellion staged by Jews during the war, and it inspired similar uprisings in other eastern ghettos, as well as concentration camps like Treblinka and Sobibor.

Another notable example is the October 1944 rebellion at Auschwitz. On 7 October, several hundred prisoners at the camp learned that they were about to be killed and blew up the gas facility and crematorium beside it, using explosives that they had smuggled into the camp. They also killed three guards. The guards crushed the rebellion relatively easily and killed most of those involved. Some of the rebels were publicly hanged. The next month, gassing operations at the camp ceased, as the Germans prepared for the arrival of the Soviet army.

THE FATE OF OTHER MINORITIES UNDER NAZI OCCUPATION

Jews were not the only group explicitly targeted and exterminated by the Nazi regime. Any person with "flaws" who could potentially tarnish the purity of the German race was subjected to repression and annihilation. This included people with disabilities and mental illness, homosexuals, Black Europeans, and Roma people.

The Roma were also singled out on racial grounds, described as lazy and prone to crime. The Porajmos, or destruction as it is known in Romani, refers to the genocide against the Roma. The fate of the Roma is understudied and under-memorialized. The repression of the Roma became German policy in the summer 1936, when a special camp for them was built just north of Berlin. The camp, called Berlin-Marzahn, was opened in conjunction with a governmental decree for "Combating the Gypsy Plague". Just one month later, in July 1936, hundreds of Roma were rounded up and forced into the camp. In total, about 1200 people lived in the camp between 1936 and 1945. The camp was in an unpleasant location, bordering a cemetery and next door to a sewage treatment plant.

The Roma were subjected to forced labour, and the residents of the camp lacked adequate food and shelter. In the winter, the three water pipes in the camp were frozen solid, and there were only two toilets that were shared between over a thousand people. As such, conditions in the camp were extremely unhygienic and many people became sick. The guards who were responsible for the camp were very cruel to internees. They frequently beat them and even allowed their guard dogs to bite them, which resulted in terrible injuries. Similar to the Jewish experience in concentration camps, Roma prisoners were also used in medical experiments which amounted to torture. Thousands of Roma, at the camp and beyond, were also forcibly sterilized.

In 1943, most of the prisoners were deported to Auschwitz and other eastern death camps, where the majority of them were gassed. Just over 100 prisoners remained at Berlin-Marzahn, but most of them died of starvation. Only about a dozen Roma prisoners are thought to have survived. Thousands of other Roma faced similar conditions in the Nazi-occupied territories. Like the Jews, the Roma were also ghettoized, and many died from terrible conditions in the ghettos. About 23,000 Roma in total were deported to Auschwitz, where they were kept in a separate compound in horrible conditions that encouraged the spread of disease. About 19,000 of them died. In 1944 an order was given by the Auschwitz leadership to murder the Roma prisoners. As the guards approached the compound, the Roma armed themselves with pipes and shovels and prepared for a fight. The guards retreated and sent the most able-bodied internees to work elsewhere in the camp, and then proceeded to murder thousands of the leftover prisoners.

In occupied Poland, and elsewhere in Eastern Europe, tens of thousands of Roma people were arrested and killed in mobile vans or shot and thrown into mass graves in the forest. 30,000 Roma were killed in the Baltic States alone. While it is difficult to track down exact statistics, experts estimate that of the approximately one million Roma living in Europe before the war, 25 percent, or 250,000 people, were murdered by the Nazi regime. After the war, it was decided that the Roma had not been targeted on racial grounds, which made them exempt from restitution, and it was not until 1979 that Roma people were eligible to claim money for abuse they had experienced during the war. Memorials to the fate of the Roma are not common in Central Europe. The Czech city of Brno has a modest museum to Roma life in Central Europe. It is an exception to an otherwise often ignored story.

The Nazis took specific interest in eradicating those with physical and mental disabilities as well as mental illness, to save the gene pool from "contamination" by defective individuals. Those with disabilities were seen as useless members of society and a drag on the system, given that they consumed state resources, and could not provide anything in return. Rejecting the "Jewish" practice of individual rights, Hitler argued that people who could not benefit society were of no use to it. The policy was written into official law in 1933, with the passage of the "Law for the Prevention of Progeny with Hereditary

Diseases", which stipulated that those with mental illnesses and disabilities were to undergo forced sterilization.

Starting from 1934, nearly half-a-million "feeble-minded" Germans were sterilized. The majority of them were Aryan. Roma people and homosexuals were also targeted, but Jews were exempt from this practice, likely because Hitler had a greater plan for them. The "Euthanasia" programme followed the sterilization policy. Starting from Germany, and spreading throughout Eastern Europe, thousands of institutionalized people were murdered under the policy, including disabled children and babies, starting from the late 1930s. The euthanasia programme started in summer 1939, and it was officially authorized in October of that year, when doctors and nurses in hospitals were encouraged to neglect disabled patients, allowing them to die from disease and hunger. The programme was nicknamed "T4" after the headquarters of the euthanasia operation, Tiergartenstrasse 4 in Berlin.

Initially, hospital staff and doctors were made to report children who showed signs of "retardation" and disability. Parents were asked to surrender disabled children to special clinics, where doctors promised to care for the patients, but actually killed them with lethal injections or starvation. At first, only children under three were targeted, but as the scope of the operation expanded, children under 17 were included, and later, adults. The practice was justified as necessary for the war effort.

Later on, consultants started to visit hospitals, looking for victims who were to be euthanized. This mass murder spree preceded the Holocaust by several years, and it is seen as the first time mass murder tactics were tested during the Second World War.

By 1941, more than 70,000 Germans and Austrians had been killed. However, mounting public criticism led Hitler to declare an end to the euthanasia programme, although the practice was continued in secret throughout the war.

Between 1940 and 1945, more than 200,000 physically and mentally handicapped individuals were murdered in the programme. Many of them were gassed with carbon monoxide at six hospitals across Germany and Austria, though others were given lethal injections or starved to death. The bodies of victims were burnt in industrial-sized ovens called crematoria which were attached to the hospitals. This practice is generally seen as a precursor to the Holocaust, as SS members who managed extermination camps were trained in the euthanasia programme before being sent to places such as Belzec, Treblinka, and Sobibor. Families of victims were usually told that the patients died in a medical episode related to their affliction.

By the end of the war, the regime expanded the euthanasia programme to include elderly patients, people who had been injured in bombing raids, and foreign prisoners and workers. The emptied hospitals were needed by German troops, who used them as medical clinics for wounded soldiers, barracks, and storage centres. The practice was carried out in Germany, Austria, the Czech lands, Poland, and the occupied Soviet territories.

While homosexual conduct was outlawed in Weimar Germany, it was generally tolerated in society, and Germany's LGBTQ activists were prominent proponents of social acceptance for gay existence. Under the Nazi regime, however, gay men were imprisoned and even interned at concentration camps, because they were deemed useless to society. Lesbian women were usually not persecuted by police, and the regime was even somewhat lenient towards gay men as long as they were not "actively homosexual", and resisted their "natural impulses".

Nonetheless, the 1930s saw the widespread erasure and destruction of LGBTQ culture in Germany, from the closure of gay clubs to the burning of books on human sexuality. Between 1933 and 1945, about 100,000 men were arrested and imprisoned for homosexual conduct. Oftentimes, men were imprisoned without cause, but because police thought they might engage in homosexual acts. The repression of German homosexuals peaked in 1937–39. Police put forth considerable efforts to infiltrate gay circles and used a network of informants to hunt guilty parties.

In internment camps, gay men were made to wear pink triangles on their clothing to symbolize homosexuality, and they faced extremely abusive treatment by other prisoners. They were sometimes kept separate from the other prisoners so as not to "spread" the homosexuality. The Nazi regime believe that it was possible to cure homosexuality, so the men were ridiculed and forced to perform hard labour in an effort to cleanse them. As such, gay men were often given the most difficult and dangerous tasks, such as working in mines. Sometimes, gay men opted to be castrated to get a shorter sentence, since castration was seen as a cure for perverted sexual desires. Nazi scientists were known to perform medical experiments on gay prisoners in concentration camps in an effort to find a cure for homosexuality. These experiments often resulted in mutilation and death. Experts suggest that death rates for gay men in the camps was around 65 percent. The Nazis also targeted religious groups, such as the Catholic and Lutheran churches, and Jehovah's Witness members, along with people with criminal records and alcoholics, and anyone else who could be deemed disruptive to society. Hitler was particularly harsh towards Eastern Europeans, as previously discussed in the chapter. Anyone suspected of being a partisan, or aiding the partisan movement, was eradicated. This practice led to millions of deaths of Polish and Soviet civilians who were accused of fighting against the Nazi regime. More than 58 percent of all Soviet POWs died in Nazi captivity.

Liberation

Starting from February 1942, the British Air Force engaged in a sustained bombing campaign against German civilians, major cities, and important industrial sites. They were aided by the United States Air Force. Thousands of bomber planes dropped explosives on German cities, destroying tens of thousands of buildings and killing German civilians. The campaign was conducted to defeat German morale and the raids significantly hampered German industrial production, which no doubt slowed the war effort. However, large civic unrest, which the Allies expected following massive bombing campaigns, never materialized. This may be explained by the totalitarian nature of the Nazi regime. While Germans were allowed to live in relative comfort, the secret police were always nearby, even at the peak of the war years, which may have discouraged German civilians from acting out. Nonetheless, the devastation that the civilian population faced was harrowing.

In Cologne, 36 factories and more than 3000 houses were destroyed in a single night in May 1942, leaving more than 45,000 people homeless. Fires burned throughout the city and could be seen from hundreds of kilometres away. Only a few hundred people were killed in the Cologne bombing but the city was not levelled, but other German cities fared much worse. The worst examples of German civilian death tolls include Hamburg, where 42,000 died (35,000 in one night); Berlin, where 35,000 died; Dresden, where 25,000 were killed; in Kassel 10,000 deaths, and Pforzheim 21,000 deaths—equivalent to 22 percent of the population. In Hamburg, the heat from firestorms caused by heavy bombing was so bad that many residents jumped into canals to avoid being burnt. Some civilians were forced to stay in the canals for hours until the fires died down, but even then they suffered burns to the neck and head. Some cities saw 80–90 percent of their housing and infrastructure destroyed. In fall of 1943, there were 400,000 homeless people in Berlin whose housing had been wrecked by bombs. Less than half a year later, by March 1944, that number rose to 1.5 million in the capital alone. It is estimated that about 410,000 German civilians died in Allied air raids throughout the war. The Allies lost 80,000 air crew. The practice of targeting civilians, by both Allied and Axis powers, was the first time in modern warfare that wartime conventions were ignored. This was total war.

The Germans were facing problems elsewhere too. After the German defeat at Stalingrad in early 1943, the tide started to turn, and the Soviet Union became more successful at winning battles and driving the enemy back. By August 1944, the Soviet forces entered occupied Poland, and started to liberate German-occupied territories. In early 1945, the Western Allies began to liberate concentration camps and found evidence of Nazi genocide. The liberation of Auschwitz by Soviet troops on 27 January 1945, has been International Holocaust Remembrance Day since 2005. Many of the camps had already been evacuated by the Germans, who either sent the remaining emaciated prisoners on death marches or executed them before departing.

During this time, the Red Army entered German territory, and in January 1945, it stood barely 100 kilometres away from Berlin. By April 1945, the Soviet army captured and liberated Vienna. The final push to take Berlin started that spring. Stalin was in a hurry to reach the German capital before the Allies, so he ordered that no lives be spared as the Red Army advanced into the country. As a result, thousands of Soviet soldiers died, who may have survived if the army had proceeded more tactfully. 300,000 Wehrmacht soldiers stood against a massive Soviet army, but they were determined to fight due to their fear of retribution from the Soviet forces. By the time the Red Army reached Berlin, there were only 90,000 German troops, many of them older or more poorly trained than those who had fought on the eastern front, left to defend the city, facing over a million Soviet soldiers. The final weeks of the war were marked by brutal fighting in the streets of the Nazi capital. More than 70,000 Soviet soldiers died during this time, partially because of the haste and carelessness with which the battle was carried out. On 30 April Hitler committed suicide in his underground bunker. German troops in Berlin surrendered on 2 May and the war was proclaimed officially over on 8 May 1945. Prague was one of the last major cities to be liberated, which occurred on 9 May when the Red Army entered the city.

Although the Soviet army had liberated a considerable part of Europe by winter 1944, and had already seen some of the Nazi's crimes against humanity, the concentration camps were an unprecedented new discovery. Most of the larger camps were in occupied Poland, so the Soviets came across them first. The first major camp to be liberated was Majdanek, which was near the city of Lublin. The Soviet forces arrived there on July 23. While the Germans attempted to hide all traces of the genocide they had committed, the camp was found practically intact, including the gas chambers, as the staff had fled in a hurry when they heard that Soviet troops were approaching, and had not bothered to disassemble it. That summer, the Soviet army also found Belzec, Sobibor, and Treblinka, though they had been abandoned in 1943, and the Jews there had already been murdered. The Soviets invited journalists to the camps to document the horrors that transpired there and spread the world, so by the end of the world much of the world knew of what the Nazis had done.

As already noted, Auschwitz, the largest camp complex, and the last one operating during the war, was liberated by the Soviet army in January 1945. While the Nazis had forced most of the prisoners to march towards Germany, about 6000 inmates were left when the Red Army arrived. The Germans had destroyed many parts of the camp, but the Soviets found evidence of what had occurred there in several warehouses, including over a million pieces of men's and women's clothing, tens of thousands of shoes, and 14,000 pounds of human hair. Despite the efforts to save the inmates, about half of them died in the days following liberation from sickness and starvation.

During this time, especially in the winter of 1944–1945, the camp prisoners were subjected to "death marches" by German troops, who were tasked with evacuating the camps near the front and moving the prisoners into the German interior so they could be used for forced labour, as well as hiding the evidence of genocide. Nine days before the Soviets arrived at Auschwitz, about 60,000 inmates were forced out of the camp and made to walk over 50 kilometres in the freezing cold towards the town of Wodzisław, where they were put on trains and moved to other camps. Soldiers shot anyone who stopped or fell behind. About 15,000 people, or 25 percent of the inmates, died during the march.

One out of two prisoners died during the evacuation of Stutthof, a concentration camp in occupied northern Poland. The Germans started to evacuate the camp, which housed about 50,000 inmates, in late January 1945 in anticipation of the approaching Soviet army. They forced 5000 people to walk north to the Baltic Sea, where the prisoners were marched into the water and shot. Others were made to walk to eastern Germany, but the convoy was cut off by the Red Army and forced to turn around. The Germans tried to evacuate the camp again in April 1945 but were surrounded by Soviet soldiers. Many prisoners were again shot and thrown in the sea, and Soviet troops entered the camp on 9 May 1945. In total, over 25,000 prisoners from Stutthof died during the attempted evacuations.

In April 1945, US troops liberated the Buchenwald camp in central Germany, and found more than 20,000 prisoners there, who took control of the camp a few days before the Allied soldiers arrived. About 30,000 prisoners from Buchenwald were forced on a death march on 7 April, in which more than a third of them died. The Americans also liberated camps in southern Germany and in Austria, such as Dachau and Mauthausen. At Dachau, the Americans found thousands of bodies of prisoners who had been shot by the Germans or died from starvation and exposure, including piles of bodies near the gas chambers and crematoriums, and a train with over 30 cars full of corpses. American soldiers were blamed for executing several dozen German soldiers at Dachau extra-judicially, either in self-defence or out of anger for the conditions they discovered, although the accounts are conflicting, and it is unclear how many people died in the incident. The US military court investigated the matter but chose to dismiss it given the conditions under which it occurred.

During the same month, British forces liberated camps in northern Germany, including Bergen-Belsen, where they found about 50,000 prisoners, nearly half of whom were critically ill. Many others were suffering from typhus and emaciated. A large number of the prisoners at Bergen-Belsen had been deported there from Auschwitz late in the war. This was the camp where Anne Frank had died just a few weeks before the British arrived. The camp was rife with horrors—the British discovered approximately 20,000 unburied corpses around the barracks. The emaciated and dehydrated inmates were skin and bones and looked like "living skeletons". The dying and exhausted inmates reportedly crawled around on all fours in search of any shred of food or water, though the water pump had been broken during an Allied bombing raid six days earlier. More than 13,000 of the inmates perished in the weeks following liberation from sickness and malnutrition. Others ate too much too quickly and died of digestion problems when their emaciated bodied could not handle the food.

The British made captured German and Hungarian soldiers carry the 20,000 dead bodies to open pit graves which had been dug with bulldozers. To punish the soldiers for their crimes, the British troops did not permit the enemy soldiers to wear gloves while they went about their task, so some of the Axis soldiers caught typhus and died as a result. Despite the efforts to handle the dead respectfully, carrying them to the graves proved too slow-going, so the bodies were eventually bulldozed into the pits. Once the camp had been somewhat cleaned, local Germans were brought to the area so they could see the evils perpetuated by their government. Like many other concentration camps, Bergen-Belsen was burned after liberation to prevent the spread of disease, but this erased valuable evidence of what had transpired there.

The surviving inmates were washed and deloused and doused with DDT powder to disinfect them. They were taken to makeshift hospitals where doctors attempted to rehydrate and stabilize them. They were then moved into housing that had been misappropriated from German civilians. For the survivors of the camps, freedom was difficult. They were sick and traumatized, had lost many loved ones, and often had nowhere to go.

Allied Crimes During the Liberation

Although the Soviet liberation effort has been credited with rescuing a massive part of Europe, and contributing overwhelmingly to the defeat of Hitler, it must not be forgotten that the Red Army was complicit in terrible war crimes as it marched through the formerly occupied territories on its way to Berlin. The majority of the crimes were committed against innocent German civilians, though the Red Army also targeted ordinary Russians and Poles, and Central Europeans along the way. Brutal actions such as mass rape and massacres of entire villages were committed by soldiers who were driven by revenge. The soldiers murdered and pillaged with impunity, and archival documents show that taking "an eye for an eye", and "treating them like they treated us" was sanctioned from the very top of the army leadership. Soldiers were also given the green light for "having fun with women" as a reward for the extreme conditions they had fought through in previous years.

Largely, this was motivated by the horrors the soldiers had witnessed and experienced on the Eastern Front. Driven by a policy of annihilation and conquest, German soldiers treated Slavic civilians with exceptional cruelty and murdered millions of innocent people. The war in the East was much more violent, vast, and personal than the war in the West, as two regimes fought one another for eradication. Once the tide had turned and the Red Army was on the offensive, they first passed through the occupied territories of the east before their arrival in Germany and witnessed what had occurred there. By the time the Red Army arrived on German territory, the soldiers were primed for retribution. They saw their invasion of Germany not only as an opportunity to liberate the German people from Nazism, but also as one to destroy the country and make the Germans pay for what they had endured. Unfortunately, this meant that millions of innocent civilians were targeted and abused.

Thousands of Germans were subjected to torture, mutilation, and murder. The Red Army brought with them a vengeance and violence unlike anything that they had ever seen before. The Soviet forces murdered and pillaged indiscriminately, without waiting to find out who had supported the Nazi regime, and who had quietly or actively opposed it. They even raped and murdered women who were fleeing in convoys of refugees.

Thousands of women fell victim to Red Army brutality, and there were many instances of gang rape, oftentimes followed by murder. As a result, many women also opted to kill themselves when they heard that the Soviet army was approaching. Other women were raped repeatedly, as many as 70 times. The abundance of alcohol supplied to the soldiers likely made it easier for them to rape and murder. The Germans had also left hundreds of litres of alcohol in Berlin, in the hopes that it would impede the Soviets' fighting ability, but it only served to make them more brutal. It is estimated that about two million women were raped by Red Army soldiers, 100,000 of them in Berlin alone, an estimated 70,000 to 100,000 in Vienna, and 50,000 to 200,000 in Hungary in the last six months of the war. Some of the victims were as young as seven years old. Many women were raped in front of their husbands and family members, contributing to a sense of collective trauma. About 240,000 women died as a result of the rapes, and another 10,000 likely died from complications of subsequent abortions. In 2011, information came to light that Hannelore Kohl, the wife of former West German Chancellor Helmut Kohl, had been gang raped by Soviet soldiers in May 1945, at the age of 12, and then thrown out of a window. She suffered life-long back problems as a result, as well as mental health issues, and committed suicide in 2001.

There are various theories on why the Soviet forces were so driven to participate in mass sexual violence. The often-cited theory of revenge, and of making the enemy suffer as the Eastern Europeans had suffered is prominent, but experts also speculate that drunkenness, PTSD, and "deprivation" after living without female contact for years may have contributed to the mass violence. Other accounts detail Soviet hatred for Germans, perhaps stemming from propaganda, and feelings of anger and inferiority after witnessing the elevated standard of living in the West, despite the wartime ruin.

Although the Soviet case is the one most often cited, other liberating powers were also complicit in violence against women. Although popular media and films would have one believe that American soldiers were gentlemen who gave German women cigarettes and danced with them, they are not free of guilt either. One source estimates that 190,000 German women were raped by American soldiers between 1945 and 1955, though most of the crimes were committed during or in the immediate aftermath of the liberation effort. Other figures show that at least 11,000 instances of rape were prosecuted by the military police by November 1945, but who is to say how many complaints were ignored or dismissed? There are at least five recorded instances of German women being found dead in US army barracks, and complaints from hotel managers in German cities of women screaming and being passed around by soldiers in some rooms. In some instances, American soldiers were tried by court martial, and in extreme cases, even shot, but the degree of punishment depended on the whim of the commanding officer. There are recorded instances of rape by British and French soldiers as well, though as with the American and

Soviet cases, not all claims of rape were properly investigated, and there was a general attitude by army leadership that those who had been raped likely had it coming. The troops' conduct was often written off as drunken merrymaking and post-traumatic stress, and officers were reluctant to discipline their soldiers after what they had been through during the war effort. The issue was exacerbated further due to a decree that was given which forced German residents to post lists of the names and ages of inhabitants on their front door, making it easy for soldiers to find young women. Many female survivors never spoke of their experience, and although testimonies were collected from victims after the war, they were not published until years later.

Various journalistic accounts of the time, including works by Osmar White and Aleksandr Solzhenitsyn, all allude to a great deal of sexual violence on the part of the liberating soldiers. But overall, the mass rape was written out of both Western and Soviet history, whose accounts largely celebrate the liberation and the salvation of Europe from Hitler. Many Russians deny the Soviet involvement in mass sexual violence because they argue that it tarnishes the soldiers' hard-earned reputation as the saviours of Europe, for which they paid with millions of lives. There is humiliation on the part of the Germans as well, because some contend that if the Nazis had not behaved so brutally towards the Slavs, there would have been no reason for the Red Army to abuse the German population so terribly.

The Soviets were also complicit in driving millions of Germans from their homes in Poland, Bohemia and Moravia, and Germany-proper, as they prepared to give the territory of what was once Eastern Germany over to the Polish government. In the Polish territories, ethnic Germans were stuffed into train cars and shipped to the West. Many of them died en route. But it was not just Germans being forced to migrate. Both during and after the war the Red Army deported thousands of people from Poland and other Soviet-occupied zones.

In occupied Bohemia and Moravia, which was one of the last places to be liberated, three million ethnic Germans were targeted and abused. The new Czechoslovak government pursued a policy of elimination against the German minority, and they were aided by the Czech partisan forces—the Svoboda (or Freedom) Army, who had fought with the Red Army. Germans were interned, forced to work for long hours each day, fed the bare minimum, and punished if they scavenged for food in trash cans. Given the fate of the Czech lands and the hostility to Germans wherever they were, it was easy to incite frenzied violence against the Germans, and sometimes thousands would die because they were accused of sabotage. The Czech laws, called Beneš Decrees, for the Czechoslovak president in exile and later president of liberated Czechoslovakia were issued during and after the war which legally authorized the expulsion of ethnic Germans and Hungarians and the confiscation of their property. Of note later, the Liechtenstein family, a royal house that had been part of the Habsburg Empire who owned vast amounts of property in interwar Czechoslovakia, were declared as Germans and thus collaborators by default. The family lost nearly half-a-million acres of land, including two castles—Lednice and Valtice—which are now UNESCO World Heritage Sites. In 2020, tiny Liechtenstein, which is smaller than the land confiscated, brought a case to the European Court of Human Rights to seek return of the territory.

Ethnic Germans were pushed out of Central Europe and forced to go on death marches to the West or sent to the East by the Soviets. More than two million Germans had been expelled from Czechoslovakia before the Potsdam Conference, which effectively divided Europe between the Western and Soviet spheres of influence, and established postwar rules, had even been concluded. About 700,000 Germans were also placed on trains and deported to Siberian gulags in the Soviet Union.

The Allies did little to stop the Soviet brutality. The postwar world order was one of chaos, and there were many Nazi operatives and collaborators to try. Additionally, the Soviet Union had consistently pressured the Western powers to concede in many aspects of the postwar diplomatic process, such as allowing them to "temporarily" put Poland under its sphere of influence. Although the Allies demanded a more humane resettlement for the ethnic German minorities in Central Europe, they were still subjected to great abuse and humiliation by the Soviet forces. This can partially be blamed on the fact that Stalin was promised reparations at the 1945 Yalta Conference which preceded Potsdam. Before Germany officially surrendered, the overrun and encumbered German troops also did little to protect the civilians from the advancing Soviet army.

After the war, and in some cases even before the conflict was over, German forced labour camps were established in many parts of Eastern and Western Europe. In Poland, hundreds of thousands of Germans were made to work more than 60 hours per week and paid very little.

About 200,000 German workers died in Soviet-run work camps in Poland. Germans were also forced to work in camps in Czechoslovakia. Tens of thousands of East Germans were made to work in Soviet camps and uranium mines, digging up materials that the Soviets could use to build a nuclear bomb. The work was gruelling and difficult and was compared to gulag labour in Siberia. Thousands of German prisoners were also sent to work in the United Kingdom, the United States, Norway, and France, but the majority of them were released by the end of the 1940s. The Soviets were much harsher to the German workers given that they saw their labour as reparations for the absolute destruction German forces had brought upon the USSR during the war. The Soviets also saw the forced labour as retribution for what the Nazis had done to the Soviet civilians, given that they had forced millions of people to work for the Reich during the war. The full extent of German forced labour in the Soviet Union was hidden until the USSR fell apart in the late 1980s, and the Soviet archives were opened.

Conclusion

Central Europe was arguably ground zero during the Second World War—the conflict started and ended there. By the War's end, Europe had lost its ability to shape events and the United States stepped into the role of moral beacon. The most significant milestones in the lead-up to the conflict occurred there, such as the annexation of Austria and the destruction of Czechoslovakia, and it was the invasion of Poland that started the war. The main aggressor in the war was Germany, a major Central European nation. The other countries were either totally or partially erased (such as Austria, Czechoslovakia, and Poland), or sided with the Nazi regime (such as Croatia, Hungary, and Slovakia).

Despite years of Nazi occupation, the Central European nations all participated in some sort of resistance, whether it was overt action with rebel forces, or quiet subversion of Nazi rules by reluctant collaborator governments. Nonetheless, the Central European nations also had contradictory elements in their societies—while the states had robust rebellions and participated in armed uprisings, they also had flourishing fascist parties, and citizens who were often hostile to Jews. Throughout the war, Central Europe housed the most ghettos and death camps, and its territories and resources were vital to the Third Reich and the Nazi war machine. The most Jews were killed in Central European territories as indeed it was where Hitler had his most authority to implement the Final Solution and where Jews faced their worst fate. Nonetheless, locals helped the German occupying forces, and these acts are a stain on many peoples and a source of continued controversy in national histories. Aside from parts of Eastern Europe, major Central European cities such as Warsaw, Budapest, Dresden, Hamburg, and Berlin faced the worst wartime damage. The war also ended in Central Europe, with the battle of Berlin, Hitler's suicide in April 1945, the subsequent capitulation of Nazi forces in Germany, and the postwar Nuremberg trials.

During the war, Central Europe continued to experience domination by two major powers, an issue it had faced in the past exposing its vulnerability and perpetuating the notion of victimhood which would re-emerge in the years following the collapse of communism. It was not only the Central European governments that faced this issue, but the civilians as well, who were pushed, pulled, deported, resettled, and expelled to and from various territories. Central Europe was the space that lay between the Soviet Union and Germany, and it was repeatedly trampled and traumatized by the two great powers as they fought each other. For this reason, Central Europeans faced greater destruction, abuse, and trauma than what the Western nations had ever experienced. In a period of total war, Central Europe was the ground upon which Germany and the Soviet Union did their absolute worse and where some of the most significant developments of the war occurred.

After the war, the region continued to be torn between East and West, although it was under the Soviet sphere of influence. In the case of divided Germany, this tension between two systems was represented literally. Despite subsequent repression under Communism for much of Central Europe, the idea of Central Europe persisted best illustrated by the multiple rebellions against communist rule. Under Soviet occupation and later Soviet hegemony after the war, Central Europe essentially disappeared and a new Eastern Europe appeared which seemed, at least temporarily, to solve the region's contested and vulnerable situation.

For Further Study

Books (Fiction and Non-fiction)

Bergen, Doris. *War and Genocide: A Concise History of the Holocaust*. Third Edition. Washington: Rowman and Littlefield, 2016.
Demetz, Peter. *Prague in Black and Gold: Scenes from the Life of a European City*. New York: Hill & Wang, 1997.
Hansen, Randall. *Fire and Fury: the Allied bombing of Germany, 1942–45*. Toronto: Doubleday Canada, 2008.
Kennan, George Frost. *From Prague After Munich: Diplomatic Papers, 1938–1940*. Princeton, NJ: Princeton University Press, 1968.
Kurtz, Glenn. *Three Minutes in Poland: Discovering a Lost World in a 1938 Family Film*. New York: Farrar, Straus and Giroux, 2014.
Snyder, Timothy. *Bloodlands: Europe Between Hitler and Stalin*. New York: Basic Books, 2010.
Zweig, Stefan. *The Royal Game*. London: J. Cape, 1981.

Films

Ashes and Diamonds (1958). Directed by Andrzej Wajda. Poland.
Closely Watched Trains (1966). Directed by Jiří Menzel. Czechoslovakia.
Operation Daybreak (1975). Directed by Lewis Gilbert. Czechoslovakia.
Musíme si pomáhat [*Divided We Fall*] (2000). Directed by Jan Hřebejk. Czech Republic.
I Served the King of England (2006). Directed by Jiří Menzel. Czech Republic.
Son of Saul (2015). Directed by László Nemes. Hungary.
1945 (2017). Directed by Ferenc Török. Hungary.

CHAPTER 4

Making Most of Central Europe Communist

Maybe the best place to start a discussion of the communization of Central Europe is to look at monuments. One of the hallmarks of the Central European memory landscape are Soviet liberation memorials as the Red Army liberated Berlin, Bratislava, Budapest, Vienna, and Warsaw. We have already come across Liberty Square in Budapest with its cornucopia of mixed messages: Soviet liberation, US President Ronald Reagan, German occupation, Trianon, and Miklós Horthy. Vienna has a huge Soviet liberation monument in Schwarzenbergplatz, not too far from the plaque marking the place where Stalin stayed in January 1913, where he wrote "Marxism and the National Question". One might have assumed that with the end of Soviet hegemony in 1989 these monuments would have been banished. Indeed, some were, but most remain. Hungarians, who were willing allies of Germany, tend to present themselves as almost helpless victims. The Poles, not surprisingly, went the furthest in transforming the memory landscape and sent the Russian stuff away, with a new emphasis on Polish resistance.

The Czechs, who spend far less time embellishing or amending the past than the Hungarians or Poles, tell a different story. In Prague, in April 2020, Czech authorities in Prague took down a statue in of General Ivan Konev, who led Red Army troops liberating the city in 1945. The Russians were furious and asked for the statue to be sent to Russia. For Russian President Vladimir Putin, the destruction of Soviet war memorials was symptomatic of a trend to equate Nazi rule during the war with Soviet rule after the war. Prague's other such monument—a tank in Kinsky Square dedicated to the Soviet tank crews that rolled into Prague on 9 May 1945—met its fate already in the early 1990s. A controversial artist, David Černý, painted the tank pink, and after he was arrested, members of parliament replicated his act in protest. The monument was quickly dismantled, and the tank moved to a museum. Decidedly Czech memorials tend to emphasize Czech resistance.

© The Author(s), under exclusive license to Springer Nature
Switzerland AG 2021
R. C. Austin, *A History of Central Europe*,
https://doi.org/10.1007/978-3-030-84543-8_4

For Czechs, as we saw in Chap. 2, two of the major foci of memorializing the Second World War in Czechoslovakia and its successor states have stemmed from the same event—the assassination of Reichsprotektor Reinhard Heydrich in 1942—though the nature of this memorialization shifted significantly with the regime change in 1989. As we saw, the assassination had led the Nazis to massacre the population of the village of Lidice and raze it to the ground in retaliation, and the Communist leadership after 1948 heavily manipulated the story of this tragic event for its own purposes. Lidice, not the assassins, became a major symbol of Communist-style anti-fascist resistance and the triumph of socialism. The survivors of the massacre—mostly women—were heavily exploited to this purpose. After 1989, the Lidice memorial site was no longer front and centre and focus shifted to the members of the resistance who had parachuted into the country with British help, carried out the assassination, hidden in the crypt of an Orthodox church in Prague, and ultimately committed suicide in the face of capture by the Nazi authorities. Because they had parachuted in from Britain under orders from the Czechoslovak government-in-exile in London, the Communists, who seized power in 1948, later considered them to be collaborators with the so-called fascist West as it was the RAF that parachuted them in and essentially erased them from history for 40 years. The many Czech pilots who served in the RAF during the war and, as collaborators with the fascist West, faced prison sentences after the communists seized power in 1948. The crypt in the Cathedral Church of Saints Cyril and Methodius is home to the National Monument to the Heroes of the Heydrich Terror.

Poland also found itself with a plethora of out-of-date Soviet memorials that were antithetical to the principles of the new regime after the peaceful regime change in 1989. Over time, hundreds of these Soviet monuments have been removed but not without controversy as in the case of the Czech Republic, particularly because of a 1994 agreement with Russia regarding the preservation of memorial sites. While the Poles argue that this agreement pertains only to cemeteries for soldiers, Russian authorities interpret it as a blanket agreement covering monuments as well and consider the removal of these memorials as a significant affront to their revisionist narrative of the war.

Still, the removal of communist-era memorials has intensified in recent years. The Institute of National Remembrance, established in Warsaw in 1998 as a state organization investigating crimes from the Second World War to the end of Communist rule, is the body that oversees the removal of these monuments. The Institute's policies are often heavily influenced by the party that is in power in the Polish government, which has been the right-wing nationalist Law and Justice Party since late 2015.

While hundreds of monuments have been removed since 1989, some have received heightened attention in the media. For example, Warsaw's Vilnius Square used to be the home of a monument to wartime Polish-Soviet brotherhood that was erected in 1945. It was dismantled in 2011 in order for a subway line to be constructed, and local residents protested its planned return. In

2015, city councillors banned it from being returned amidst renewed Polish-Russian tensions over the conflict in Ukraine. Elsewhere in the city, a monument in Skaryszewski park commemorating the death of Soviet soldiers in 1944 was frequently vandalized with paint before being taken down in 2018.

Also in 2015, the authorities of the western Polish town of Nowa Sól decided to remove a prominent monument to Polish-Soviet brotherhood, which sparked vehement protests from Russia. Other monuments whose removal has received outrage and protest from Russia include a mausoleum memorializing Red Army soldiers in the town of Trzcianka, a monument of gratitude to the Red Army in the city of Szczecin, and a large memorial to Red Army soldiers in the city of Legnica, among many others.

The election of the Law and Justice Party to power in late 2015 brought with it a rise in nationalist and anti-Soviet sentiment, supported by new legislation and an official campaign of "de-communization", which has certain revisionist elements itself. In 2016, the government announced plans to move Soviet-era monuments to an educational park at the former Soviet military base of Borne Sulinowo, in northwestern Poland. In 2017, the Polish parliament passed a new law requiring the removal of any monuments glorifying the communist era, and since then, the dismantling of these monuments has escalated. Several hundred monuments were marked for removal by the new law.

One major site harkening back to the Soviet-dominated past that still remains is Warsaw's imposing monumental Palace of Culture and Science. Designed by a Soviet architect, it was built by Soviet workers during the early 1950s amidst the rubbles of a totally destroyed Warsaw and features an imposing clock tower. As a "gift" to Poland from Joseph Stalin, it was also supposed to bear his name before the process of de-Stalinization commenced after his death. Various politicians have called for the demolition of the building, proclaiming that it stands for everything Poland rejected in 1989. As such, the imposition of communist rule remains complex and contested.

Wartime Conferences

As a start, in 1945, Central Europe became Eastern Europe and the region was lost to Soviet rule until 1989. Recalling the words of the Czech/French writer Milan Kundera, Central Europe was kidnapped. Only Austria and what would become West Germany, or the Federal Republic of Germany, would escape Soviet hegemony. The story of how this happened is largely straightforward and very much part of the Cold War that gripped Europe between 1948 and 1989. Prior to the Yalta Conference in February 1945, the Allies met several times to plan the war and postwar strategy. The fate of Central Europe, which had very much shaped the war's origins, was highly contested. The Casablanca conference in January 1943 included US President Franklin D. Roosevelt and British Prime Minister Winston Churchill. Stalin was invited but remained in Moscow. Most importantly, the conference settled on the Allies' policy of "unconditional surrender" which was to become a cornerstone for the rest of the war. Churchill, Stalin, and Roosevelt met together in the Tehran conference in November/December 1943. There the focus was very much on the war with Japan, but discussions started over the fate of Central Europe, especially Germany. Stalin was already pushing for a revision of Poland's eastern border. The Baltic states, grabbed illegally in the 1939 Nazi-Soviet Pact, were destined to remain in the USSR despite pledges for referenda in Estonia, Latvia, and Lithuania. The USSR had already planned for that outcome and engaged in extensive ethnic cleansing by deporting 40,000 people in June 1941 just as the Germans were invading. Talk of a United Nations was also mooted to replace the failed League of Nations. The success of Tehran suggested that the USSR was, in a way, converging with the other allies and that postwar cooperation was possible. One tiny indication was that Stalin shut down the Communist International in May 1943. The ideological confrontation of the period prior to the war seemed to be, at least potentially, a thing of the past.

Another major landmark for the fate of Central Europe was the infamous "percentages agreement" of October 1944. In this agreement, which included only Churchill and Stalin, the two agreed to share out spheres of influence in Central Europe. It is an extremely strange agreement and ultimately it proved worthless. Stalin originally got 90 percent of Romania, 75 percent of Bulgaria, Churchill got 90 percent of Greece while they went 50/50 on Hungary and Yugoslavia. Albania did not merit a mention. In the end, Stalin only kept his word on Greece, in the rest of the countries, at the end of the war his control was much closer to 100 percent.

For Central Europe, even though its fate was already decided, the Yalta Conference was held in Crimea in 1945 between the "Big Three": Joseph Stalin, Winston Churchill, and Franklin D. Roosevelt where the facts on the ground were made concrete. The leaders aimed to negotiate measures to end the war, divide Europe effectively, re-establish occupied nations, and handle the war in Asia. The negotiations, while at times tense, were considered to have generally gone well, though the agreement made in Crimea that winter has been seen as another major betrayal of Central Europe on the part of the Western leaders.

The main point of disagreement was between Churchill and Stalin, whose views opposed each other on the question of governance in Eastern and Central Europe. Churchill insisted that the countries there be governed democratically, while Stalin demanded that they fall under the Soviet sphere of influence for security reasons. Stalin, an avid reader of history, viewed Central Europe through the paradigm of the 1930s. Outside of Czechoslovakia, he saw a region of states that were completely hostile to the USSR during the period where even communist parties were banned. Stalin's notion of "friendly" governments in the West was clearly different than what either the United Kingdom or the United States envisioned.

Ultimately, it was Stalin who won the battle because he controlled the territory. In the past, there was ample debate that centred on Stalin's ambitions for the region with some historians arguing that Stalin's intentions were more benign than many had assumed. In the end, with access to documents that came with the collapse of communism and the disintegration of the USSR, we know that Stalin's vision for the region was defined in the 1930s and that he set out to communize much of Central Europe and the Balkans. As we saw with Habsburg disintegration in 1918, the facts on the ground, that is the presence of the Soviet Army in Austria, Bulgaria, Czechoslovakia, Germany, Hungary, Poland, and Romania was a the most essential tool for ensuring Stalin's long-term vision and Soviet security needs. Only Czechoslovakia, as shall see, ended up in the Soviet sphere by choice. Albania and Yugoslavia went communist too but without the aid or presence of the Red Army. This, to a degree, provided those regimes with a degree of legitimacy that was missing in Central Europe.

At Yalta, the topic of Poland was also a contentious one. For Stalin, Poland (along with Bulgaria and Romania) was simply too important for Soviet security needs to be anything but a satellite. The Western leaders supported the Polish government-in-exile in London, while the Soviet team tried to push them to accept the Communist-backed government which had been set up in Lublin, and neither party was willing to budge. While Stalin promised to allow the country free elections, the other leaders were sceptical of him, but eventually conceded. Stalin argued that Poland was critical to the Soviet Union because it was the main route through which the Germans had attacked the USSR, but that he felt the Poles deserved freedom and dignity because the Soviet forces had treated them poorly and unfairly. After this impassioned speech, the Western leaders felt inclined to believe him. Churchill famously said that Chamberlin had been a fool to trust Hitler, but he felt that he could count on Stalin on the topic of Poland. Of course, he was tragically wrong. Stalin's true intentions are shown in records of how he discussed the issue with his foreign minister, Vyacheslav Molotov. Molotov told the leader that he was concerned the agreement at Yalta would impede their intention to establish a sphere of influence in the region, to which Stalin replied, "Nevermind, we'll do it our way later." Stalin began to consolidate control of the country almost immediately after the Yalta Conference. When elections were finally held in 1947, a Communist government was installed. After the war, the entire Central European region, as well as former Axis powers such as Bulgaria and Romania, were turned into the Soviet Union's satellite states.

While the leaders signed the Declaration on Liberated Europe, which outlined that the governments of all occupied countries would be reinstated, the Soviet Union held most of Eastern and Central Europe with a military force much larger than that of the Western nations, so there was a sense that Russia was calling the shots at the conference, and that while the leaders agreed to certain terms, the Soviet Union ultimately had the final say. James F. Byrnes, a member of the American delegation, aptly observed, "It was not a question of what we would *let* the Russians do, but what we could *get* the Russians to do."

Hitler was dead on 30 April 1945 and the Germans offered their unconditional surrender on 8 May 1945 at midnight—*Stunde Null* in German—or "zero hour". Germany was the most important postwar question and therefore the fate of Germany is really the principal source of the Cold War. The Allies agreed to divide Germany and Berlin into four occupied zones, which were to be given to the United Kingdom, the United States, France, and the Soviet Union. The French section was cut out of the British and American territories, but it was not looked upon kindly by French President Charles de Gaulle, who was very displeased that he had not been invited to the Yalta Conference. De Gaulle tried to occupy Stuttgart, but was deterred by the Americans, who threatened to sanction France. It was decided that Germany would pay reparations partially through forced labour. The Allies also debated whether Germany should be dismembered into various smaller countries. Various solutions were on the table to deal with the "German" problem including the Morgenthau Plan, named after Hans Morgenthau, the US Secretary of the Treasury, who advocated stripping Germany of any potential to make war in the future. Stalin's suggestion that he was amenable to a neutral and unified Germany was not sincere.

Finally, the leaders agreed that Nazi war criminals would be tried and some Nazi leaders would be executed. Stalin also agreed to participate in the creation of the United Nations, and guidelines for voting at the Security Council were drafted. Stalin pushed for the Western powers to grant all of the Soviet republics membership in the UN General Assembly, but this right was only given to Ukraine, Belarus, so the USSR had three seats in total.

The conference, while well received at the time it was held, became a contentious topic after the start of the Cold War, and is seen by Central Europeans as a second betrayal of Munich-level proportions. The Western leaders were criticized for handing the region away to a dictator again, albeit a different one. The countries that fell under the Soviet sphere of influence during the time faced Communist occupation for decades into the future, so the agreement at Yalta was critical to the long-term postwar order of Europe.

Relations between the leaders at the Conference are described as being amicable, and in the immediate aftermath of the meeting, the agreement was celebrated as proof that US-Soviet relations would last into the postwar period. Today, the event is generally regarded as being the last time that the Eastern and Western leaders were on good terms until the fall of the Soviet Union. Roosevelt died just two months after the conclusion of the Yalta Conference, and was replaced by President Harry S. Truman, who became responsible for handling the conclusion to the war.

The Potsdam Conference occurred in the last two weeks of July in 1945, in Potsdam, a suburb of Berlin, and it was the last meeting of the Big Three before the end of the Second World War. No doubt the visit was an eye opener as the delegates got to see first-hand the results of the Soviet siege and the unrelenting Allied bombing campaign. Berlin was field of ruin. By then, Roosevelt had died and was replaced by his vice-president, Harry Truman. During the conference, Winston Churchill lost an election was replaced by Clement Atlee. No doubt Stalin was perplexed by this as he was not subject to any elections that mattered. While relations in Yalta had been seen as amicable, the environment at Potsdam was considerably different. The conference was regarded as less successful compared to the Yalta Conference before it, given that the Allies did not have a common enemy to deal with, which made them more impatient, competitive, and self-interested than before in their negotiations. Although the leaders disagreed on many topics, they managed to agree again that Germany was to be divided between the American, British, French, and Soviet forces, and that all Nazi influence and laws were to be removed from the country. They also demanded unconditional surrender from Japan, discussed the atomic bombing of the country which for some later historians introduced the notion of atomic diplomacy in that the United States tried to encourage the USSR to play ball or face atomic weapons, and eventually permitted the United States to pursue this course of action. The leaders also agreed to implement the five "D's" across Germany and Austria: demilitarization, deindustrialization, decentralization, de-Nazification, and democratization. Austria, as we saw in the preceding chapter, had somehow slipped into the victim camp due to the *Anschluss* of 1938. Austria too was under four-power occupation but Stalin would show some flexibility towards Austria's partition that would, under his successors in 1955, permit Austria to achieve what many thought impossible: the end of occupation and the beginning of an entirely new era of neutrality and prosperity aided by healthy doses of amnesia.

At Yalta, Stalin had pushed for massive economic reparations from Germany for what they had done to the Soviet Union and its civilians, and Roosevelt agreed to the leader's demands, but the same request was rejected at Potsdam by Truman and Churchill. The two Western leaders saw the Soviet demand for money to be dangerous, given that harsh economic sanctions after the First World War had contributed to the rise of Hitler and the start of the Second World War. Despite this rejection, the Soviet Union was allowed to take 10–15 percent of the industrial equipment from Western Germany in exchange for raw materials and agricultural products from the USSR.

The leaders also debated about how to redraw the borders of Europe, and what to do with the Germans who had been settled in the Central European states before and during the war. It was decided that the Soviet Union would take a large portion of Polish land, which they had occupied in 1939, ending at the Curzon Line, but in return, the Poles would be granted land from Germany. Poland was given large chunks of Germany to the Oder-Neisse Line, along the Oder and Neisse rivers.

Even before the Conference had started, Poland, the Czech Republic, and Hungary began to expel Germans from their territories, and the mass migration worried the Western leaders, who feared that the influx of refugees would destabilize Germany. As such, they asked the Central European states to pause with the expulsion and treat the Germans humanely. However, this did not occur, as the Central European states exacted their revenge on the Germans, whom they saw as an extension of the Nazi state which had subjected them to so much injustice.

The leaders again failed to agree on what to do with Poland. The concept of making the country democratic was disputed and contentious. The Big Three eventually recognized the Soviet-backed government in Poland, meaning that the Polish government-in-exile in London became defunct. Like Berlin and Germany, under the Potsdam Agreement, Austria and Vienna were also divided into four sections, which were managed by the Allied countries. The Agreement was signed on 12 April 1945.

The Nuremberg Trials

In 1943, the Allies advised the Germans that their leaders would be tried when the war was won, in the Declaration on German Atrocities in Occupied Europe. The decision to punish Nazi leaders was reiterated at both the Yalta and Potsdam Conferences. The number of Nazis to be executed was discussed at the 1943 Tehran conference, where Stalin said 50,000 to 100,000 officers ought to be killed. Roosevelt reportedly joked that 49,000 was enough, and Churchill vehemently opposed any such action and advocated to persecute only the leadership.

The Allies had plans to execute all major war criminals, but this plan was unpopular amongst American and British voters, so it was abandoned. Upon his arrival on the scene, the new American President Harry Truman advocated for a legal process, and the trial of war criminals was planned. The trials started on 20 November 1945 in Nuremberg, Germany and set a new standard for international criminal justice which was later applied following other conflicts such as the wars in the former Yugoslavia in the 1990s. Stalin had advocated for the trials to be held in Berlin, as the capital of the Nazi regime, and Luxembourg and Leipzig were also considered, but Nuremberg was the winner in the end because its courthouse was mostly intact, and also because it was the birthplace of the Nazi Party.

The judges at the Nuremberg trials were from each of the major Allied countries. The defence lawyers were mostly German. Twenty-four indictments were brought against war criminals, as well as six organizations who were seen as having committed war crimes, such as the Nazi Party, the Schutzstaffel (also known as the Protection Squadron or the SS), and the Gestapo. They were accused of committing crimes against peace, initiating war of aggression, participation in war crimes, and committing crimes against humanity.

More than ten different trials took place are Nuremberg, the most prominent being the Major War Criminals' trial, which occurred between 1945–1946. Twelve other trials were held afterwards, from 1946 to 1949. The later trials included special categories for doctors who had carried out medical experiments on victims, and legal servants who had proposed, advocated for, and implemented eugenics laws in the Third Reich. At the trails, evidence was presented that showed the Nazi crimes had been premeditated and targeted specific racial groups such as Jews and Slavs. A number of high-ranking officials of the Einsatzgruppen and SS admitted to the premeditated murders of thousands of Jews and Slavs, as did the managers of major concentration camps such as Auschwitz. During the trial, as already noted, the Soviets also blamed the 1940 Katyn massacre on the Germans, though their accusations lacked sufficient evidence, and the Germans strongly denied it, the Allies accepted the Soviet version it as truth, since they had bigger issues to worry about at the time and did not want to risk upsetting the Soviets. The Soviets denied responsibility for the crimes until 1990, five years after Mikhail Gorbachev came to power.

Unfortunately, it proved impossible to try most of the top Nazi leadership because they were already dead. As noted, Adolf Hitler had shot himself inside his Berlin bunker on 30 April 1945. Joseph Goebbels (the Nazi minister of propaganda) killed himself that spring as well. Heinrich Himmler, the leader of the SS, tried to go into hiding, but was captured, and ingested cyanide in British captivity in May 1945. As noted, Reinhard Heydrich, the "butcher of Prague" and the mastermind behind the Holocaust, was assassinated by Czech and Slovak partisans in June 1942. Adolf Eichmann was detained and put into a camp by US troops after the war, but his true identity as one of the main facilitators of Nazi death camps remained unknown, so he escaped, obtained falsified papers, spent the better part of a decade in hiding, and moved to Argentina. Although he had successfully escaped from Europe, he was eventually captured by the Israeli secret service. He was tried and hanged in Israel in 1962. His trial, chronicled by Hannah Arendt first for the *New Yorker* and later in her book *Eichmann in Jerusalem: A Report on the Banality of Evil*, are ground-breaking studies of the mindset of Nazi functionaries. Out of all top-ranking Nazi operatives, Albert Speer, Hitler's chief architect and the minister of war production, was the only one to take personal responsibility for his actions at Nuremberg. During his trial, he told the court that he had become increasingly disillusioned by Hitler towards the end of the war, and even plotted to kill him in February 1945. He was sentenced to 20 years in prison.

Overall, the Major War Criminals' trial lasted nearly a full year, with the final sentences read out on 1 October 1946. Twelve defendants were scheduled for execution, seven were given prison time, three were acquitted, and two were not charged. The Allies debated the best way to kill those condemned for execution. The French wanted to execute the guilty by firing squad, but the Soviets argued they were not deserving of a traditional military death. It was eventually decided that the men would be hanged.

Hermann Göring, the first Gestapo boss and later the head of the Luftwaffe (Nazi Air Force) was scheduled to be hanged but committed suicide with a cyanide pill the day before his execution. In one of his suicide notes he said he would have accepted death by firing squad but refused to be hanged. Martin Bormann, Hitler's private secretary and the head of the Nazi Party Chancellery had died in 1945, so he was convicted in absentia. The others facing the death penalty were largely Nazi cabinet members, and included Nazi Foreign Minister Joachim von Ribbentrop; Hans Frank, the sadistic head of the Polish General Government; Wilhelm Frick, Nazi minister of the Interior and governor of the

Protectorate of Bohemia and Moravia; Wilhelm Keitel, chief of the Nazi Armed Forces High Command; Nazi Colonel General Alfred Jodl; SS General Ernst Kaltenbrunner; Alfred Rosenberg, an ideologue of the Nazi Party; Julius Streicher, a Nazi Party propagandist; Alfred Seyss-Inquart, an Austrian Nazi official alluded to earlier; and Fritz Sauckel, a Nazi politician.

The ten men were hanged in the gymnasium of the Nuremberg Prison on 16 October 1946, by John Clarence Woods, a US army sergeant. There were some technical difficulties with the gallows, however, including that the ropes were apparently too short, which caused many of the victims to suffocate to death, which took up to half an hour in some cases, instead of the intended humane and quick death from a broken neck. The trap door was allegedly also too small, so some of the convicts hit their heads and were cut during their descent. The dead were burned in a crematorium in Munich and their ashes were scattered over the Isar River in Bavaria.

Although at the time of the trials many legal bodies dismissed them as an abuse of power on the part of the Allies, Nuremberg is now widely regarded as an important milestone in the development of international law. Not only did the process try and convict war criminals, but it was the first-time war crimes were persecuted in the modern era. It presented a new approach to law, and the framework of the war crimes laws were later used by the United Nations in similar cases and led to the creation of the International Criminal Court. It was also the first time that genocide was mentioned in the context of modern law. Others were less happy. For some, it placed blame right on the top leadership without a meaningful bottom-up assessment of ordinary Germans in the Nazi enterprise. That type of reckoning would have to wait until the 1980s. For now, many Germans could engage in forgetting or assume that their country was hijacked by a gang of murderous criminals. But to be sure, a new albeit Western Germany, did emerge. With help from the United States, Germany came to grip with its past far better than any other country. Collective responsibility for the crimes of the Nazi regime is very much embedded in the German psyche. Most importantly, the education system ensures that all students know, in an unforgiving way, what happened between 1933 and 1945.

Postwar Refugees and Population Transfers

During the war, Nazi/Axis and Soviet policy had already changed borders dramatically and actively resettled whole groups of people. This was over and above the near total destruction of Europe's Jews. For example, as a result of the August 1939 Nazi-Soviet Pact, the Soviets deported thousands of Estonians, Latvians, Moldovans, Lithuanians, and Poles. The Poles of eastern Poland were particularly hard hit by the USSR's attempts to reshape the ethnic landscape of their new territories. After the war, forced migration intensified as Europe was filled with millions of displaced people. It is estimated that the war had displaced between 11 and 20 million people from their homes, and Germany alone housed seven million of them. Various forced migrations were taking place. Occupants of concentration camps had been liberated and did not know where to go. Eastern Europeans, especially those who had collaborated with the Nazis, tried to flee to the West. Westerners who had lost their homes during bombings had nowhere to live. Poles and other groups who had been forcibly resettled by the Germans had no homes. For the "feel" of at least a part of Europe after the war the best film is Carol Reed's *The Third Man* (1949) which captures Vienna under four-power after 1945. With a screenplay by Graham Greene, Orson Welles as the black marketer Harry Lime explains the end of European morality in stark terms and how worthless life had become.

It was initially decided that the best course of action was simply to repatriate the displaced people as quickly as possible, but this soon proved difficult. Jews who had been deported were often afraid to return home. In some countries, such as Poland and Slovakia, there were anti-Semitic pogroms in which Jews were harassed, beaten, and even killed. The largest took place in the Polish town Kielce in 1946, where 42 Jews died. Jews who tried to return home often found that their houses and belongings had been confiscated by strangers. Sometimes, they were occupied by Aryan neighbours who had denounced them in the first place. The scene in Hungary was no better where Jews returning home had to essentially bury their experiences. Possibly one of the better film portrayals of this time is *1945* (2017). It tells the story of two Jews who return to a village after the war. The locals are terrified. Some of them are compromised by bad behaviour towards the Jews. Why are they there? Do they want their property back? The people of the village are forced to confront their own shameful roles in the fate of the Jews.

Some population movements, especially in the Soviet-occupied territories, contradicted the repatriation policy. Over a million refugees, usually of Eastern European descent, were left homeless because they could not be repatriated due to fear of returning to their homes in the Soviet Union. Under the conditions agreed upon during the Yalta Conference, the Soviet Union felt entitled to the return of their civilians and demanded that the Allies comply. Many Eastern European refugees, and some Soviet prisoners of war, refused to go back to their home countries to avoid the Communist regime. While some were sent back forcibly, breaking the United Nations' rules on *nonrefoulement*, others managed to escape and make new lives in Canada, the United Kingdom, the United States, and Australia.

The fate of the historic community of Germans in Central Europe deserves additional detail. Between 1944 and 1947 over 12 million Germans were from Central (and Eastern Europe) and hundreds of thousands died, some say more than one million. The east German territories of Pomerania and Silesia were transferred to Poland, and the Germans there were expelled. In their place, nearly two million Poles from the eastern part of the country were settled, and the borders of eastern Poland were changed to give the territory to Ukraine and Belarus. Half-a-million Belarussians and Ukrainians were removed from Poland and resettled in the Soviet Union. German writer Walter Kempowski's novel *All for Nothing* (2006) is a good entry point to understand the fate of

Germans sitting in East Prussia (now Kaliningrad) as the Red Army approached, their lives progressively unravelled and their world got turned upside down.

The two cases that stand out are the fate of the Germans in Czechoslovakia and Poland. In the former case, the postwar Czechoslovak moved to expel the Germans and the Hungarians. Given the perceived role of the Germans in events leading up to the Munich agreement of 1938, the postwar Czechoslovak President Edvard Beneš had his own rationale for expelling the Germans: it was humane in that in protected the Germans from random acts of a people who might see justified revenge. In any case, first Germans were forced out in violent "wild marches" usually driven by locals. In Czechoslovakia, fines were imposed on anyone who intervened on behalf of the Germans. For others, the notion of ethnic homogeneity was something to be embraced as it would prevent another war. For the German expellees in Poland in what the new communist government called the "recovered territories" their experience was the same as the Sudeten Germans. The German city of Breslau, which became Polish Wrocław after the war, tells this moment in twentieth-century history as the communist bosses did their best to prove their Polishness over the centuries. Apologies or restitution did not exist, and the issue persisted well into the twenty-first century. In fact, the expulsion of the Germans was often hardly mentioned in a world where it was impossible for Germans to be victims. But the facts remain, it was largest case of forced migration in recorded history.

Reconciliation, often halting, was a long time coming. In Poland, though, it was the Church that took the first step. In a letter from the head of the Archdiocese of Wrocław Bolesław Kominek in a 1965 letter to German bishops wrote, "We forgive and ask for forgiveness." Poland's then communist rulers were not happy with the Church making foreign policy. In 2005, 15 years after the communists departed and on the 40th anniversary of the letter, Kominek got a statue in Wrocław. Czechoslovakia's first post-communist President Václav Havel also offered an apology to the German expellees in 1989. The allies learned after that fact too that the population transfers had been a disaster and vowed not to let them occur in further discussions down the road with Germany. Despite that, population transfers did not die as a means to solve minority problems as lots of serious people offered them up again during the Yugoslav wars in the 1990s.

Elsewhere in Europe, other changes were underway, and although the war had ended, the events were often tragic. The northern German city of Königsberg, now known as Kaliningrad, was annexed by the Soviet Union, and the Germans there were expelled. Conditions in the city deteriorated terribly in 1945—there were serious food shortages, and people sometimes resorted to cannibalism. Thousands of German refugees fleeing from the east died when their overcrowded ships sank in the Baltic Sea. Other Germans were brutally deported from Central Europe. While many had been resettled there under the Nazi regime, others had been living there for generations and were part of a minority group, but they were ruthlessly cast out of the area as well. In total, 2.2 million Germans were expelled from the Czech Republic, and their belongings and property were confiscated. About 60,000 fled from Hungary before the war had even ended. Many Germans who remained in the Soviet-occupied Central European countries were deported in trains to labour camps in eastern Ukraine and Russia. Meanwhile, millions of Soviet prisoners were released from captivity in Germany and returned to the Soviet Union. Unfortunately, the Soviet state, still run by Joseph Stalin, was paranoid about enemy agents, and suspected the returnees of having been "turned" by the Germans, so many of them were arrested and deported to the gulags in Siberia for even more time in terrible conditions, after they had already spent years barely surviving in German prisoner of war camps.

Displaced persons (DP) camps were set up by the Allied powers and the United Nations, largely on the territory of Germany and Austria. About 250,000 Jews stayed in the DP camps, sometimes for years, until they were granted the right to leave Europe. Many of the displaced Jews were from Poland, but there were also citizens of Czechoslovakia, Hungary, and the Balkans represented there. The camps, and Europe's displaced people, were overseen by the United Nations Relief and Rehabilitation Administration (UNRRA—the precursor to the UNHCR) starting from October 1945. Prior to the UN's takeover of the camps, refugees there lived in dire conditions, facing shortages of food and harsh treatment from camp guards. The conditions were considered especially bad in American camps. Even under the UN administration, conditions for refugees were difficult. Food rations were scarce, medical, and hygienic supplies were often unavailable, and the refugees themselves were traumatized, emaciated, and prone to sickness.

Meanwhile, governments were in disarray, and immigration papers were difficult to obtain. Many Jews aimed to go to Palestine, and various attempts to send refugee ships there were foiled by British forces in the late 1940s. A large number of Jews were forced to stay in the DP camps until the state of Israel was created in 1948, after which Jews moved there in the hundreds of thousands. Israel accepted over 600,000 Jewish refugees by 1950.

In the years following the war, many countries started immigration programmes. The United States took about 400,000 displaced persons between 1949 and 1952. Only a small fraction of these were Jews though, and the total amount of those resettled in the United States was a drop in the ocean compared to all the refugees in Europe. At this time, the United States also opened the Escapee programme, which took in victims of repression from Communist countries. Canada took more than 150,000 refugees, and Australia took over 180,000 people, the majority of whom were Eastern Europeans. Many Latin American countries also took considerable refugee populations.

The latter half of the 1940s saw the creation of vital humanitarian organizations that still exist to this day, such as the United Nations High Commission for Refugees (UNHCR). The organizations were not perfect however, and there was a great deal of bureaucracy and political manoeuvring, especially due to the outbreak of the Cold War. Despite the difficulties, about six million refugees were successfully repatriated by the end of 1945. By the end of the 1950s, the Western states took in nearly a million Second World War refugees. While most of the DP camps closed in the late 1940s and early 1950s (only two remained after 1952), it wasn't until 1960 that all of Europe's refugee camps were closed.

The Marshall Plan to Rebuild Europe

The Marshall Plan, or the formally the European Recovery Programme, was a large funding package offered to the postwar European countries by the United States announced in June 1947 and launched 1948 to promote democratization, stability, and economic prosperity across the war-ravaged continent. Named after Secretary of State George Marshall who was horrified about Soviet hegemony in Central Europe and the potential for economic collapse in Western Europe that could only strengthen already strong communist parties in France and Italy, the United States gave $13 billion (worth about $100 billion in 2018) to the European nations to help their economies. The United Kingdom took more than a quarter of the funding, France took 18 percent, and West Germany took 11 percent. The Soviet Union was invited to take the money as well, but they refused, since it was offered with the stipulation of economic cooperation and the purchase of American-made products, and because Stalin was suspicious that the money would come with Western meddling attached. Stalin also blocked the Soviet-backed governments in the Eastern Bloc, including Poland, Hungary, and Czechoslovakia from taking any help, though they were eager to get assistance in rebuilding their countries. In exchange, Stalin offered the Central European countries $450 million along with machinery, grain, and the establishment of manufacturing in those countries. The denial of Western funding by the Soviet Union broadened the economic divide in Europe and had lasting implications on the continent which are still felt today. While the West was able to cooperate economically and rebuild and faced several decades of resurgence and growth after the war, the East, which was considerably more war ravaged by default, struggled and fell behind.

Communist Takeovers

As the Marshall Plan transformed parts of Western Europe but terrified the Soviets as a tool for undermining their hold on the region, Central Europe disappeared for the next 45 years and became Eastern Europe. In broad strokes the communist takeovers in the region bear some startling similarities. Fundamental, as already noted, was the overwhelming presence of the Red Army everywhere except in Hoxha's Albania and Josip Broz Tito's Yugoslavia. In both cases, the communists won hard-fought civil wars. This gave both countries a degree of mobility within the Soviet bloc that was denied to Central Europe. In addition to the Red Army there were hundreds of Soviet "advisors" on hand in the army, the police and various ministries and the Red Army was in the driver's seat. As important, local communist party leaders were totally obedient to Moscow. Austria will be discussed in detail in the next chapter, but we can say that it avoided a communist takeover largely because Stalin decided it was unnecessary although Austria remained under four-power occupation until the State Treaty of 1955. Strangely enough, in the case of Austria Stalin rejected partition and even restrained local communists who pushed for partition and prolonged Soviet occupation. It was good politics after all. The West controlled the richer west of Austria and any partition might invite the merger of the other occupation zones with West German occupation zones.

It can be easy to forget that while larger forces, primarily the Red Army, were deciding the fate of the region, ordinary people were still recovering from the devastating destruction of the war and even the years that preceded it. Central and Eastern Europe were the hardest hit regions in Europe. The interwar experience with People capitalism had utterly failed the region, and change needed to occur. Soviet intentions for the region were reasonably clear and understood. But installing communists in power would not be that easy as there were very few places where Communists had popular support, yet the Soviets and local Communists were able to accomplish the task in just three years. While in some places, as we will see, the Soviets had to manipulate political structures, such as in Hungary and Poland, in other places, like Czechoslovakia, the Communists were able to come to power through the system already in place, with genuine popular support.

In 1945, it was obvious Central and Eastern Europe needed a restructuring plan, and as the occupiers, the Soviets and the Red Army took advantage of that fact to increase their power and influence. With the West abandoning the region already by 1938, and distrust of the West at an all-time high, the Soviet Union and local Communist organizations promised they could lead the region to recovery. It is easy to understand why people believed that when one re-examines the region's fate between the wars and why Stalin was so terrified that unfriendly governments on the USSR's western borders had to be avoided. Remember, outside of Czechoslovakia, there no Soviet-friendly governments. Precisely the opposite in fact. Regional Communist organizations led by hard core fanatics had also played an important role in many countries' liberation efforts, including Hungary, the Czech lands, Slovakia, Romania, and Yugoslavia, giving them credibility not found in other political parties and organizations. Often these organizations had a large number of dedicated and enthusiastic youth, who helped campaign for Communism after the war had ended. Even before the Communists attempted to seize power, the state was heavily involved in the effort to rehabilitate the region, providing food and shelter to those that needed it, and "abandoned" property falling into state ownership. Indeed, the Second World War but a decisive change in the role of the state in all of Europe. Ordinary people relied on state intervention in the postwar recovery effort, and the Communists were able to step in as the most organized political party in many countries, with help from the Soviet Union. Communist propaganda talked about a restructuring plan, peace, and a continued fight against fascism more efficiently than others. With the addition of long-awaited land reform, the Communists were able to gain support of many rural populations across the region.

The Soviets had also arrived in Central and Eastern Europe well-prepared. They knew the world of propaganda. Early on the controlled the message (and the police) as they took control of radio stations when they occupied these countries. Along with the political organizations on the ground, the Communists were able to spread their postwar plan over the radio and make their case for why they were the right course to avoid the death and destruction the war had brought upon these countries. With the introduction of policies such as enhancing workers' rights and safety, which had not existed in most parts of the region, the Communists were able to gain favour as they gained power. They also helped with education reforms, including expanded access to higher education and programmes to help adults catch up on their educations. Of course, there was some resistance to the Communists in places like Poland, but overall, the people of Central and Eastern Europe were too tired—or perhaps, didn't even care—to fight the increasing hold Communists had on their governments.

While the allies haggled over the composition of the coalition governments that emerged after the war, Stalin implemented a policy that served largely Soviet interests and had already been evident with the Nazi-Soviet Pact of August 1939 with the creation of a stable sphere of influence. With Western leaders calling for democratic governments, the Soviets knew that they could not win at the ballot box. What happened between 1945 and 1948 largely followed a similar pattern: sham coalition democracy with communists in key positions that did not attract a lot of undo attention, steady destruction of pre-war political elites and wartime real and perceived collaborators, elimination of competing centres of loyalty such as the church, except in Poland, and civil society organizations, atomization of society through informer and secret police networks, rigged trials, and rigged elections. Outside of Czechoslovakia, the regional communist parties were extremely small existing on the margins with members moving in and out of jail often. But the communists in each place did have a fairly strong school of hard knocks inner circle that was prepared to do the bloody work required to seize and maintain power in what were extremely unfriendly environments. How else can communist parties with often less than 2000 members in 1945 end up with 95 percent voter support by 1948. This meant that their main tools were covert and overt terror and repression. While the top-down story is important, as we shall see there were lots of reasons why ordinary people willingly embraced the new order on offer from Moscow.

The Hungarian communist leader Mátyás Rákosi, by all accounts a despicable person, who called himself "Stalin's best pupil" and was fiercely loyal to the USSR was in many ways typical of the type of local communist the Soviets needed to solidify control. He remains the most emblematic of the type of people who rose to the top of the communist hierarchy between 1945 and

1948 in Central Europe. School of hard knocks hardly scratches the surface. Born in 1892 in what is now in Serbia, Rákosi was a capable student who excelled, served in the First World War, and later as a prisoner of war in Russia and even served in the Kun government in 1919. He remained a well-travelled and polyglot communist activist between the wars and was sentenced to prison but was later exchanged for some flags from the 1848 revolution and sent to the USSR in 1940. When he returned to Hungary in 1945, he brought a special love of violence to his rule over Hungary between 1948 and 1956. His notion of "salami tactics", whereby the communists sliced off, bit by bit the parties they were in a coalition with became a simplistic albeit useful way to understand the basics of communist takeovers. It was a highly fluid milieu where even the top could end up in jail or dead in a world where you could be a hero one day and traitor the next.

As Horthy had maintained some democratic trappings in the period between the wars, Rákosi and his inner circle went against the non-Horthyite political parties such as the Smallholders Party and Social Democrats. Horthy's Unity Party and the Arrow Cross were eliminated to a degree by executions and by the fact that many former Arrow Cross party members joined the communists. Horthy fled Hungary in October 1944 after the German/Arrow Cross takeover and headed to Vienna and then placed under house arrest in Bavaria. He was later arrested by US troops, testified in Nuremburg but was never charged with war crimes, even for the ones he committed when his troops invaded Yugoslavia in 1941. He was later given sanctuary in Portugal where he died in 1957. He was reburied in Hungary in 1993. Arrow Cross leader Ferenc Szálasi was arrested and executed in 1946. Three former prime ministers, László Bárdossy, Béla Imrédy, and Döme Sztójay, were also executed. Plus, as noted, everyone agreed to expel the Germans. Land reform finally came which obtained its desired result: the elimination of the pre-war landowning class and an equally harsh blow against the church.

During the period of consolidation there were three elections—1945, 1947, and 1949. In the 1945 elections the communists got 17 percent of the vote but held four ministries including the Interior Ministry, the most important since it controlled police, border guards, and state security. In the last "free government" the Soviets, who called the shots politically and economically, ensured that the Interior Ministry was held by Hungarian Communists, who also controlled mass media and the courts. Control of what were called the People's Courts proved especially effective to ensure your enemies faced certain conviction. In the 1947 election, the last free election in Hungary until 1990 they got 22 percent. Between 1947 and 1948, they ramped up their attacks on the opposition so that in the 1949 election they had 96 percent. The Smallholders Party, until then the biggest party, eventually imploded, tarred with false accusations, led by László Rajk, the communist interior minister and later foreign minister, in the communist-controlled media. The once powerful Social Democratic Party, usually aligned with the communists, ceased to exist and the communist party became the Hungarian Workers' Party in 1948, destined to rule Hungary as a "People's Republic" until 1989.

Unlike in Hungary where Stalin took his time, the Poles and Poland were doomed from the start. They did not even get the sham democracy of 1945–1948. The Polish story is simple. The postwar government was dominated by the Communists (called the Polish Workers' Party until 1948) and their allies—Social Democrats and others. They confronted only one opposition party in their midst, the Polish Peasants' Party. The communists destroyed them with false accusations or simply murder by the secret police. The party's leader was smuggled out of Poland fearing for his life. But the Poles did get some exceptions. As noted, collectivization never happened and the Catholic Church did not suffer the same fate as in Hungary.

Given the justifiable anti-Russian sentiment in Poland, the Soviet Union's communization project in Poland was a tough sell. Unlike its neighbour Czechoslovakia, the Polish population did not have many Communist sympathizers; this, coupled with a weak democratic tradition, resulted in the Communists undergoing an illegal seizure of power. Throughout the war, Polish Communist parties re-emerged, eventually coming together in a coalition known as the Lublin Committee in 1944, consisting of the Polish Workers' Party (PWP) and the Union of Polish Patriots. The PWP, led by Władysław Gomułka, was founded during the Second World War and was the most influential and powerful of the leftist parties in postwar Poland. Gomułka was certainly the most important of all of Poland's communist party bosses. He was a classic worker and trade union activist, jailed in the 1930s for his activities, who also studied in Moscow. The Soviet-approved Lublin Committee opposed the Polish government-in-exile in London, which was recognized as the official government of Poland by the Western powers. By January 1945, the Soviet Union recognized the Lublin Committee as the Provisional Government of the Republic of Poland.

Poland began its postwar period without a genuine attempt at democracy, as the ruling coalition was already formed of only Communists and their sympathizers. The coalition consisted of the PWP, the Polish Socialist Party, the Democratic Party, the Labour Party, and the Peasant Party (PPP). The leader of the PPP, Stanisław Mikołajczyk, and his party were the main threat to the Communist coalition. However, the Communist coalition also had some genuine support, as they had helped in popular resistance during the war, and compared to his eastern European counterparts, Gomułka's ties to the Soviet Union and Stalin were not as strong. Gomułka openly criticized Soviet troops for their behaviour as they liberated Poland from German occupation and acknowledged that the United Kingdom and the United States had played a large role in defeating Germany. While Gomułka's public attitude towards the Soviet Union aided the Communists slightly, popular support remained minimal.

The process of the Communist takeover in Poland began immediately after the war, when the coalition first targeted the Polish economy. As part of the postwar nationalization decrees, in January 1946, most industry in Poland was nationalized and the property of Germans and collaborators was taken away. One sector that was not nationalized and would remain largely that way throughout the Communist period, was agriculture: while other countries were unable to stop all sectors of their economy from being nationalized, Poland maintained some independence and privatization in its agriculture throughout the entire Communist period. The Polish Communists also controlled key ministries, such as the Ministry of the Interior, the Ministry of Public Security, and the newly created Ministry of Regained Territories (run by Gomułka).

The Polish Communists had to rely on disingenuous democratic movements in order to gain control of the entire government; despite the Polish Communists openly criticizing aspects of Moscow's decision-making, popular support for the Communists in Poland remained scarce. In 1946, the State National Council held a referendum, dubbed the "Polish People's Referendum", that dealt with three issues: abolishing the senate, the nationalization of the economy, and Poland's new borders (Poland's borders had shifted westwards into Germany following the war). Unofficially, the referendum was intended to see if the Polish people accepted Communism as their new form of government; under this assumption, the coalition campaigned for a "three times yes" referendum result, where they would receive a vast majority of support on all their proposed questions. While the majority of Polish citizens voted yes on all three questions (with the borders issue having 90 percent support), the usual intimidation and threats had been a large part of the communist coalition's campaign. The Communists targeted those who opposed the measures in the referendum, and even switched votes in the ballot box. The manipulation of the voting in the referendum resulted in a call for democratic elections the next year.

Like the results of the referendum, the 1947 elections showed the extent of power the Communists already held in Poland, through the way they were able to exert influence over voting and the election process. Many of the same intimidation tactics were used on those who opposed the communist government. The 1947 elections saw attacks against Mikołajczyk's Polish Peasant Party, since they had the largest political following in Poland. Almost a fifth of the PPP candidates were disqualified, and the PPP was given limited access to the communist-controlled radio for campaigning. The Communist coalition won 80 percent of the vote and shortly after their win they made a new constitution on 19 February. While the parties maintained the guise of a coalition for a couple months, on May Day Gomułka announced that the PWP was the only party that needed to represent the working class. The Communist takeover of Poland was now complete, but would face a bumpy road ahead, including the largest anti-Communist movement Eastern Europe would see.

Czechoslovakia was the only country in the Soviet sphere of influence with genuine support for the Communists, as well as the only country with a successful interwar democracy. The situation for the Communist takeover in

Czechoslovakia was unique: Soviet troops left Czechoslovakia by December 1945, unlike in neighbouring countries, where Soviet troops stayed while the Communists took over the government, and even after. The democratic tradition from Czechoslovakia's interwar period carried over into the postwar period, where Edvard Beneš, an interwar leader, once again became president of a reunited Czechoslovakia. With the memory of the Munich Agreement fresh in the minds of both the government and the people, Czechoslovakia's relationship with the Western powers remained shaky following the war. Beneš, despite wanting to keep Czechoslovakia's democratic tradition alive, believed that the Soviet Union would act as the main influential power in central and eastern Europe. Fearing a revanchist Germany, he considered the USSR as protector of Czechoslovak sovereignty.

While other countries faced issues between their wartime governments-in-exile and the Communists in Moscow, the different Czechoslovak parties made an agreement shortly before the end of the war. The leader of the Communist Party of Czechoslovakia, Klement Gottwald, had been the Chairman of the Party since 1929; he was a dedicated follower of Stalin and had close ties to Moscow (one could even call him a "die-hard" Stalinist, as he passed away less than a week after Stalin's funeral in 1953). He had spent the duration of the Second World War in the Soviet Union and returned to Prague following the Soviet liberation of Czechoslovakia. In April 1945, the government-in-exile, which the Western powers recognized as the legitimate government of Czechoslovakia, and the Czechoslovak Communists in Moscow created a genuine democratic coalition between Communists and non-Communists called the National Front in Košice. The Košice Programme created a framework for the postwar National Front, where all parties agreed on the expulsion of Germans and Hungarians from Czechoslovakia. The programme also confirmed that Czechoslovakia's foreign affairs would focus on its relationship with the Soviet Union, rather than with the Western powers, which both Beneš and Gottwald supported. Following the 1946 elections, Gottwald became the prime minister of Czechoslovakia, while Beneš remained president.

Following the elections, the ministries in the government were evenly split between the Communists and the non-Communists. The Communists sought their usual key ministries: interior, information, education, defence, and agriculture, while most of the other ministries were controlled by non-communists. Some of the non-Communist ministers had a Communist leaning, which resulted in the Communists controlling approximately half of the Czechoslovak ministries. Unlike the other countries in the Soviet bloc, the Communists in Czechoslovakia did not attempt an illegal seizure of power; while in countries like Poland the Communists struggled to gain popular support, there was a large portion of the Czechoslovak population that actively supported the Communist Party. In the May 1946 elections, for instance, the Communists gained 40 percent of the Czech votes and 30 percent Slovak votes, which totalled 38 percent of the total votes in Czechoslovakia. However, these elections prevented "collaborators" and "traitors" (i.e., Germans and Hungarians) from voting, and two popular interwar parties, the Czech Agrarian Party and the Slovak People's Party, were not permitted to run.

Despite the popular support for the Communist Party, 1947 was a difficult year for the Communists, as the Soviet Union forced a struggling Czechoslovakia to reject Marshall Plan aid which they desperately needed. As well, while at first the minister of the interior, Václav Nosek, worked with Beneš on the common goal of expelling the country's Germans, by 1947, most of the Germans in Czechoslovakia had been forcibly removed. By January 1948, public support for the Communists had dwindled, and the Communists no longer held common ground with Beneš and his supporters. When the non-Communist cabinet ministers accused Nosek, of filling the police force with Communists, he refused to discuss the issue, and all the non-Communist ministers from three of the four coalition parties, except the foreign minister Jan Masaryk, the son of interwar President Tomáš Garrigue Masaryk, resigned; these ministers thought that their resignation would force another round of elections, which they believed the Communists would lose due to the decrease in support. Starting in the fall of 1947, the Communists began organizing strikes in response to their blocked proposals in parliament. Beneš had made some efforts to curb the Communist power grab when he supported the non-Communist ministers in their initial opposition to Nosek; however, he did not create a new administration that excluded the Communists after those ministers resigned, as they had hoped.

Following the general strike, it was clear that the Communists had power over the police, politics, and, to a degree, the people. At the same time, the Soviet Union openly pledged support to the Czechoslovak Communists if the Western powers intervened in the takeover, and the Red Army surrounded Czechoslovakia along its borders. With the Soviet threat of force and the popular display of support for the Communists, Beneš capitulated to Communist demands and supported Gottwald's appointment of new Communist ministers and creation of a new administration. The strikes acted as a display of Communist power over the general population and the massive support they had on the ground. These strikes hit their climax in February 1948, when the Communists organized a general strike in support of Gottwald's leadership. Over two million citizens took part in this strike, which forced Beneš to accept not only the Communist's social power, but their political power.

Despite all Czechoslovak national organizations still being legal and the legacy of the democracy in the country, there was no formal attempt to stop the Communists from seizing power in 1948 in what was later called a coup that was really not. Referred to by the communists as "victorious February" the seizure of power did reflect just how much power the communists had. In fact, Beneš swore in Gottwald's replacement ministers for the ones that had resigned. Beneš would resign by 6 June and was dead in September. The Czech communists, in power until 1989, began to Stalinize the country immediately, hastening the pace of nationalization which had started under Beneš and collectivized agriculture.

However, it was not Beneš with which Tomáš Garrigue Masaryk's democratic dream for Czechoslovakia died; shortly after the Communist takeover, on 10 March, Masaryk's son, the much beloved Foreign Minister Jan Masaryk, was found dead below his window. The Communists claimed he had died by suicide; however, it was widely believed that his death was at the hands of the Communist government. Sometimes referred to as the "Third Defenestration of Prague" by those who believed it was a murder, subsequent "investigations" have followed political currents in Czechoslovakia, where Jan's death was ruled an "accident" during the reforms of the 1968 Prague Spring, and murder after the 1989 Velvet Revolution.

East Germany remained an occupation zone until 1949 when the German Democratic Republic appeared. A currency reform in West Germany, initiated by the United States in an attempt to stabilize it, forced the Soviets to blockade under four-power occupation in June 1948. The blockade lasted a year and, in the end, the vision of Chancellor Konrad Adenauer—West Germany anchored itself to the West with a new capital in Bonn and dramatic de-Nazification was put off. The Soviet zone suffered the same fate as the rest of Eastern Europe: rampant looting of its industrial infrastructure by the Soviets, Stalinization, the population terrorized by the largest secret police, the *Staatsicherhiet*, or Stasi, living by its motto as the "shield and sword of the Party". Its leaders argued they represented the real Germany, not the American-run "fascist" state in the West.

Conclusion

With Stalinist-style People's Republics in place by the end of 1948, Central Europe not only embraced political Stalinism but its economic variant too. The latter was especially stark given the differences between countries from the already industrialized and relatively advanced Czech lands to the largely agrarian Poland. This meant copy-pasting the template in all aspects: centralized decision-making, nationalization of everything that was not already public, class struggle, emphasis on heavy industry, collectivization in some places but never on the scale or with the violence that characterized the USSR, and five-year plans. The issue of collectivization is an important one. It was a hallmark of Stalinism in the USSR where exporting grain was the key to getting hard currency to pay for mega-industrial projects. Soviet-style collectivization led, among other things, to a forced famine in Ukraine that killed almost four million people. It was applied differently in Central Europe. In the Balkans, with the exception of Yugoslavia, private farming disappeared instantly while Czechoslovakia, Hungary, and Poland held on to some aspects of it and the Poles never ended up on collective farms. By any measure, collective farms were total failures. By 1948 there was hardly any private business left in Central Europe. Everybody got a Stalin-city to make steel: *Nowa-Huta* near Krakow in Poland; *Sztalinvaros* on the Danube in Hungary; and *Stalinstadt* in East Germany. Even Albania had its *Qyteti* Stalin. Czechoslovakia got off with just a few housing estates named after him. The Stalinist systems would survive, in various forms, until Stalin died in March 1953 when modest reforms became possible. In some places, like Albania and Czechoslovakia, hardline Stalinism would survive long after Stalin's death.

Despite the deviousness of Soviet tactics in Central Europe, one cannot assume that the entire populations of the region were mere objects or simply fools who slipped easily into Soviet-style totalitarianism. Lots of ordinary, decent, educated, and uneducated alike bought into the ideology that promised to finally put them on the right side of history. Indeed, the attraction of Marxism to many was genuine as an appropriate answer to the failed dogmas of the twentieth century. Many of the regime's later opponents were of course first good and devoted communists. For one thing, the Soviets and the Red Army did defeat the Germans and, this was especially true for the Czechs, the Soviets would be better able to protect them from a revanchist Germany than anyone else especially given the legacy of 1938. Sure, Edvard Beneš wanted postwar Czechoslovakia to be a bridge between east and west but if he had to choose, he would choose the Soviets. Many people would agree that there needed to be change after the interwar failures and the devastation of the Second World War. The Communists and their dedicated followers were able to capitalize on that desire and take power. Plus, they were never afraid to employ violence and terror. As we have seen, support varied across the region, and the Communists had genuine support in countries like Albania, Yugoslavia, and Czechoslovakia. The question, then, is not how the Communists came to power, but how they managed to stay there for 40 years.

If the Americans later had to convince the Europeans the USSR was a mortal threat, Germany was for most Europeans the real threat and fear of Germany was very real. The ideology was also attractive in its own way. The interwar and wartime experiences were unmitigated disasters. The capitalist systems of the interwar period were total failures for the vast majority of the populations. For many people, the new regimes offered new opportunities for some, simple careerism or the chance to learn to read for others. Even better, given the swelling ranks of willing informers, the chance to get even with your neighbour by denouncing him. Plus, outside of the Czech lands, the region was still premodern. Stalinism was a path to modernity and even long-awaited upward mobility. Could a planned economy be any worse? People wanted stability too and made the accommodation necessary to preserve their families and livelihoods where possible. Finally, just as important, there was limited concern in the West for the fate of the region.

The communist parties that took power were not only predatory towards ordinary citizens but the consolidation of their rule in Central Europe witnessed a form of internal consolidation as well which reflected wider international trends within the emerging Soviet bloc of satellite states. But it proved to be events in the Balkans that would jolt the regimes in Central Europe in some unexpected ways. As noted, both Albania and Yugoslavia had achieved "communist" liberation largely on their own although both liberation movements benefitted from aid from the Allies in the struggles against German occupation. In the Albanian case, help for them came largely from Tito's communist forces in neighbouring Yugoslavia. In the end, the relationship between Albania and Yugoslavia would accelerate communist party consolidation in Central Europe and bring fresh waves of violence brought about by intra-party struggles.

The close ties between the communist leaderships in Albania and Yugoslavia developed during the war morphed into a kind of unification movement that could have seen Albania join Yugoslavia. Moreover, Tito was eager to play a larger-than-life role in the Balkans and he dreamed of a much larger Balkan federation that he would run. Tito's big dreams ran counter to Stalin's vision. Although initially willing to let Tito "swallow" Albania, the ever-capricious Stalin changed his mind. Tito was called out, kicked out of the bloc and Stalin tried repeatedly to have him assassinated. Tito's "national communism", which rejected much of Stalinist-style political and economic trappings, was a certainly a virus that threatened the entire Soviet bloc. Nationalism of any type could not be tolerated within the bloc. The charge of Titoism or Titoite was a death sentence within the communist parties. While the violence was worse in Albania, where you actually could be a Titoite, outside of there, trials against alleged Titoites became the order of the day and heads did indeed roll. The purging of top echelons of the party leadership no doubt sent a chilling message to ordinary people in 1949 and after. Once in power, as we shall see, the period of high Stalinism between 1948 and 1953 was marked by its extreme violence.

It is important to remember that there is not so much discontinuity between the 1930s and the communist period. First, as we saw in Chap. 2, the regimes of the interwar were hardly democratic, leaving aside Czechoslovakia, and were almost always run by strongmen like Horthy in Hungary, Piłsudski in Poland, King Alexander in Yugoslavia, King Zog in Albania, Franco in Spain, or Hitler in Germany. The political space was extremely small with the Left almost completely destroyed. The communists would destroy the pre-war Right-wing political structures and would bring in another crew of strongmen: Bierut in Poland, Tito in Yugoslavia, Hoxha in Albania; Rákosi in Hungary; Gottwald in Czechoslovakia, or Ceauşescu in Romania. Sometimes these men were nothing more than wily peasants like Ceauşescu or had the cosmopolitan veneer of Hoxha who had spent time studying in France. What the new communist leaders had in common was an incredible capacity for violence. Neither the Germans nor the Soviets destroyed democracy, as it never really existed and the highly centralized, oppressive, violent, and autarkic policies of the interwar and wartime periods continued after the Soviets finalized their takeovers by 1948. With the exception of the temporary banishment of the exclusive nationalism that poisoned the region prior to 1945, not much had changed. The servile obedience of the region's leaders ensured the USSR had total control. But political control, unsurprisingly, never led to economic success. The new Eastern Europe, which as Central Europe had measured up reasonably well to Western

European economic standards, endured the Soviet failure to make successful economies. Estonia had the same GDP per capita as Finland in 1939, in 1989 Estonia's was a third of Finland's. Czechoslovakia was better off if only by a bit in 1937 than Austria. In 1989, Czechoslovakia's GDP was only 20 percent of Austria's. Poland was even worse off.

On the international front, the new Eastern European satellites assumed their usual role: objects of the Great Powers in the Cold War which was a reality by early 1947 when much of the US government had decided that cooperation with the USSR was impossible. Noting the absence of free elections and the general disappearance of non-communist parties, in 1947, President Truman addressed a joint session of Congress and announced what became known as the Truman Doctrine. It stipulated that the United States would support "free peoples who are resisting attempted subjugation by armed minorities or by outsides pressures". It was obvious he was talking about communists and Moscow. Decisions of significance were also made in Moscow: In 1947 the defunct Comintern re-emerged as the Communist Information Bureau or Cominform. The United States lamented the fake elections in the region and the Soviets warned of the Americans imperialist designs. Two camps emerged. East Europeans would need to wait until 1989 to become Central Europeans again and for their actions to have any meaning.

For Further Study

Books (Fiction and Non-Fiction)

Buruma, Ian. *Year Zero: A History of 1945*. New York: Penguin Press, 2013.
Djilas, Milovan. *Conversations with Stalin*. London: Penguin Classics, 2014.
Judt, Tony. *Postwar: A History of Europe since 1945*. New York: Penguin Books, 2005.
Kovály, Heda Margolius. *Under a Cruel Star: A Life in Prague 1941–1968*. Cambridge, MA: Plunkett Lake Press, 1986.
Lukša, Juozas. *Forest Brothers: The Account of an anti-Soviet Lithuanian Freedom Fighter, 1944–1948*. Budapest: Central European University Press, 2009.
Anonymous. *A Woman in Berlin: Eight Weeks in the Conquered City: A Diary*. New York: Picador/Henry Holt, 2006.

Films

Somewhere in Europe (1948). Directed by Géza von Radványi. Hungary.
The Third Man (1949). Directed by Carol Reed. United Kingdom.
The Berlin Airlift: First Battle of the Cold War (1998). Directed by Robert Kirk. USA.
The Innocents (2016). Directed by Anne Fontaine. France.

CHAPTER 5

Communists in Power, 1948–1988

We left off with Eastern Europe's communist parties devouring themselves through violent purges as they consolidated their hold over society. Stalin willed all of this, especially the anti-Semitic hue that dominated some of the purges in his later years. In Hungary, the trial of former Interior and Foreign Minister László Rajk is a good place to start and the gold standard of show trials for high communist officials. Since national communism à la Tito was the virus, Rajk was charged with being an Anglo-American agent, a fascist collaborator, and stooge of Tito. Tortured by his former best friends, nobody can ever tell what went through Rajk's mind. Rajk's successor at the Interior Ministry was János Kádár, destined to play an over-sized role in Hungary's dark twentieth century. Rajk's fate brings us back again to the character Rubashov in Koestler's *Darkness at Noon*. Koestler's book, based largely on the purges in the USSR and the resultant show trials, exposed the communist system as essentially a fraud. Rajk, like the fictional Rubashov, remained a good communist until he was hanged in October 1949, apparently calling out "Long Live Stalin, Long Live Rákosi" before his hanging. But the march of history meant he had to die. There are countless other stories just like that where good communists died extolling their love of their leaders, their fealty to the party, and some even walked to the gallows carrying a book by the party leader. Rajk's fate was determined long before the torture and trial began. Rajk's trial and execution unleashed a series of other trials with pre-determined outcome. Sándor Zöld, another Interior Minister, saw the writing on the wall in 1951 and went home after losing his job at Rákosi's behest, killed his whole family then took his own life too. For Rákosi, who more than anyone in the Hungarian Party felt he could see the future, did not then realize that the dead could come back, especially in Hungary where a burial or even better, a reburial, could bring some unforeseen consequences. In Rákosi's case, it was László Rajk whose spirit would return in the early 1950s to undo Rákosi's legitimacy. In any case,

© The Author(s), under exclusive license to Springer Nature
Switzerland AG 2021
R. C. Austin, *A History of Central Europe*,
https://doi.org/10.1007/978-3-030-84543-8_5

trials throughout the region were designed to educate a population that needed to know what was in store for anyone who opposed the party line.

Due to Soviet pressure and the insistence that there were threats in the Communist Party of Czechoslovakia, Klement Gottwald turned on his longtime ally and the General Secretary, Rudolf Slánský. Along with Slánský, 13 prominent members of the Communist Party were accused of Titoism, Trotskyism, and Zionism (11 of the defendants were Jewish). Arrested in 1951, while in prison, Slánský attempted suicide, while the other accused and their families were threatened and even tortured into confessing. Eleven of the accused were hanged in 1952, while the three that survived endured humiliation and became social pariahs following the trial.

The story of Milada Horáková, the only female to be hanged as a victim of the show trials in Czechoslovakia, is equally telling and chilling. She was active in Czechoslovak politics in the interwar period, fighting for women's equality, and one of Masaryk's followers. During the German occupation, she joined an anti-fascist organization, resulting in her arrest in 1944. She spent the remainder of the war in the Terezín concentration camp, until Allied forces liberated the camp in 1945. She became more directly involved in politics following the war when she joined the Czechoslovak parliament as a member of the Czech National Socialist Party and led the Council of Czechoslovak Women. She was a very vocal member of parliament, where she often criticized the Czechoslovak government for its pro-Soviet position. Following the Communist takeover, she was expelled from the Council of Czechoslovak Women and resigned from parliament. While she understood the risk of staying in Czechoslovakia because of her anti-Communist activism, she refused to leave her country. In September 1949, shortly after her husband escaped Czechoslovakia, Horáková was arrested, and along with the other defendants in her trial, underwent both psychological and physical torture at the hands of the State Security (StB). The Communist government made the usual accusations: espionage on behalf of Yugoslavia, the United States, Great Britain, and France. During her trial, world leaders and political advocates in the West sent petitions for her pardon, but despite the international pressure, Gottwald upheld the guilty verdict. On 27 June 1950, Horáková was executed by hanging and then immediately cremated; her ashes were never given to her family and their location remains unknown. Her letter to her daughter written in prison is heart-wrenching. She gives her daughter some important insights, foremost among them is "Choose your friends carefully", In the present-day Czech Republic, the anniversary of her death is now marked with the "Commemoration Day of victims of Communism".

Domestic political control, which included Soviet imposed cultural and social norms, also included the Cominform albeit without Yugoslavia, plus Stalin's own East European integration project. In January 1949, the USSR established the Committee for Mutual Economic Assistance (CMEA) or Comecon. It was ultimately designed to counter the American Marshall Plan for Western Europe and serve as a means to further isolate Tito. It generally served the USSR's economic interests and often pigeon-holed bloc countries into playing very specific roles in bilateral trade and would never evolve into a true customs union along the lines of what Western Europe established first with the European Coal and Steel Community in 1952 and later the European Economic Community in 1957. In April 1949, with American leadership, the anti-Soviet North Atlantic Treaty Organization (NATO) was formed. NATO proved to be the most important guarantee of European security and allowed Western Europe to rebuild economically. As already noted, the division of Germany entered a new phase with the establishment of the Federal Republic of Germany in West Germany and the German Democratic Republic in the East. The Soviets would wait until 1955 before adding a defensive military alliance, the Warsaw Treaty Organization of Warsaw Pact, to their list of "holds" on the peoples of Eastern Europe.

In the years between 1948 and 1953, the Cold War intensified but wars were avoided in Central Europe and instead fought in Greece, Korea, Vietnam, and elsewhere. The satellite countries worked diligently to implement Stalinism. Only Tito's "National Communism" offered a separate path with its workers' self-management alongside substantial decentralization and the relative ease of travel for its citizens. Rest assured, Tito's Yugoslavia was still a dictatorship but in its critique of Stalinism it did suggest an alternative path to communism which, to Stalin's dismay, resonated elsewhere in the bloc.

Systems that outwardly appeared resilient were ultimately dependent on what was going on in the USSR. That said, Stalin's death in March 1953 suggested that a break from the violence and rigidity of Stalinism suggested alternatives. After all, Tito was still alive and Yugoslav socialism seemed to offer an early version of what would come to be known as "socialism with a human face". While still a dictatorship, Yugoslavia seemed to offer a way out of Stalinist economic planning. Stalin's death sent shockwaves of chaos and uncertainty throughout the USSR, the eastern Bloc, and communist parties around the world. The new collective leadership there, which replaced the all-powerful single ruler in charge of party, government, and state, expected the same from its satellites. The new Soviet elite may well have looked at their "bloc" with disdain. Dated, ageing, and hardline Stalinists dominated. Plus, dissent was already in the air in Czechoslovakia, East Germany and Poland especially. What we see in all three places is increasing labour unrest and popular dissatisfaction among broad parts of society. In the end, the Soviets had to encourage a broad relaxation of pressure and modest changes in party leadership.

If the fates of Czechoslovakia, East Germany, Poland, and Hungary (as well as Albania, Bulgaria, and Romania) were similar, Austria surprisingly ended up on the right side of history. At the end of the war, Austria, at least in hindsight, was never a real priority for Stalin. Hungary, which was totally occupied, worked as reasonable compensation. Plus, the West occupied the richer and more prosperous parts of Western Austria. The Soviet sphere was small, had few inhabitants, and was not worth it. As we saw in Chap. 3, Stalin had already warned his people in Austria that they were not to pursue partition. Moreover, a division, along the lines of what happened in Germany in 1949 could result in a new *Anschluss*. Austria got lucky. It was treated as a liberated country, not merely as a part of Germany. It had to de-Nazify but only to a point, and the process stalled not long after the war ended. The Marshall Plan, on a per capita level, was extraordinarily generous. Plus, the emerging Cold War increased Austria's significance. In keeping with the new atmosphere following Stalin's death, Khrushchev found in Austria a place he could improve relations with the West in the very busy 1955. The Soviets played the key role in negotiating the State Treaty ended occupation and, added to the treaty Austria would declare neutrality. It all worked, and Austria really started with a clean slate. Whatever nastiness that had occurred in the past was quickly swept under the carpet. Austria began, through innovation, industry, and tourism a remarkable economic recovery that produced spectacular results. The *proporz* system of government, mindful of the conflicts of the interwar period, entailed permanent compromises between the two major parties—the People's Party and the Social Democrats—brought permanent political peace. Neutrality saved money too and allowed Austria to build a sustainable social democracy. As the bridge between east and west that Hungary hoped to be, and later home to part of the international infrastructure of the United Nations, Austria was set to become one of Europe's most prosperous states. It was also best position to profit from the collapse of communism.

The Nazi past and even the Nazis still lurked in the shadows. Confronting the past, which came to Germany in the 1960s and 1970s, bypassed Austria almost completely. Monuments to victims came late and were often sometimes generic enough to conflate the suffering of all Austrians to the detriment of the main victims, the Jews. Austria's duality, captured in the creation of a new identity of Sisi and the Habsburgs, the Mozart candies that appealed to people inside and out, the tidiness of it all, and the picture-perfect villages existed alongside something dark.

Telling of the duality of Austrian identity is the story of Kurt Waldheim, a key figure in the Austrian Foreign Ministry. Elected as Secretary General of the United Nations in 1972 he served until 1981. When NASA sent out the two Voyager probes in 1977 to tell any extra-terrestrials willing to listen that "*we come in peace*", it was Waldheim's voice on the recording. While running for Austrian president in 1986, with slogans like "The Man the World Trusts" his past service in the German army came to light. Waldheim had clearly erased his past service in the German occupation armies in Greece and Yugoslavia. Austrians, many also eager to erase the past, defended Waldheim and argued that Austria was being picked on or the victim of a Jewish conspiracy led by the World Jewish Congress. Despite the evidence and calls from leading public figures in Austria to step aside, Waldheim stuck to his lies, claimed he was injured and discharged, was that he was just "an honest soldier". Plus, Austria never went through any process of assessment of its complicated past. Waldheim was just one of more than 500,000 registered Nazis who simply slipped back into normal lives. The Waldheim affair did have the benefit of starting a much-needed critical discussion of the victim theory. Waldheim's presidency left Austria briefly as a pariah state. Oddly enough, Austria would not learn much from the incident, in 1999, the far-right Freedom Party of Jörg Haider, known for his weird praise of Hitler and the SS, joined a coalition with the mainstream Austrian Peoples Party. That too earned Austria a time-out, that time from the European Union which they had joined in 1995. The Freedom Party would end up back in power, again with the Austrian Peoples Party in 2017–2019.

1956 IN HUNGARY

Let's return to the dog-eat-dog world of Hungarian communism and introduce János Kádár, destined to become the key figure there between 1956 and 1988 and likely the most emblematic of Eastern European communist leaders. He was poorly educated and liked to see himself as a simple person. He was a bit like the chess playing peasant Czentovic in Stefan Zweig's *Chess Story*—like him, Kádár only knew how to do one thing well. Kádár, along with Rákosi, was inner circle and indeed we encountered him in László Rajk's downfall. In 1951, Kádár was arrested and sent to prison for life in 1952 for treason. Stalin's death and the potentially new climate got him out of jail and back in the game. In June 1953, Rákosi was "called" to Moscow and more or less demoted and told to collectivize the leadership. For the new post-Stalin era Rákosi was simply an anachronism plus his violence was no longer the order of the day. He kept his party leadership post but gave up the premiership to Imre Nagy, a promising young agronomist in the Politburo who people actually liked and who had very little blood on his hands. This begins a period of intensive party infighting as Rákosi was not one to go easily. Plus, there were clear divisions about the future of Stalinism after Stalin.

Hungary, never ever happy to be a mere replica of the Soviets or their other satellites, started tinkering with reform. This was good news for a country that had experienced a decade of terror. Copying his Moscow masters, Nagy promised many things: easing up pressure on peasants; slowing down industrialization; fewer people in prison and an almost entirely new cabinet freed of some of the worst perpetrators of excess violence. In power until 1955, Nagy confronted a difficult internal and even more perilous external situation. Rákosi's people worked tirelessly against him and in 1955, things outside his, and Hungary's, control took a toll.

1955 is watershed year for a number of reasons. To be clear, in the battle for supremacy in the USSR's new collective leadership, Nikita Khrushchev won. In the next decade in power, Khrushchev would undertake some truly bold initiatives only to be ousted in 1964 for taking bold initiatives and what were deemed "harebrained schemes". In early May 1955, West Germany joined NATO, later the same month the Soviet formed the Warsaw Pact to ensure the bloc stayed the bloc. As important, also in May, Nikita Khrushchev, as Soviet Communist Party General Secretary and first among equals in the new collective leadership, mended fences with Tito in Yugoslavia. This was a major step not just for the USSR when you consider how many communist parties in Eastern Europe had used the Tito trope to shape their very legitimacy. It was the latter fact that in many ways forced the creation of the Warsaw Pact to inhibit any future "Titos and undid Nagy at the same time. In April 1955 Nagy was ousted and Rákosi was in charge again but time was running out for him too. But Stalin's best pupil could not survive what lay ahead despite the fact that he restored all the previous levels of oppression.

1956 was a real watershed year for communism. Khrushchev took to the podium at the 20th Soviet Party Congress in February and denounced, in somewhat muted ways, the once untouchable Stalin. That the bloc survived this incredible blow remains surprising as two countries attempted to use the moment to reform socialism. The Secret Speech, as it become known, is a major turning point. Protests occurred throughout the bloc—in Plzeň in Czechoslovakia, and Łódź and Poznań in Poland. In Poland, the once-jailed Gomułka, the Polish version of Imre Nagy, was back.

In the Hungarian context, it re-opened a few good doors. On the one hand, Rákosi was out and this time for good. He started an exile in the USSR where he died in 1971, aged 78. He was lucky enough that the system he helped create, at least in Hungary, had softened enough that political opponents no longer needed to be murdered. For Rákosi, it was the once dead Rajk who came back as the door on the past opened leaving him exposed. Rajk's rehabilitation, in communist parlance, was Rákosi's end. Rajk even got a massive reburial in October which made clear the depravity of the regime and the utter confusion in the people. After all, Rajk was hardly a role model. In October, Nagy was back in the party. With Nagy in power, he unwillingly set off a chain of events that led to the Hungarian Revolution of October/November 1956. It is often referred to as the first anti-Totalitarian revolution. Sensing an opening, Nagy set out not to destroy the system but to correct it. It was a version of socialism with a human face and Nagy was a true believer. The year 1956 was not 1989, at least in hindsight, although it could have been. At the forefront of the demands for change were students and workers. Rallying around the nineteenth century hero Sándor Petőfi with his "National Song" as its calling, students pushed for their 16, not 12, points adding calls for real national independence, Soviet withdrawal, free elections and Nagy not just back in the party but in power. On 24 October Nagy was back as prime minister in the fall and he re-introduced his reform plan. The ultimate fence-sitter, Kádár, was General Secretary.

Street fighting became the norm as the country's young revolutionaries attacked the institutions of the state especially the media and the secret police. Nagy hoped to calm things down and offered amnesty to those who would stop fighting. But he finally gave in to the logic of the revolutionaries and started to take steps to meet them at least halfway. He called for the abolition of the much-loathed secret police. The regime was actually disintegrating—multi-party democracy was back if only for a week. In the end, just like in

1848–1849, the Hungarians went maybe too far. On 1 November, Nagy announced Hungary's exit from the Warsaw Pact, signalling Hungary's neutrality. János Kádár, who had declared himself on the side of the revolutionaries, fled to Moscow to re-group and choose a different side. The United States sponsored anti-communist Radio Free Europe broadcasts from Munich encouraged the people to fight on. What is clear now is that the United States was not all that informed about events in Hungary and was never prepared to do anything to save the revolution.

Obviously, it was decisions in Moscow that would decide what happened in Budapest. At the start, the Soviets seemed willing to accept the changes in Hungary. National communism was not in the cards. They opted for force and invaded on 31 October and decisively crushed the revolution. Could 10,000 freedom fighters defeat the Red Army? The Hungarian situation was truly impossible. János Kádár was installed as the Soviet's new puppet. Nagy and the top leadership had to make some choices. Where to flee? They chose the Yugoslav embassy in Budapest. Tito, it turned out, could not be relied upon. In any case, the revolution's top leadership was arrested by the Soviets and taken to Romania where the torture started over again and Hungary entered another era of violence, show trials and executions, all at the behest of Kádár. The group was returned to Hungary and tried in secret—death sentences, despite even Soviet pressure to spare their lives, were decided well in advance. They were hanged for treason in June 1958.

If Rajk's reburial was a kind of catalyst because it questioned the legitimacy of the party's rule, 1989 would see another one, that of Imre Nagy. It would be equally cathartic and de-legitimizing once again for Hungarian communists as Kádár's regime would rest on a very hollow legitimacy. For Kádár, 1956 had to remain a counter-revolution, planned by the "black hand" of the West, even though ordinary Hungarians never bought it. Given the depth of reprisals that followed and were as bad anything that came from the Rákosi era, it was a hard sell. Surely a survivor like Kádár feared that someday he too would be forced to account for terrible repression he sanctioned and like Rajk, he would have to answer for Nagy's murder. More than 20,000 sentences were handed out for alleged crimes with long prison sentences the norm. Others went to internment camps. Plus, more than 200 people were executed. Equally significant, Hungary experienced a massive brain drain. More than 200,000 people fled the country. These 56ers, as they were called, were scattered around the world, and they enriched places they went, especially Australia, Canada, and the United States.

Kádár was as good a stooge for the USSR as Rákosi had been—he would never question the Soviet's control over Hungary even if he did try to loosen it. In the aftermath of the revolution, once martial law had been lifted and Hungary started to exit from the shadow of 1956 another side of Kádár began to appear that worked as long as you could forget he was a murderer. Kádár the reformer appeared, and two new isms arrived too: Goulash Communism and Kádárism. He would become the folksy communist populist and make Hungary the envy of the rest of the bloc for its shopping and tourism for bloc states but the West as well. The ugly hotels on the Pest side of the Danube, some built in the 1980s, tell that story. For Kádár, looking at Hungary's truly hopeless economic performance, he decided that in order to prevent further troubles he needed to raise living standards dramatically or face another uprising. He started in the early 1960s with changes to agricultural policy and even declaring an amnesty for prisoners from 1956. His biggest innovation was to allow some free markets to co-exist with planning. By 1968, the same year as the Prague Spring, he introduced Hungary's New Economic Mechanism. Everything was new except it was still a one-party state, 1956 was a counter-revolution, and the Soviets were there to stay. The essence of the new Hungary, which was broadly social peace through consumerism, introduced a soft authoritarianism, especially when compared to neighbouring Czechoslovakia, based on the idea that those who were not against the communists were with the communists. In short, buy a fridge, maybe a car, a small cottage, lie low, and say nothing public against the regime. Kádár hoped that if people's existential needs were basically met, they would opt out of politics. But Kádárism could not last. It bred despair, alcoholism, low life expectancy and suicide and, most tellingly, extraordinary debt. The West lent the communists just enough money to destroy them.

Kádár financed his big initiatives by integrating Hungary into the global financial architecture of the West. Hungary joined the International Monetary Fund and World Bank in 1982. Western investment came—you can still see its legacy on the Pest side of the Danube embankment in the ugly hotels as Hungary became a relatively mainstream tourist destination. Kádár the torturer and murderer became Kádár the statesman travelling around the world and received with honours everywhere as the spokesman of East-West dialogue and friendly socialism. Even the crown of Saint Stephen came home from the United States. The crown and the coronation regalia had been removed from Budapest due to the advance of Soviet troops and later handed over to American forces in occupied Austria in 1945. As Hungary drifted away from the West and the violent crushing of the 1956 revolution worsened relations even more, the Americans dismissed thoughts of returning the material and instead stored it in Fort Knox. Better relations in the 1970s and the new administration of President Jimmy Carter sent the crown home in January 1978.

The crown aside, if Kádár's goal was a genuine improvement in the standard of living and the popularity of the regime, people's lives did get better—wages rose, people could advance even without being party members, tolerance in artistic life came, harassment of political opponents lessened, private life was to a degree respected and, just like in neighbouring Yugoslavia, Hungarians started to travel from less than 5000 mostly officials in the 1950s to well over 500,000 in the 1980s. Elsewhere in the bloc, exit was nearly impossible. No passports and a plethora of bureaucracy stood in the way of an exit visa. Kádár eased the restrictions over time so that Hungarians started travelling and even coming home after their trips. Currency restrictions, plus arbitrary exchange rates in the favour of the state were obstacles but by the 1980s hundreds of thousands of Hungarians were going places.

For sure 1956 was a failed revolution but it did lead to Goulash Communism which was far softer than anything elsewhere in the communist bloc. But outside of Hungary it had serious implications. It served as a guide, especially for what would happen in Czechoslovakia in 1968. It served even as a guide for 1989 in a way. But most importantly, it told would-be reformers that change would have to come from Moscow. Plus, it told the men and women who made the revolutions of 1989 that socialism with a human face was simply out of the question. The system could not be reformed but only destroyed. Legitimacy of the systems would slowly disappear and even Kádár's Goulash Communism could not save Hungary. Grumbling conformity was how the Stasi would characterize the DDR in the 1970s. That assessment applied everywhere.

Czechoslovakia: 1968 and Normalization

In East Central Europe, the 1960s were generally a decade of a kind of liberalization, communist style. This was especially true in Czechoslovakia which resulted in the Prague Spring. At the beginning of the decade, the country was still among the most Stalinist in the Eastern Bloc under the leadership of Antonín Novotný, who desperately sought to avoid a 1956 repeat under his rule. With the leadership in Moscow moving in a new direction, reform-leaning Communist leaders in the satellites had more leverage to push their respective regimes away from Stalinism as well. In 1962, the Czechoslovaks took down the world's largest statue of Joseph Stalin, whose granite form had towered over Prague from a massive concrete pedestal in the city's Letná Park since 1955. They also dismantled the mausoleum of the first leader of Communist Czechoslovakia, Klement Gottwald.

The leader of the Czechoslovak reform movement was Alexander Dubček, a Slovak member of the Communist Party. In 1963, unhappy with the hardline policies of the regime, Dubček and his allies fought for and took over control of the Slovak branch of the party, initiating the country's reform movement in Slovakia. They eased censorship and allowed criticism of the Communist Party and of Stalinism in Slovak newspapers. A few years later, Ota Šik, a member of the Communist Central Committee and the head of the economics institute at the Czech Academy of Sciences, proposed his "new economic model". It was similar to Hungary's Goulash Communism in that it would ease up central planning and rely more on market forces in what Šik called the "third way" between communism and capitalism. Novotný, who was still in power at the time, opposed the plan, and the government only partially adopted it in 1967.

The 1960s also somewhat allowed for the rebirth of cultural life in Czechoslovakia, though complete freedom of expression was still lacking. This development is particularly evident in the New Wave movement in the film industry. This movement, frequently featuring dark and absurd humour, pushed the boundaries of biting social and political commentary in subtle and often surreal ways, playing with the newly relaxed censorship laws. It was headed by directors who have since become familiar worldwide, such as Miloš Forman (who also directed *Amadeus*—filmed in Prague to look like Vienna in the late 1700s and an absolute treasure), Věra Chytilová, Ján Kadár, and Jiří Menzel.

In May 1967, the Fourth Congress of the Union of Czechoslovak Writers took place, with leading authors Ivan Klíma, Milan Kundera, Pavel Kohout, and Václav Havel in attendance. They criticized Novotný for insisting on the continuation of Stalinism in the country despite the liberalization movements occurring in other Eastern Bloc countries and pointed to the continued suppression of cultural life at the time. One author, Ludvík Vaculík, even went so far as to state that the party's leading role, the basis of the entire system, was no longer necessary and that it had not solved any social issues in its 20 years in power. He was correct but also subsequently expelled from the Writers' Union. But in 1967 Kundera published his first novel, *The Joke*, which, among other themes, is anti-totalitarian. Miloš Forman's satirical film *The Firemen's Ball* also appeared.

That same year, the Central Committee experienced a major shake-up of power when Dubček and Šik accused Novotný of adhering to Stalinism long past the time when its policies should have been dropped. Šik, not foreseeing what China would someday do, claimed that authoritarianism and a successful economy could never exist. Dubček also accused Novotný of attempting to consolidate too much power in his own hands, verging on dictatorship. Eventually, under immense pressure, Novotný resigned as First Secretary of the Czechoslovak Communist Party at the beginning of January 1968. The Czechoslovak Central Committee voted to replace him with Dubček, setting off the period known as the Prague Spring. Dubček, like Imre Nagy, was later characterized as being a sincere, honest, and devoted communist. In a sense, just too nice for such a bad system that favoured cynics, crooks, and mostly opportunists. Dubček was likely none of those, but he could not have gotten where he was on just sincerity alone.

In January 1968, Dubček's policies were taken to the public. The following month, on the twentieth anniversary of "victorious February", the Communist coup in 1948, he gave a speech about the need to do things differently. Keep in mind that by then things were different in the USSR. Khrushchev was ousted in October 1964 by his once loyal underling Leonid Brezhnev. No doubt Dubček hoped for some of the same tolerance to different roads to socialism that Khrushchev had tolerated to follow under his successors. In March, his government almost entirely abolished censorship and implemented policies that aimed to regain the confidence of what was largely a fed-up public. It was the first time in 20 years that people could speak more freely and openly that would in some ways foreshadow what Mikhail Gorbachev would try to do in the USSR nearly 20 years later.

In April 1968, the government revealed its new *Action Program*, which contained plans for widespread and far-reaching reforms. Its authors proposed injecting the system with more freedom and human rights—a move they deemed essential for a real and successful socialism. Among others, the Action Program set out plans to set up new structures for local debate and self-government, to decentralize the oversight of workers, to allow freer travel abroad and religious practice, and to introduce elements of competitive economy. Dubček coined this movement "socialism with a human face". The lessons of 1956 were not lost on him either. But the writers wanted more than that. In June 1968, the author Ludvík Vaculík took advantage of the relaxed atmosphere to publish his "2000 Words" manifesto, signed by 70 other writers and public figures. He criticized the proposed reforms for not going far enough and condemned the past actions of the Communist Party.

In July, the Czechoslovak leadership declined to attend a meeting of the Warsaw Pact countries, whose delegations demanded that Czechoslovakia attack "the rightist, anti-communist forces" it had allowed to develop a voice earlier in the year. At the end of the month, the Czechoslovaks entered into bilateral talks with the USSR in Čierna nad Tisou, where the two parties negotiated a deal to allow the Czechoslovak leadership to shift courses and avoid an outside intervention. The talks continued with other parties in Bratislava, and on 3 August, Eastern Bloc leaders pledged to allow each socialist state to follow its own path but with the caveat that other states could intervene should the necessity arise. Meanwhile, Brezhnev, who had replaced Khrushchev in 1964, made his displeasure with Dubček's refusal to use force against dissenting voices known. Czechoslovakia's communist neighbours worried that Czechoslovakia's virus would spread to them too.

Throughout the month, the Warsaw Pact's armies amassed to pressure Dubček into acquiescence, and the Soviets found it difficult to find conservatives in Czechoslovakia to oppose him. They badly needed their Kádár. Finally, they found an ally in Vasil Biľak, a hardline member of the Communist Party and General Secretary of the Slovak Central Committee. He asked Brezhnev to intervene with all the means he had at his disposal, opening to doors to the Warsaw Pact invasion of Czechoslovakia, or "Operation Danube". During the night from 20 August to 21 August 1968, tens of thousands of troops poured over the borders of the country to significant popular resistance. Protestors tried to protect the radio building on Vinohradska Street so that it could continue to broadcast and inform people about the evolving situation, tampered with signage to disorient the invaders, and employed characteristically *Švejk*-like strategies, such as politely giving misleading directions, to otherwise hinder their progress. The secret police refused to cooperate, and prisoners refused to be released in exchange for helping suppress resistance. In many places, the protests turned violent. At the same time, Biľak attempted to carry out a coup, which failed miserably. News had already arrived of the invasion, some conspirators backed out of the plan, and President Svoboda refused to support it.

On 21 August, Dubček and several colleagues were arrested and taken to Moscow, while the Czechoslovak Communist Party Congress met in secret in the Vysočany District of Prague the next day, destroying the legitimacy of the conspirators. The Soviets were forced to negotiate with a Dubček that had not been deposed by the expected coup. In reality, the negotiations were mostly a front, and the Soviets psychologically battered all but one member of the delegation into signing the secret Moscow Protocol. The Protocol essentially returned the country to its pre-reform status, invalidating the Vysočany Congress, reversing most liberalization reforms, and legitimizing the presence of the invading troops. Dubček would, however, remain in power for the time being.

Autumn 1968 marked the shaky beginning of a 20-year period known as normalization. At first, the leadership attempted to stabilize the country, placate the invaders, and maintain at least some of the reforms implemented earlier in the year. Censorship was restored and the Action Program was delayed. Popular mobilization remained intense and many people, both domestically and internationally, continued to believe in the "third way". Unlike Imre Nagy in Hungary, Dubcek was not executed but instead went into a kind of internal exile in his hometown of Bratislava. He was lucky enough to see the end of communists in 1989 and was briefly involved in Czechoslovak politics again. He died in 1992 as a result of injuries from a car crash. In April 1969, however, Gustáv Husák replaced Dubček in power and brought any hopes of reform to an end. Husák, a Slovak from Bratislava, like so many of the region's communist leaders spent time in prison—first under the German-backed puppet government in 1940 and again but this time by how own communist party in the 1950 He would remain boss of the party until 1987 and president of Czechoslovakia until 1989. His regime's hallmark was old-style intolerance and conservatism: normalization—two decades during which socialism was to seep into every corner of everyday life and become the unquestioned "normal". Regular public life under normalization was relatively innocuous for ordinary people—certainly less tense than during the Stalinist 1950s—but was still entirely saturated with Communist propaganda and calls to centre life around socialist ideals and slogans, such as "build the nation—you will strengthen peace!"

The Pioneer organization for children attempted to instil these values from a young age and raise "good socialist children" and future leaders. Organizations at all levels, from the highest offices of the government to universities to the smallest community groups, were led by people who supported the regime and promoted its values to its members. Workplaces had mandatory unions and people's militias—paramilitary organizations within the workplace to keep everyone in line. Museums promoted the "right" narratives and schools implemented a militarized education with curricula containing East-West ideology and conspiracy theories about "the West" and Americans in particular. Russian was mandatory.

Life under normalization was generally more comfortable than it had been in the 1950s. The shortening of the work week from six to five days meant that people had more free time, and the socialist system meant that most people had a decent income, universal health care, and a developed social infrastructure in general. That being said, the centralized economic system meant that people often had little to spend their available money on. What was available was also often of poor quality. People often waited for months or years on a waitlist for the infamously flimsy and unreliable Trabant cars, for example, simply because nothing else was available. For other items, they relied on personal relationships with shop owners, who would hide stock under the counter for favoured customers, and on extensive networks of friends and family to obtain scarce goods. It was a culture of home invention and resourcefulness, in which people learned to make do with what was available and cultivated their own skills to make what they could not buy. Women were also saddled with what is called the "double burden". Under the guise of full equality and employment, they were expected to have full-time jobs. At the same time, they also shouldered most of their traditional responsibility of raising children and keeping the household running.

Of course, the supposed equality of socialist society was a ruse in other ways as well. Loyalty to the regime was substantially rewarded. Those who had the regime's trust managed firms and other organizations—the *nomenklatura*—were able to move up the social ladder to better-paying positions that came with other benefits, such as travel and access to luxury items in special stores. It all came at a price, however, of voluntarily giving up freedom of speech and thought and subscribing fully to the party line. Most people unsurprisingly made big and small compromises to get a job, earn a trip abroad or a place in a university for their children.

The darker side of the normalization era was the infiltration of all levels of society with state surveillance, overseen by the secret policy and the Ministry of the Interior. In Communist Czechoslovakia, the secret police was called the *Statní bezpečnost/Štátna bezpečnosť* (StB/ŠtB). Although not as large as the notorious East German *Stasi*, its methods were similar; agents often employed criminal and extra-legal methods with little punishment. The organization itself employed a large number of agents whose lives were dedicated to spying on the people in Czechoslovakia, but the state also encouraged neighbours to spy on each other, and the secret police had an extensive network of civilian informers. They developed sophisticated systems of hidden cameras and recording devices that they used to track the activity of people they suspected of anti-state activity; these devices were sometimes hidden in people's apartments as well, often in walls or doors. In turn, people who knew they were under surveillance developed techniques to try to evade the secret policy. For example, they would turn on the tap or play music while discussing sensitive information at home in an effort to mar recordings. The secret police kept meticulous records of all this activity and amassed an extensive archive of files on individuals that can now be partially accessed.

In 1975, the Helsinki Accords of the Conference on Security and Co-operation in Europe affirmed the importance of respecting human rights. Signed by the USSR and most other Eastern Bloc countries, they inspired civic opposition groups in the region, which now had a new tool for attempting to hold their respective governments responsible for their actions. In Czechoslovakia, a centralized and persistent civic opposition to the regime began to develop in earnest the following year. In 1976, several members of the rock band *The Plastic People of the Universe*, whose songs contained subversive lyrics, were arrested following their performance at the Festival of the Second Culture. The state, hoping to make an example of them, prosecuted and jailed them. One Canadian bandmate, Paul Wilson, was deported. Subsequent protests sparked the creation of the Charter 77 document, which called on the government to respect basic human rights as agreed to in Helsinki. The protests soon turned into a civic initiative of the same name, headed by the playwright Václav Havel. Other notable signatories of the Charter included the philosophers Jan Patočka and Václav Benda, the actress Vlasta Chramostová, the writer Ludvík Vaculík, and the former foreign minister from the pre-invasion government in 1968, Jiří Hájek. Signatories came from all walks of life and professions, but many were involved in intellectual life and the arts. Charter 77 was an important symbolic milestone, but it was hardly a national movement.

The Charter was immediately censored, and the initiative's members were frequently harassed by the police and thrown in prison. In 1978, an offshoot organization called the Committee for the Defense of the Unjustly Prosecuted (VONS) was formed and continued activity alongside Charter 77 through 1989. During this time, Havel wrote his most famous essay, *The Power of the Powerless*, which discusses concepts that are central to his philosophy, such as living in truth and bearing personal responsibility for one's actions. It is the essay from which his famous greengrocer analogy for citizens passively reinforcing oppressive state structures by not thinking for themselves comes. It is a must read for understanding life under these regimes. Throughout the years after the Charter's formation, its members continued to organize gatherings and other events for sharing ideas, information, *samizdat* publications, and more. They were constantly watched and periodically punished, but activity persisted.

Czechoslovakia and the GDR continued to be the most hardline regimes in central Europe, and members of the opposition did not attain any real political power the way some of their counterparts did in Hungary, for example, where communism would collapse in stages and eventually through negotiation. Nor was the Charter 77 network as widespread or even as influential as Poland's Solidarity which had the character of a real mass movement as membership approached ten million. Still, its members were active, passionate, and determined. It was only towards the end of 1989, with the establishment of the Civic Forum social movement, that the Charter's members were swept into true leadership positions as the Velvet Revolution progressed. Czechoslovakia, after Hungary and Poland, began the transition to democracy largely because of people power as we shall see in the next chapter.

POLAND: PERMANENT OPPOSITION

Khrushchev's secret speech resonated in Poland too. That same month, the Stalinist General Secretary of the Polish United Workers' Party, Bolesław Bierut, died, opening new opportunities. Since Stalin's death in 1953, Poland had been slow to adopt the economic policies of the Khrushchev's New Course, but this series of events in 1956 signalled a turning point in the country's path forward.

In June of that year, tens of thousands of workers began protesting in city of Poznań after new, higher work norms were announced. Workers not only resisted this increase in work demands but also demanded appropriate compensation. The crowd grew to over 100,000, and after the government sent in troops to quell riots, many people were left dead and injured. It was clear that the Party needed new leadership and Poland needed a new plan to move forward. While 1956 in the Eastern Bloc is most widely known as a year of turmoil and upheaval in Hungary, Poland also went through a period of significant change, known as Polish October, which ushered in a new period in Polish political culture. As usual, the Poles were at the forefront of opposition to communist rule.

The survivor Władysław Gomułka was back on the scene, a Polish communist who had led Poland from the end of the war until 1948. Recall that having resisted Stalinist collectivization, he had been expelled from the Party in 1949 and imprisoned from 1951 to 1954. He held a certain level of popularity among many different factions of the Polish population as a result, and in the reform-oriented atmosphere of 1956, he was politically rehabilitated. In October 1956, amidst talks about the new leadership of the Party, the secret police refused pressure from conservative members of the Politburo to arrest him. He was named General Secretary despite significant protests from the Soviets, who arrived in Warsaw in person to interfere with the course of Polish politics. Khrushchev eventually acquiesced, recognizing that an uprising in Poland over Soviet interference would be difficult to suppress, especially because Polish leaders stated that the Polish military would resist a Soviet military intervention.

The period of Gomułka's leadership went forward, putting an end to collectivization and stressing Poland's independence from the Soviet Union, though not to an extent that would create further problems with the leadership in Moscow. Workplaces remained the centres of a push for economic change. The Party wanted to maintain peaceful relations with workers and thus allowed for some negotiations regarding wages, norms, and other working conditions. Gomułka remained in power until 1970.

The 1970s ushered in another new decade of workers' strikes in Poland. They began with a series of strikes along the Baltic coast in 1970, where violent government suppression brought Gomułka's tenure in power to an end. The year 1976 saw yet another wave of strikes due to an increase in prices. Like in other parts of central Europe, the year also brought an increase in activity among intellectual dissidents. The strikes spurred the creation of an organization of lawyers and intellectuals called the *Komitet Obrany Robotników* (KOR), or the Workers' Defence Committee, which cooperated closely with the Catholic Church and lent financial and legal assistance to workers and their families. It also published otherwise unpublishable works by dissident authors from Central Europe such as Jerzy Andrzejewski, Bohumil Hrabal, Czesław Miłosz, and banned Western authors such as George Orwell and Hannah Arendt. While the organization was obvious to the authorities, its members made a point of working within the Polish legal framework and the guidelines set out by the Helsinki Accords in an attempt to avoid arrest and harassment from the police. Despite these tactics, KOR members were arrested in the spring in 1977, but protests and pressure from the West led the Polish government to grant the arrestees amnesty and back off. By the end of the decade, KOR, renamed *Komitet Samoobrony Społecznej KOR* (KSS KOR), or the Committee for Social Self Defence KOR, was publishing many works every month, including ones by the well-known thinker and author Adam Michnik, who would go on to be a major figure in the events of 1989. It was also organizing cultural and intellectual events, strengthening civil society, and in effect building up a grassroots opposition movement to the regime.

Alongside secular dissidents, the Catholic church was one of the main long-term targets of Communist regimes throughout the Eastern Bloc. It came to play an important role in dissident circles, particularly in Poland, where a high proportion of the population is Catholic. For some, Catholicism provided guiding principles separate from the Communist regime and the impetus to resist the regime, both actively and symbolically in mind and spirit. In other cases, Catholic clergy actively cooperated with secular dissidents and offered church space for people to meet, especially in the 1970s and 1980s, when all the different streams of dissidents were beginning to come together to form a tangible movement.

Especially after Cardinal Karol Wojtyła, formerly the archbishop of Cracow, became Pope John Paul II on 16 October 1978, the Catholic Church came to play a large part in galvanizing popular resistance to the regime throughout Poland. John Paul II's position as pope made him a particular threat to the Communist Party leadership. He was Polish, charming, charismatic, and provided the many Polish Catholics with an attractive figure in leadership outside of the Party. In fact, the Party debated whether he should be allowed back into the country, before ultimately allowing him to visit in 1979. It was during this visit that he delivered a famous speech in Warsaw's Victory Square, which some historians see as the beginning of the end of Communism in Poland, if not in all of Central Europe. The pope's presence attracted a massive crowd that acted with harmony, peace, and order without the threat of force or police interference. It demonstrated to many that self-organized mass mobilization was possible and helped foster a partnership between religious and secular intellectuals, as described in the works of the Polish dissident and historian Adam Michnik, particularly *The Church and the Left*. It was an undeniable turning point for Poland.

Towards the end of the 1970s, Poland, just like Hungary, was in an extremely precarious situation economically and needed to solve its problems with rising foreign debt. The policies chosen involved a cut in imports and yet another increase in the centrally controlled domestic prices of goods and services. Inevitably, the situation led to another series of strikes as workers demanded a raise in wages to mirror the increased prices. The strikes began in July 1980 and escalated to the most famous Polish strike of the Communist era, which took place on 14 August at the Lenin shipyard in the city of Gdańsk on the Baltic coast. This particular strike began as a protest against the firing of a woman named Anna Walentynowicz mere months before her planned retirement—an act that would lower her pension. It was at this strike that a man named Lech Wałęsa spoke, urging workers to keep protesting. The strikes spread and came to encompass a much wider set of demands, including the freedom of the press, the release of political prisoners, and free trade unions. On 16 August, the strike committee at the Lenin shipyard agreed to accept a pay raise and end the strike, but other unions who had joined the protests felt betrayed. At the shipyard, a woman named Alina Pienkowska, who had been instrumental in spreading the news of the strike outside of the shipyard, called on the workers to stand together in a broader fight for their rights. She subsequently led a push to draw up a list of 21 demands, and this series of events became the genesis of the well-known *Solidarność* (Solidarity) movement that came to lead Polish dissidence over the following decade.

In the immediate aftermath of these protests, the government was unsure how to respond. It found itself in the peculiar situation of leading an ostensible workers' state whose workers were rebelling against it. Solidarity and its capacity to mobilize nation-wise was a significant and unprecedented threat to the regime's stability and authority. The regime thus sent negotiators to meet with Solidarity's leaders. The result was the Gdańsk Agreement, in which the regime agreed to recognized Solidarity as a free and independent trade union. It also acquiesced to a number of demands, including an increase in wages and freeze in price increases, a limit on exports, additional social services and increased (but still limited) freedoms for workers, and a change to a five-day work week. Over the following year and half, the Solidarity movement, with Lech Wałęsa as its chairman, spread and rooted itself in every corner of the country, gaining millions of members.

The year 1981 was turbulent for Poland. The previous fall had seen continued protests from Solidarity over a variety of issues, including the legal registration of the organization with the state. In March 1981, tensions arose again when the state declared that farmers were ineligible for membership in the union, but the issue was eventually settled by making the rural branch of Solidarity an association instead of a union. The summer consisted of turnover and limited liberalization in the political leadership, a bad harvest, and continually growing foreign debt. In October, Solidarity held its first national congress, voicing demands for freer and fairer politics and liberalization of the market economy—a radicalization of the workers' demands the previous year. Throughout the entire series of events, the USSR was growing increasingly nervous, as it had in 1956 over Hungary and in 1968 over Czechoslovakia. It became clear that a military intervention was not out of the question, though the Soviets were reluctant to act due to Poland's size and questionable support from the rest of the Warsaw Pact countries.

The situation came to a head at the end of 1981. General Wojciech Jaruzelski, who had taken over the Party leadership the previous month, made the decision to enact martial law on 13 December, which would last until 1983 but have consequences for years afterwards. It was and continues to be a controversial decision. While the imposition of martial law undoubtedly prevented a Soviet invasion, it also destroyed all of the progress made by Solidarity over the previous two years and crushed the liberalization movement. Poland turned into a police state, Solidarity was forced to go underground, and many of its leaders were imprisoned. The group still continued to function, however, printing and distributing newspapers and samizdat publications thanks to a group of women called *Damska grupa operacyjna*. Refusing the idea that women had the capability to run such an organization, the investigating authorities failed to figure out how everything continued to run.

Despite the tightening of state control in the 1980s, Polish civil society continued to develop. Old groups, such as Solidarity and KSS KOR, cooperated with each other and with organizations in other Eastern Bloc countries, such as Czechoslovakia's Charter 77. Together, they secretly translated *samizdat* publications and distributed them across borders. New groups sprang up as well, targeting a variety of issues, including the environment and the military draft.

The Catholic Church also continued to be involved in dissent, though not in its entirety. While some of the clergy cooperated with the regime in exchange for funding and peace, a radical wing developed as well. This wing included the priest Jerzy Popiełuszko, who urged civil disobedience and participated in radio broadcasts of Radio Free Europe. In 1984, after one assassination attempt failed, Popiełuszko was kidnapped by the secret police, brutally beaten, and dumped in a reservoir to drown. The Ministry of the Interior, which controlled the secret police, investigated the murder, indicting and imprisoning the policemen involved, but this act was not altruistic. Throughout the trial, Jaruzelski controlled news headlines and manipulated the story to improve the relationship between the regime and Polish society in advance of coming austerity measures. Like most authoritarian regimes, blame got pushed down as would be the case after the Chernobyl disaster in 1986. Nobody higher up was held accountable.

Despite the enmity between the West and the USSR and their satellites, there were some breakthroughs prior to the collapse of communism in 1989. The Helsinki Accords, also known as the Helsinki Final Act, were signed in

1975 by 35 states, including the United States and Canada, and all European countries aside from Albania and Andorra. The Accords were the epitome of the East-West detente policy which was popularized in the late 1960s and early 1970s. Although the agreement was highly controversial when it was first established, in the decades following this historic moment, many argued that the Helsinki Final Act was a key ingredient in undermining the Soviet regime, and that it played a significant role in its later downfall especially since the bloc states had to acknowledge the unthinkable: human rights. Additionally, the Accords directly led to the creation of the Organization for Security and Cooperation in Europe (OSCE), an agency which frequently addresses human rights problems, among other pressing matters. It can therefore be said that the historic agreement made in 1975 has had a significant role in influencing European and global history.

The Helsinki Final Act was the culmination of years of intense negotiations between the major Western powers and the Soviet state, but its inception can be traced to 1954, when the Soviet Union first raised the issue of starting a "pan-European security conference". Under the guise of Khrushchev's "peaceful coexistence", the Soviet Union saw this proposal as an opportunity to gain Western acknowledgement of its post-war borders and values, which would carve in stone a terrible status quo. The early proposals were unsuccessful because they were seen by the West as a Soviet attempt to legitimize its conquest of East Central Europe (which is not wrong), and because the Soviets had not extended the invitation to the United States, as they sought to limit American influence in Europe. The Finnish government made its own proposal for a European security conference in May 1969, this time inviting North Atlantic Treaty Organization's (NATO) North American members to the table, which served as a catalyst for the negotiations. The early half of the 1970s were characterized by talks between foreign ministries on both sides of the Cold War. Then Soviet leader Leonid Brezhnev sought recognition of his state's hegemony in Eastern and Central Europe, based on the 1968 Brezhnev Doctrine, while the West hoped to hold the Soviets accountable to international human rights law and promote freedom of travel and flow of information.

Much of the talks were held in Helsinki, Finland, a country which had a long history of withstanding Russian and Soviet aggression, and which had branded itself as a neutral state in the context of the Cold War. This commitment was upheld by a treaty which Finland signed with the Soviet Union in 1948, called the treaty of Friendship, Co-operation and Mutual Assistance (FCMA), which essentially asked that Finland be treated as a neutral party and remain "outside the conflicting interests of the Great Powers", while pledging to defend the Soviet Union if it was ever attacked by Germany or one of its allies, in exchange for the same protection. That was likely something Central European states dreamed of way back in 1945.

The Helsinki Agreement was laid out in separate "baskets", one for European security, another for cooperation in economics, science, technology, and the environment, a third for humanitarian and cultural cooperation, and a final basket for a follow-up conference. The Western negotiators worked hard to omit any line that could be mistaken as endorsing the "Brezhnev Doctrine". The West fought to include Principle VII of Basket I, which stipulated that participating states were to respect "human rights and fundamental freedoms" and that this acknowledgement was vital to the "peace, justice and well-being necessary to ensure the development of friendly relations and cooperation among themselves as among all states". Although the Soviet Union attempted to include a hierarchy of rights, placing sovereignty and non-intervention above individual human rights, the West pushed them until they accepted that all the principles were of equal importance.

At the time the agreement was signed, many criticized the West for what they saw as a concession to the Soviet Union, and a second "betrayal" of Eastern Europe after the Yalta Conference in 1945. But the critics turned out to be wrong. The West's efforts to uphold human rights law in the agreement served as a catalyst for the development of dozens of human rights monitoring groups, both in the West and, more surprisingly, in the East. Almost immediately after the Accords were signed, advocacy and monitoring organizations called Helsinki Groups sprung up across most major Communist countries, including Russia, Ukraine, Czechoslovakia, Poland, Armenia, and Georgia, motivated by the principles laid out in the agreement. The agreement not only inspired dissent, but also gave the dissidents the technical language with which to articulate their abuses at the hands of the state. Although the Soviet government made efforts to crack down on these groups, they faced condemnation from the West. These Soviet-era activists inspired generations of human rights workers, who continue to fight for equality and justice to this day.

The Soviet Factor

The years 1956 and 1968 and the events in Poland in the 1980s proved a few things for would-be regime opponents. Socialism with a human face à la 1956 or 1968 was simply a waste of time. The system was totally broken and could not be repaired. For many, there were no third ways. As well, it was understood that meaningful change had to first come from the USSR. By the mid-1980s, it was clear that legitimacy of the regimes had been eroded. A snapshot of the regime leaders in 1984 says it all. A greyish 73-year-old Constantine Chernenko in the USSR replaced the ailing Yuri Andropov after he survived only two years in office, a 72-year-old Kádár in Hungary in power for 28 years, a 71-year-old Husák in Czechoslovakia in power for 15 years, and a 72-year-old Honecker in power for 14 years in East Germany. The Balkans were no better off. Tito had died in 1980 after 35 years of absolute power, leaving ageing hacks like the 76-year-old Hoxha running Albania since 1944, Bulgaria's 73-year-old Todor Zhivkov running the show for 30 years and the ultimate villain, Romania's somewhat youthful 66-year-old Nicolae Ceauşescu in power for 19 years. Everyone was born before the First World War. Only Poland's military leader, Jaruzelski, was born after the First World War. When Gorbachev assumed power in March 1985, he was the first Soviet leader born after 1918 but he was still surrounded by largely old and grey men. He made the other bloc leaders look especially old and no doubt what he saw in the bloc depressed him. Hoxha would die in April 1985 while the rest of the leadership would be ousted in various ways by the wave of fresh ideas coming from Moscow. An aged and demented Kádár and Zhivkov would be eased into retirement by reform communists in palace coups, Husák would succumb to people power, Honecker was forced to resign by his own party in October 1989, Ceaușescu also fell in a palace coup to his former stooges and, to ensure he never spilled the beans, was executed on Christmas Day 1989 along with his even more dangerous wife, Elena. The execution was not shown to Romanians until three months later. But more on that in the next chapter.

Gorbachev proved to be in the long run to be the most important catalyst for the subsequent liberation of the bloc states. No doubt he did not see this coming, but he unleashed a series of events that hit the region in unimaginable ways. Gorbachev did believe, like Nagy or Dubček, that the system could be saved through dramatic economic reforms and that the bloc states could also reform but also retain a pro-Soviet position. Gorbachev never gave up on Stalin's notion of a buffer for the USSR, but he was prepared to accept a version of the 1945 version of Soviet-friendly states on its borders. Among the many unforeseen consequences of Gorbachev was the return of nationalism which he unleashed both in the USSR and the bloc, as Marxism had never really solved the national question. Nationalism was very much part of the Soviet project, but they hoped it would disappear. It did not.

A huge amount has been written about the end of the Cold War and its causes. The United States tends to take too much credit, to the expense of the very important roles played by Gorbachev but also the various figures in the bloc who appeared to challenge communist rule. As noted earlier, the states of Central Europe had been largely extremely vulnerable objects in a Great Power game. The events of 1985–1989 gave people a role that is sometimes underestimated.

Gorbachev unleashed a series of initiatives that proved somewhat durable. The first, *uskorenie* in Russian which meant acceleration, aimed to save the system by injecting more dynamism in the economy. While the USSR and the bloc state economies were weak by Western standards, they were not total catastrophes and could have probably limped along. East Germany, for example, had a GDP that was only 40 percent lower than West Germany. East German statistics do need to be viewed with some scepticism, as it become quite clear when West Germany got the bill for reunification after 1990 that things were not always as they seemed. But things were bad, nonetheless. In terms of GDP, the communist years had set them years behind. GDPs that had been close in 1939 were now below half, in the case of the always far richer Czechoslovakia, or a third in the case of Hungary and Poland, of Austria's. The failure to make viable economies remained the biggest shortcoming of the entire enterprise as viable economies simply eluded them from the forced austerity of Romania where there was no debt but only one light bulb to the free spending Hungarians eating and drinking their way to an early death. Declining living standards, high corruption, rampant nepotism, high infant mortality rates, low productivity, long waits for poor quality consumer goods to say nothing of the environmental degradation that was totally unprecedented even by the low standards of the time. Keep in mind that the USSR also spent some 20 percent of its GDP on the military.

Life expectancy also tells a sad story. In 1989, life expectancy for a male in the USSR was 64 years. It went up only briefly in the mid-1980s after Gorbachev, as part of his reforms, cracked down hard on the country's main cause of early death: excessive alcohol consumption. As an indicator, tax on vodka sales was 35 percent of the Soviet budget in 1988. Gorbachev's new alcohol policy included higher taxes, limited shops where it could be sold and banning it before 2 pm in restaurants. As hard as it is to believe, things got even worse for Russians after the collapse of the communist order with life expectancy for males dropping to 57. In 1989, Czechs, East Germans, Poles, and Slovaks could count on a few more years but not the Hungarians. Poor diets, cheap booze and cigarettes, limited exercise and a general feeling of powerlessness contributed to the miserable state of affairs. Life expectancy was roughly 75 years in North America and Western Europe at the same time.

Gorbachev's managed reform process, which was very much a square peg in a round hole, later included perestroika (restructuring) and glasnost (openness) which were critical for undoing the communist monopoly on power. By far it was glasnost that served to rot the systems from within, particularly in the USSR. Outside the USSR, Gorbachev's new thinking brought mixed opinions from the old men in Budapest, Prague, and Warsaw. Hungary, laden with debt, was already where Gorbachev wanted to be in some ways but without the despair. Poland was a mixed bag. Czechoslovakia wanted nothing to do with reform, East Germany too, also heavily indebted, did not even see themselves as a satellite state but almost as a partner with the USSR. In the Balkans, where various forms of national communism prevailed, Gorbachev was not welcome.

But before glasnost and perestroika which came in 1987, there was Afghanistan and Chernobyl. The USSR had invaded Afghanistan in 1979 and Gorbachev needed to find a way out without provoking a reaction from the Army. The war cost a fortune and alienated most of the population. The withdrawal was complete by 1989. But it was the Chernobyl nuclear accident in the Ukrainian Republic in late April 1986 that exposed the near total failure of the Soviet system at home and abroad and forced Gorbachev to take far bolder steps. In what was supposed to be a routine turbine test in a Soviet-made reactor an explosion happened and one of the station's four reactors began to meltdown sending a nuclear cloud north and west. First detected by Sweden, the Soviet leadership did its best to cover the whole thing up and Gorbachev really only spoke on the disaster almost three weeks after the explosion, inviting criticism not only from the West but from their own citizens too and those of the neighbouring bloc states. It revealed just how authoritarian states responded to crisis: denial, cover-ups, and then scapegoats. But Chernobyl was just one of the ecological disasters that defined the communist system.

For the bloc states, it certainly emboldened opposition movements even more. The official reactions in the Bloc countries of Central Europe unsurprisingly copied Moscow's response: deny and then downplay the impact. The reaction was the most subdued in then still hardline Czechoslovakia. A brief report noted that there had been an explosion, but authorities maintained that there was no threat to Czechoslovaks. After several days of a media blackout on the subject, during which May Day parades took place (as they did all around the Eastern Bloc and in the USSR despite obvious dangers) and radioactive rain fell, another news report stated that radiation levels were falling. There was no guidance on what measures to take in terms of health or hygiene, and people were not instructed to stay indoors. News reports in East Germany were similar, downplaying the severity of the explosion. Experts attempted to reassure people that there was no danger. The Polish and Hungarian media were slightly more expansive in their reporting on the topic, but they still attempted to convince their audiences that there was no significant threat to their health and safety. Poland was, however, the only country to distribute doses of iodine, which is used to protect the thyroid from the effects of radiation, to children. After all, Lithuania had two of the same reactors, while Bulgaria, East Germany and Slovakia had similarly dated and potentially dangerous reactors. All of these reactors were later closed as part of the European Union's accession process.

The most important impact on Central Europe was on media trust which was already low. People attempted to listen to Western radio broadcasts, which were often jammed, and rumours spread among family, friends, and neighbours about the true severity of the issue, what not to eat, what medicines to take, and the like. Organizations such as Charter 77 published complaints about how the situation was being handled. It is now clear that the explosion had a severe impact on the region, increasing the rates of cancer and thyroid diseases, impacting pregnant women and their unborn babies, and contaminating soil throughout the region. One lasting peculiarity is that a large portion of Central Europe's wild boars continue to be radioactive at levels unsafe to eat—a concern in a region where boar meat is part of the traditional cuisine.

But even before Chernobyl, the Hungarians had used the environment to push for political change. Representative of the strength of civil society, activist Hungarians formed the Danube Circle in 1984 to challenge a major dam project between Czechoslovakia and Hungary on the Danube in what was near an extremely pristine area of the river called the Danube Bend. The group not only succeeded in preventing the dam by 1989, but also became a place for regime opponents to channel their opposition.

Conclusion

In June 1987, US President Ronald Reagan gave a speech at the Brandenburg Gate, the divider between East and West Berlin. Gorbachev and Reagan had already met twice—once in Geneva and once in Reykjavik. Speaking directly to Gorbachev, Reagan took the bold step to tell him to "open this gate" and "tear down this wall". No doubt East Europeans were emboldened but they had already done a lot by then anyway. Reagan's intervention was likely not decisive as we shall see because local actors were doing the heavy lifting as lots of people had successfully carved out a space outside of government control. Many had taken Havel's advice and stopped living the lie. In any case, by the end of 1988, the writing was on the wall, even without the benefit of hindsight. The surveillance state could not survive forever. A good entry point for the period might be best captured by the film *Lives of Others* (2006), directed by Florian Henckel von Donnersmarck. The film tells the potentially unlikely story of a Stasi agent who decides that this time around, the regime is wrong. Above and beyond that, it explores the insidiousness of what were morally and ideologically bankrupt regimes. Keep in mind that it was easier for East Germans to get visas to go to the West in the 1980s than to go the fraternal socialist Poland for fear citizens would catch the virus of Solidarity. Plus, opposition to Gorbachev was strong in Czechoslovakia and East Germany. East Germany even banned the Soviet publication *Sputnik* in December 1988. As a modernization project, the communists had largely failed. Genuine allegiance was no longer a goal, just conformity.

But let's return to Hungary which was always on the frontlines of systemic change. Hungary was bankrupt for sure, but things in neighbouring Romania eroded the governing communists' legitimacy even more. Ceaușescu played the nationalist card in the 1980s with pleasure and ramped up his attacks on the minority Hungarians. The fact that the communists could really do nothing to help their brethren did not go unnoticed. In May 1988, János Kádár was forced out of office by a clique of reform communists led by Karoly Grosz and Imre Pozsgay. Hungary even introduced a kind of multi-party democracy. He kept a largely ceremonial post. No charges, no jail. Kádár's departure told a bigger story of hubris for the region's communist leaders. Some felt that house cleaning, without the jail sentences, executions, or unmarked graves but with the usual amount of historical falsification could save the party and their power. As we shall see in the next chapter, the West would provide some help to the would-be communist reformers. Indeed, 1989 unleashed a number of possibilities and not all of them good. The West wanted to ensure that 1989 did not become 1929. This was to be the challenge and, like so many times in the past, it was better the devil you know. One of the big questions was what role would nationalism play? While Marxism-Leninism was explicitly international, the region's communist leaders used nationalism when they had to. While this was most obvious in the Balkans, it was elsewhere too. The West was concerned about that, especially the European Community (one of the many forerunners to the EU) which was enjoying to a degree the hubris of post-nationalism. For policy-makers in Brussels, nationalism was a direct path to war. Could Eastern Europe avoid such path dependency? Fears were not unfounded. Already in 1987 in Yugoslavia, Slobodan Milošević, the number two in the Serbian Communist party, a national branch of the Yugoslav communist party, found that in demonizing the Albanians in Kosovo he was on to something. In Bulgaria, the last breath of the regime there was to begin the "revival process" which aimed, by force, to eliminate the Turkish identity in Bulgaria. Romania's Ceaușescu never hesitated to whip hysteria against the minority Hungarians. Nobody was yet even talking about the Roma, who constituted the region's biggest minority.

For Further Study

BOOKS (FICTION AND NON-FICTION)

Applebaum, Anne. *Iron Curtain: The Crushing of Eastern Europe, 1944–1956.* New York: Knopf, 2012.
Bolton, Jonathan. *Worlds of Dissent: Charter 77, The Plastic People of the Universe, Czech Culture under Communism.* Cambridge: Harvard University Press, 2012.
Garton Ash, Timothy. *The Polish Revolution: Solidarity, 1980–82.* London: J. Cape, 1983.
Borhi, Lazslo. *Dealing with Dictators. The United States, Hungary and East Central Europe, 1942–1989.* Bloomington: Indiana University Press, 2016.
Havel, Václav. *The Garden Party and Other Plays.* New York: Grove Press, 1993.
Imre, Anikó. *TV Socialism.* Durham, NC: Duke University Press, 2016.
Sebestyen, Victor. *Twelve Days: The Story of the 1956 Hungarian revolution.* New York: Pantheon Books, 2006.

FILMS

The Firemen's Ball (1967). Directed by Miloš Forman. Czechoslovakia.
A tanú [*The Witness*] (1969). Directed by Péter Bacsó. Hungary.
The Joke (1969). Directed by Jaromil Jireš. Czechoslovakia.
Moonlighting (1982). Directed by Jerzy Skolimowski. United Kingdom.
Those Wonderful Years that Sucked (1997). Directed by Petr Nikolaev. Czech Republic.
The Lives of Others (2006). Directed by Florian Henckel von Donnersmarck. Germany.
Barbara. (2012) Directed by Christian Petzold. Germany.
The Waldheim Waltz. (2018) Directed by Ruth Beckermann. Austria.
Never Look Away. (2018) Directed by Florian Henckel von Donnersmarck. Germany.

CHAPTER 6

1989–2004: Roundtables, Street Protests, and the Long Journey Back to Europe

As we have seen, so much happened in 1988 that it suggested dramatic things would continue in 1989. However, few predicted the collapse of communism and there was nothing inevitable about what happened. However, in hindsight, it does take on a strange inevitability that was actually not there. The year 1989 is a sea of turning points when things really did change. The opening of the Berlin Wall in November 1989 is the most emblematic and TV-friendly moment of 1989, but a huge amount had happened before then. Hungary and Poland had roundtable talks that included opposition groups early in 1989. In January, Czechs commemorated the 1969 self-immolation of Jan Palach in his fight against normalization. In June, Hungarians reburied the 1956 leader Imre Nagy and Poland's communist went down to defeat in the first almost free elections. In August, to mark 50 years since the Nazi-Soviet Pact consigned them to misery in the USSR, more than two million citizens of Estonia, Latvia, and Lithuania joined hands for a Baltic chain through those states in support of independence. In Leipzig in East Germany 300,000 people took to the streets in October to demand change and Hungary opened its border with Austria to allow East Germans to travel to West Germany via Austria. Of course, on 9 November, the Berlin Wall came down. But things could have gone differently. In June 1989 the Chinese government violently crushed the pro-democracy protests in Tiananmen Square and never looked back. The communists still had massive resources and violence was always an option, at least for some of them in Albania, East Germany, Czechoslovakia, and Romania. Palace coups also held out their own allure.

What we do know for certain is that Moscow's shift to allowing extraordinary reform was the key catalyst in the success of the liberation movements of 1989 in much of the communist bloc. Plus, already in 1988 Gorbachev had made clear that the USSR would no longer technically uphold the Brezhnev Doctrine, which more or less was right to intervene to preserve Soviet-style socialism, and he also called for Soviet troop reductions in the bloc states. In the fall of 1989, a spokesman in the Soviet foreign ministry called the new paradigm the "Sinatra doctrine" as states could do things their way. The impact of these changes is telling especially given the fate of countries where Soviet influence was limited where things were nastier and less decisive. There were no Soviet troops in Albania; Romania and Yugoslavia and transitions there went a different direction costing an entire generation the promise of a normal life. The year 1989 thus became to a degree like 1919 in that the map of Europe is redrawn geopolitically with the end of the Cold War and the return of Central Europe. Four states disappeared—Czechoslovakia, East Germany, the USSR and Yugoslavia. When the dust settled, 14 new states appeared in Central Europe and the Balkans.

What took place were two types of regime change in the new Central Europe: negotiated outcomes in the case of Hungary and Poland and forced as in the case of Czechoslovakia and East Germany where both regimes tried to hold on despite growing public protests. The type of regime change would become important later on as subsequent governments would challenge the legitimacy of the transfer of power as it happened in 1989. As we saw in the preceding chapter, a top-down transition really started in Hungary with János Kádár's removal in 1988 and the triumph of reform communists. Hungary's and Poland's economic collapse was imminent, and citizens' groups challenged the regime on different levels from Solidarity in Poland to preserving the Danube to demanding a reassessment of the events of 1956 in Hungary. The Balkans did not get off as lucky as Central Europe. People there largely got what on the surface looked like the nationalist pattern of political change where former communists chose nationalism for mobilizing the population. But it was more than that—nationalism was a cynical choice that permitted these regimes to capture the state for largely private interests. With war engulfing Yugoslavia and communists retaining real power in Albania, Romania, and Bulgaria, those leaders chose state capture over reform. One needs only to compare the pedigrees of say Czechoslovakia's Václav Havel to Serbia's Slobodan Milošević or Romania's Ion Iliescu to see why things ended so differently in two post-communist settings. For one thing, Havel was never a communist. He was a playwright who urged his fellow citizens to stop living the lie. But the West rightly feared that same potential for violent disintegration, the renewal of the interwar nationalisms and contested borders.

The key Western leaders—George H W Bush in the US, Helmut Kohl in West Germany (and the first chancellor of a reunited Germany), François Mitterrand in France and Margaret Thatcher in the UK—feared instability more than anything else. Stability was more important than shaky democracy among peoples unprepared for it. Gorbachev was able to leverage their fears to buttress his own case for a new socialism at home but in the bloc states as well. No doubt few people doubted that the USSR, just like in 1945, had legitimate security goals that needed to be respected. To his credit, Bush was decidedly cautious when dealing with the pace of change in the East bloc obviously in the hope of ensuring Gorbachev stayed in power. In fact, it was very hard for the US and Western Europe not to view the region though anything other than the interwar paradigm. Most seemed to agree that the system established at Yalta in 1945 was still relevant and that there was even a place for a reformed Warsaw Pact too. Moreover, Western leaders seemed to have more faith in the reform communists' ability to maintain stability than the dissidents who were pushing for real change. After all, the West had largely made peace with the communist regimes in the 1970s and 1980s. By far the best example of this was West Germany's rapprochement with East Germany within the framework of Ostpolitik that started in the 1970s and ended with reversing the West German policy of non-recognition of East Germany among other things. The reform communists as well, used to a world where you survived through subservience, these men could be counted on if only for the sake of staying out of jail or murdered by mobs. Bush even liked General Jaruzelski—everyone just wished he would get a makeover to look more appealing.

Moreover, a hint of cultural superiority shaped things too—not everyone believed that these countries could actually become democracies—stability within the Warsaw Pact and the USSR mattered more than anything else. Plus, there was the national question and the bigger fear about re-opening border questions. The communist leaders of Czechoslovakia, Hungary, and Poland had very little credibility on these questions so they could be counted on to stay silent. But who could say for the opposition leaders in Hungary who would no doubt reject the communist mantra that one should not speak about the fate of the Hungarians left outside the Trianon borders. Hungary's first post-communist prime minister, József Antall, had already said in May 1990 that he was spiritually the prime minister to *all* Hungarians which no doubt ruffled feathers not only in Bratislava and Bucharest but in Western capitals too. Nationalism was certainly a big part of the events of 1989, but it was subdued outside of Slovakia and Yugoslavia, and skewed towards the more liberal version on offer in Western Europe. The allure of re-joining Europe allowed for the nationalist pattern of political change to take a back seat for the sake of a stable and prosperous life. But that would not always hold things together. In 1989, Central Europe therefore had something that had never happened before: a non-violent revolution. The term Velvet Revolution was later applied to Czechoslovakia, that swept the communists out of power in a year. This led some to conclude that these were not real revolutions at all but something more nefarious whereby communists became, almost overnight, mainstream European socialists, converted their political power into economic power and sold off the country's assets to foreign investors or their friends for a pittance. This was certainly the case in Russia which had a privatization process that empowered an entire new class of business people with strong ties to the security services. There is a grain of truth to this interpretation but that is a conversation for the next chapter.

In Hungary, Kádár's successors tried to manage change but were not averse to using the language of the old days: class struggle, counter-revolution, and white terror. Political pluralism was welcome but within the confines of the one-party system. But new political parties emerged like the Hungarian Democratic Forum, the Alliance of Young Democrats and the Federation of Free Democrats (Fidesz), while old parties like the Smallholders and the Social Democrats reappeared. In March, the opposition groups formed the Opposition Round Table (ORT) to create a united front to the communists who controlled the assets of the state. Of note is that Fidesz, in some senses a youthful liberal party led by Viktor Orbán, had an upper age limit. Party members, at least until 1993, had to be 35 years or younger. Fidesz would later morph into a more conservative and nationalist party that would dominate Hungarian political life after 2010.

Two more important milestones in the winter of 1989 suggested something big was about to happen. Let's return briefly to the 1950s and the question of history and legitimacy. Knowing the future gave the communists an edge but they still needed to control the past in a way that did not undermine their leading role. On multiple occasions the communists needed to "correct" the past to ensure the future stayed the same. In the 1950s, as the communists grappled with the death of Stalin, some of the foundational myths of their hold on power were questioned and re-assessments of the past became extremely dangerous. We saw that with the Rajk "resurrection" and its impact on Mátyás Rákosi. For the Hungarians in the 1980s it was 1956 that was the perpetual elephant in the room. The myth of 1956 as counter-revolution unwound and the communists were forced to acknowledge what happened was indeed a popular uprising. Historical legitimacy was thus questionable at best. After that, people wondered even aloud about the presence of Soviet troops. In February, a multi-party system was introduced but the Communists would retain their paramount position. Roundtable talks started with opposition groups in March.

But what stands out in 1989 for Hungary is the reburial of Imre Nagy and other executed leaders of the 1956 revolution held in truly epic circumstances in June. In total, 200,000 people gathered in Heroes' Square in what some say was the death blow to the communist hold on power. It was a blow, but largely a symbolic one, as the communists by then had figured that their days were numbered. Emotional to say the least, no people can do a reburial like the Hungarians. No doubt watching the proceedings was János Kádár wondering how Nagy could be back. Kádár died three weeks later. Six black coffins—five were key leaders of the revolution and the sixth for the unknown martyrs—were on display. Speeches were obviously made but the stand out there was a 25-year-old Viktor Orbán, destined to become Hungary's key political figure in the early twenty-first century and indeed a major European figure as well. Orbán's speech was later hailed for his willingness to call for the removal of Soviet troops. What stood out, and certainly set Orbán apart from everyone else, while also giving a clear indication of what his policies really were, was when he bravely called out the communists for the disgusting fraud they were. After all, communists shedding tears for the dead Nagy and his colleagues was a bit much. The same party had killed Nagy and hid behind the lie for 33 years.

Orbán's anti-communism, not the alleged liberalism he abandoned, was the hallmark of the moment. In that, he remained consistent. Liberalism, as we shall see, was not part of his DNA.

Also in June 1989, in a largely symbolic act, the Austrian and Hungarian foreign ministers had cut the border fence between the two countries but this did not mean the border was actually open. But what was happening in Hungary was crucial for the fate of the bloc. Thousands upon thousands of East Germans had been flocking to Hungary in hopes exiting through Austria and then on to West Germany. Thousands also piled into the West German embassies in Budapest and Prague. In both cases, Czechs and Hungarians were expected to return the East Germans to East Germany. This was the basis of the bloc. In both cases, that did not happen, and it thus undermined, in the most dramatic way, the very essence of East Germany's already fragile legitimacy. In the end, the East Germans in Prague left by train, through East Germany at Honecker's request and thousands tried to board in Dresden, to West Germany. In the end, the Hungarians decided to really open the border to Austria in September 1989. It was as breath-taking as it was spontaneous. Most importantly, keeping in mind that the Berlin Wall, which went up in 1961, which stemmed massive flight of East Germans to West Germany, still stood, was a turning point for the fate of East Germany. It really had no reason to exist. As we have already seen, the Hungarian communists' attitude towards borders was quite unique. Relative freedom of travel started under Kádár and in the 1980s they had already started to evaluate the viability of an expensive and largely unnecessary border control system. In 1987 the Hungarians introduced a "world passport" that allowed them to travel anywhere although currency restrictions still meant they arrived in their destination broke. Prior to 1988, most people went to Czechoslovakia for cheaper foodstuffs.

Cheaper food was not the only thing that distinguished Czechoslovakia from Hungary. While dissident activity in Czechoslovakia had increased in the late 1970s and throughout the 1980s with the formation of Charter 77, the Czechoslovak regime remained decidedly hardline almost to the end. To be sure, Czechoslovak citizens in general were fed-up and relatively resigned and apathetic in political terms after 20 years of "normalization" following the Prague Spring. Unlike Hungary, there was only limited liberalization, during this period, and while the dissident community was active and vibrant, it was much smaller than Poland's Solidarity.

Only in 1989 did any real unrest begin to brew, beginning with the twentieth anniversary of Jan Palach's self-immolation in January 1969 in protest of the regime and civic apathy. Following this act, the regime had inevitably tried to suppress the memory of his protest and prevent him from becoming a symbolic figure of opposition, exhuming his body from the Olšany Cemetery in Prague and sending his ashes back to his mother, who was prevented for several years from reburying them. In January 1989, however, commemoration of his protest developed into a series of demonstrations called "Palach Week", which criticized the regime and called for change. They were violently suppressed but, in the end, helped catalyse the popular unrest that would make 1989 a major turning point for Czechs and Slovaks too. Readers interested in learning more about Palach can watch Agnieszka Holland's three-part series *Burning Bush (2013)*.

Policy decisions in Czechoslovakia's neighbouring states were also an early catalyst in stirring up energy in the country's moribund political atmosphere. As we have seen, in May 1989, the Hungarian government announced that it would be removing the physical border between Hungary and Austria, providing unprecedented mobility between East and West and the subsequent exodus of East Germans from Hungary and Prague did not escape the notice of Czechoslovak citizens, who began to mobilize in a way that had not been seen in the country in two decades.

November came to be the pivotal month. On 9 November, the Berlin Wall—the ultimate symbol of the division between East and West—was irreversibly breeched by East and West Germans together, and the revolution almost fully engulfed Czechoslovakia fewer than ten days later. The date 17 November 1989 was the fiftieth anniversary of student protests in 1939 against Nazi occupiers and decrees that had shut down Czech-speaking universities. For this anniversary, students in Prague organized a peaceful demonstration to commemorate the death of Jan Opletal, who had been killed in the 1939 protests, and the values for which students had fought 50 years earlier. The demonstrators met a police blockade on Národní třída, a major boulevard in the centre of the city, and were violently pushed back and dispersed. The following day students went on strike to protest the violence and over the next few days new political organizations, formed mainly of dissident artists and intellectuals in the capitals, coalesced with other local leaders. The two main groups were the Civic Forum in Prague and Public Against Violence in Bratislava.

These last couple of weeks of November saw a series of powerful demonstrations, particularly on Prague's emblematic Wenceslas Square. Leaders of the dissident movement, including Václav Havel, spoke to an energized crowd and demanded significant change, truth, and freedom. Marta Kubišová, blacklisted by the government since her song, *Modlitba pro Martu* (A Prayer for Marta), an anthem of the 1968 protests, performed the same song once again for the crowd. On 25 November, the new opposition organizations began negotiations with the prime minister, Ladislav Adamec, who agreed to form a new government but still with a Communist majority, which many people still found unacceptable. That same day, and again the following day, people power sealed the regime's fate as approximately 800,000 people gathered on Prague's Letná plain for a massive demonstration. On 27 November, three-quarters of the country's population took part in a general strike, and in the following days, the Parliament, under the Party's instructions, finalized the decision to end the party-state system that had been in place for 40 years. The whole process had taken just under two weeks in a country that had not experienced any major reform over the preceding two decades like its neighbours had.

December was a month of reorganization and change in leadership. There were no roundtable discussions in these early stages like there had been in Poland. The break was much cleaner, involved fewer compromises, and the entire system was primed for turnover, although the Communist Party was allowed to continue operating as a largely ideologically unreformed party in the new system, unlike in other Eastern Bloc countries. On 7 December, Prime Minister Adamec resigned. Three days later, Gustav Husák named a new government and resigned as president. The same day, dissidents in Slovakia organized a peaceful march from Bratislava to the Austrian town of Hainburg, on the other side of the newly opened border. Over 100,000 people unexpectedly joined in, physically cutting down the barbed wire separating East from West themselves as they went.

The next task in the government was figuring out who would become the new president of the country. One candidate was Alexander Dubček, who had supported the Prague Spring as leader of the country in 1968, but after negotiations and student activism stirring up support among the population, Václav Havel was elected and subsequently sworn in on December 29. To be fair, since 1989 was a far cry from 1968, Dubček was for some really an anachronism. He was a symbol but in no way could he have been a leader for the new era.

In 1990, Czechoslovakia faced many complicated decisions and changes in its transition out of a communist regime. One of the first issues that arose was the name of the country. Havel proposed removing "Socialist" from the official name of the country, unintentionally igniting a heated debate known as the "Hyphen War". The debate was, in essence, over whether to spell the new name of the country as "Czechoslovakia" or "Czecho-Slovakia". Most Slovaks favoured the latter as it emphasized the equality of the two members of the federal country. Most Czechs opposed it on the grounds that it evoked the name the country had briefly held between the 1938 Munich Accords and the full occupation of Bohemia and Moravia by Nazi Germany in March 1939, thus serving as a reminder of one of the bleakest periods in the country's history. In the end, the compromise name was "Czech and Slovak Federative Republic".

Politically, some of the key issues related to how to handle the de-communization process. Because of the party-state system, the regime had reached into practically every corner of society and the process was complicated. One element was the issue of preventing members of the former regime and its collaborators from remaining or returning to positions in the public sector. Czechoslovakia was one of the more proactive Eastern Bloc countries on this front, passing a harsh lustration law in 1991. Both successor states later opened their respective secret police archives to the public for purposes of transparency as well. Another issue to tackle was that of restitution. Many private citizens and organizations such as the Catholic Church had had their property confiscated and nationalized in the late 1940s and 1950s. The process of returning this property to its owners or their descendants was far from straightforward and continues to be an issue in some cases to this day.

Just as political turnover had varied among Eastern Bloc countries, so did economic turnover. Czechoslovakia entered the 1990s in the advantageous position of having little foreign debt, unlike some of its neighbours, giving its leaders some leeway in their policy choices. While others converted their economies gradually, Poland had tried the "shock therapy" method of simply switching to liberal policy overnight, and Czechoslovakia followed a more gradual path, led by the neoliberal economist and Minister of Finance, Václav Klaus. Along with price changes, private citizens were issued vouchers meant to purchase shares in state-owned business that were to be privatized. Even with Czechoslovakia's relatively advantageous economic position, the change was inevitably not entirely smooth, with unemployment rising and the economy temporarily contracting.

In June 1990, Czechoslovakia held its first free and fair elections. Civic Forum and Public Against Violence won overwhelmingly in both houses of Parliament, but the path forward was not smooth. In the turmoil of the first few post-Communist years, the landscape of political parties in the country was understandably fluid and party allegiances shifted frequently among the country's citizenry. While the Civic Forum and Public Against Violence had garnered considerable momentum leading from November 1989 into the first elections in 1990, support splintered thereafter, and members of these movements began to form and join other political groupings. As citizens looked for the best possible leaders, two men in particular grasped the opportunity to position themselves as alternatives. They were the aforementioned Václav Klaus, particularly in the Czech half of the country, and Vladimír Mečiar in Slovakia. They formed two new parties: The Civic Democratic Forum and the Movement for a Democratic Slovakia, respectively. The two were quite different but they could agree that Czechoslovakia should not exist. Klaus, a monetarist, was a former banker, with a stints studying in the US and Italy. He would remain a figure in Czech politics throughout the transition even though most Czechs would eventually consider him to be a villain. Mečiar, educated as a lawyer, was a solid communist, at least until the Prague Spring saw him ousted from the Party after which he ended up in blue-collar jobs and later as a lawyer. He would be the principal figure in Slovak politics from 1990 until 1998.

In the next set of parliamentary elections, held in June 1992, these two parties won the most support despite their leaders' clashing views on the future of the country, which made it difficult to compromise and form a coalition. As a result, Klaus and Mečiar turned to the possibility of splitting the country. Such a move would have normally required a referendum, but Klaus argued that the election had served as such, even though it was evident that public opinion was largely against a split. Klaus and Mečiar went ahead with their plan, and the "Velvet Divorce" of the country into the Czech Republic and Slovakia officially took place on 1 January 1993. The terms of the divorce were largely hammered out in the Tugendhat Villa in Brno, a UNESCO heritage home built by the celebrated architect Mies van der Rohe. The villa, now state-owned and lavishly restored, also tells the story of the fate of the original Jewish owners.

While many people were unhappy with how the situation had unfolded, the breakup was ultimately remarkably smooth and peaceful, especially in the context of the violent dissolution occurring simultaneously not too far south, in the former Yugoslavia. In the end, while many lamented the absence of a referendum, the elections made clear that the forces in favour of separation had the upper hand. Klaus had other plans that meant Slovakia was merely a burden. Mečiar wanted his own state but not an independent one. Moreover, unlike in 1918 when bigger was better, in the 1990s a smaller state was a safer bet and one without minorities even better.

After the breakup of the Czech and Slovak Federative Republic on 1 January 1993, the two new countries set off in completely different directions politically. The Czechs, under the leadership of Václav Havel, as president, and Václav Klaus, as prime minister, continued on a relatively smooth path towards democratic consolidation and liberal economic policies. Under Vladimír Mečiar, the Slovaks took a brief, five-year detour back towards autocratic rule with a nationalist spin. In fact, the Slovak pattern of political change bore some striking similarities with what was happening in the Yugoslavia of Slobodan Milošević without the war. Among other consequences, Slovakia's political situation from 1993 to 1998 threatened the country's application to join the European Union and NATO.

One of Prime Minister Mečiar's early decisions in 1993 was to halt Klaus's neoliberal economic reforms and veer towards corrupt crony capitalism closer to what happened in Russia under President Boris Yeltsin with a privatization scheme that favoured his allies. He also turned to nationalism, largely with an anti-Hungarian bent but anti-Roma too, and codifying it in the language of the new Constitution which spoke exclusively to the "Slovak nation". This new political culture resulted, for example, in a series of new anti-Hungarian laws and policies. He also oriented Slovakia eastwards, favouring strong ties with Russia and signing a number of agreements. Mečiar's pro-Russia argument was based on the notion that Slovakia has more to gain from joining forces with a poorer East, where Slovakia had advantages, as opposed to a rich West. As Mečiar's policy proposals radicalized, he encountered resistance from Slovakia's president, Michal Kováč, and Mečiar's government eventually fell after a vote of no confidence in early 1994. After the parliamentary elections later the same year, however, he was back as the prime minister and newly invigorated to attack the opposition and consolidate power for himself. He often clashed with the constitutional court, and his policies threatened the rule of law in Slovakia. His popularity, which was genuine, was based on his appeal to rural and elderly voters outside of cosmopolitan Bratislava. His peasant humour also served him well.

In September 1995, as friction between Mečiar and Kováč escalated, the president's son was kidnapped in Bratislava and taken to Austria where he was left drunk on the steps of a police station. There were strong suspicions that the Slovak secret police was implicated in this episode and that Mečiar was behind the entire sordid affair, but it has never been proven. Mečiar suspiciously blocked investigation into the case during his time in power, and the statute of limitations for legal investigation has now run out.

Mečiar's leadership of Slovakia had serious consequences for the country's international standing. In 1997, the EU decided to remove Slovakia from the first wave of new accessions. It had previously been assumed to be part of this group along with its neighbours but was actively removed due to the concerning political situation in the country. It also was no longer on track to join NATO along with its neighbours, who became members in 1999.

These threats eventually helped turn popular support away from Mečiar, along with fears of a constitutional crisis and disgust in the levels of corruption that had developed in the country. The tide turned in 1998 with a new set of parliamentary elections. These elections effectively pushed Mečiar out of power in favour of a new, four-party, centre-right coalition. Moving forward, Slovakia returned to the path of market reforms and democratic consolidation. The 1998 elections in Slovakia brought a kind of everybody but Mečiar coalition that set Slovakia back on a pro-European path with remarkable success based on an extremely vibrant and resilient civil society. Unlike what would happen in Hungary, the Slovaks would not so easily surrender the gains made in 1989. Slovakia in 1998 showed that Slovakia really was different and able to go to the brink and back owing to their willingness to preserve what had been obtained in 1989. The country was also now back on track to join the EU with its neighbours, officially re-joining the group of candidate countries in 2000 and the EU itself in 2004. The Slovak story is one of going to the brink and pulling back.

In East Germany, the exodus of refugees from Hungary and Czechoslovakia spelled trouble. Honecker called the whole business a counter-revolution but he was deposed in mid-October and was replaced by the equally colourless Egon Krenz who had openly supported China's response to the democracy movement there. Krenz did not last long: he stepped down in December. The communists did change their name to from the Socialist Unity Party to the Party of Democratic Socialism but for all purposes, they were finished. East German civil society grew like mad as the demonstrations got bigger and bigger. On 9 November, an ill-informed East German official told a press conference that travel restrictions were lifted effective immediately. East Germany no longer had a reason to exist. The future president of Russia, Vladimir Putin, sat in a lonely KGB office in Dresden waiting for instructions from Moscow. German re-unification quickly became the new destination. But not everyone was on board: UK Prime Minister Margaret Thatcher opposed German unification for fear of border changes. But people power, at least to a degree, ensured the shift towards unification was really unstoppable as the slogans shifted from "We are the people" to "We are one people".

To be sure, there were reform communists and some dissidents that hoped to preserve a version of East Germany. But in the March 1990 elections West German political parties, especially Helmut Kohl's Christian Democratic Union (CDU) prevailed. Kohl put everyone's mind at ease when he accepted the

Oder-Neisse line as the eastern border and dropped the pursuit of reparations for expellees. The Two plus Four negotiations—the two German states plus the four occupying powers went well. Gorbachev hoped to keep the GDR afloat but had to recognize that it was beyond the USSR's capabilities. In October 1990 the East German state ceased to exist—the West Germans simply took it over and paid the enormous bill for re-unification.

In the latter half of the 1980s, the Polish regime of Jaruzelski loosened some of the social control it had imposed in the first half of the decade, granting amnesty to the victims of martial law, and easing censorship. Economic reform was once again on the table and open for limited public discussion. When price increases in early 1988 set off yet another round of workers' strikes on the Baltic coast, the regime turned to negotiation as its primary tactic of settling the situation. The situation in Poland was somewhere between the hardline regimes of East Germany and Czechoslovakia and the Goulash Communism reformist regime in Hungary. Still, for all, the events that transpired over the course of 1989 were unpredictable.

In early 1989, the Polish regime persisted in its tactic of negotiation, sitting down for the now famous round table talks with a variety of participants, including representatives from Solidarity. Topics of discussion included the freedom of expression, media, and the judiciary; the creation of a Senate, where all the seats would be contested; and a round of elections to fill those seats and 35 percent of the seats in the existing chamber of Parliament, the Sejm.

These elections took place on 4 June 1989 and were the first semi-free elections held in the Poland since the Communist regime consolidated its power in 1947. A fully free election was promised four years later. There were semi-free because not all seats in the new bicameral legislature were freely contested. The recreated senate was elected entirely democratically while 65 per of seats in the other house (the Sejm) were reserved for communists. Solidarity mobilized heavily and incredibly effectively for these elections, publishing a newspaper called *Gazeta Wyborcza* to inform the public, stripped for decades of any real voting power, about the candidates and the voting procedures. In the end, even with an electoral system rigged in favour of the communists, Solidarity won 99 of the 100 seats contested in the new Senate and all the independently contested seats in the Sejm. Regarding the rest of the seats in the Sejm, the Communist candidates for almost all failed to reach the requisite 50 percent of the vote to win the first round of voting. The elections were a huge victory, with Tadeusz Mazowiecki becoming the first non-Communist prime minister in decades. Elected by the parliament, Jaruzelski stayed on as president but Lech Wałęsa eventually replaced him in 1990. Eventually, the decision to enact regime change through negotiations with the old regime and its members would come to have negative consequences, but in their immediate aftermath, the elections set off a dizzying series of events in the region that would bring the Communist era to an end. Over the following months, the Communist regimes in the rest of the Eastern Bloc countries in central and southeastern Europe began to fall one-by-one like dominoes as well.

Of course, roundtable negotiations did force compromises on the opposition and who knows what the communists did with the secret police files. Like elsewhere in the region, real reckonings with past were largely sacrificed to blackmail, conspiracy theories and political gain. Even the founding leader of Solidarity, Lech Wałęsa, was caught up in this when he was accused as being an informant in the Poland's Security Service in the early 1970s when he did engage in conversations with the secret police. A court later ruled that Wałęsa had been falsely accused but the charges lingered. Wałęsa's "case" later consumed Polish society and his opponents later argued that his service to the police doomed the 1989 roundtable talks and meant that Solidarity was never fully able to exploit their total victories in 1989 and thus had "betrayed" the Polish people.

Lustration and Transitional Justice

The rebuilding of some institutions and the destruction of others was a big part of the process in EU accession. The strong, overarching state, a key feature of the communist regimes, needed to be weakened and de-centralization was the order of the day. This was especially true in states with minorities where the EU pushed for the empowerment of ethnic communities through various forms of self-government that many governments chafed at. Constitutions also needed to be revised. Most countries simply revised the old Stalinist constitutions in the short run. Poland got a new one in 1997. Hungary would wait until 2011 for a new and extremely contentious one to be examined in the next chapter. Institutions, especially constitutional courts, needed to be strengthened to prevent another slide into dictatorship. East Germany slid into the West German constitutional fold which already in 1949 had its Basic Law to ensure no repeat of the Weimar Republic that included a 5 percent threshold to gain parliamentary representation. Coming to terms with the communist past, or providing justice for the injustices of the past, proved to be more difficult than the post-1989 leaders realized. This was the process known as transitional justice which ebbed and flowed in the region and to be sure, most communists got off relatively easy. It was deemed transitional in that it was a bridge from the dictatorial past to a new democracy and meant to address past crimes to solidify the democracy. The communists were not just murderers and routine violators of rights, they had falsified history, made certain subjects simply taboo or forced people to forget things, and sowed tremendous amounts of distrust.

Indeed, the rebuilding of trust in the state and its institutions may well be the most critical part of a transition. Plus, it was not just the communist past that was an open wound, there was also the wartime experience that was not necessarily a story brave resistance to German occupiers in some cases. A full-blown conversation about the past was mandatory. The absence of violent retribution—this was another unique aspect of the 1989 moment—also tells a different story. The 1989 leaders, in their eagerness to start a new chapter, rejected the harsh reprisals that had shaped every revolution until then. While

Albania, Bulgaria, and Romania took far bolder steps towards the top bosses—Albanian jailed almost the entire last politburo on almost spurious charges related to over consumption, Bulgaria jailed Todor Zhivkov and Romania's Ceaușescus were executed after a bizarre and highly flawed trial—the communist leaders in Central Europe got off relatively easy. East Germany's Honecker was an exception. After being forced out, ill with cancer, Honecker and his wife briefly hid out with a Protestant Pastor in Brandenburg before they secretly fled to the USSR to avoid arrest. Once in Moscow, he sought further refuge in the Chilean Embassy where he stayed until July 1992 before returning to Germany to face trial. The trial, which focused on charges related to the killing of people trying to flee East Germany, never really finished. Honecker's illhealth ended the trial and Honecker was permitted to join his wife in exile in Chile where he died in 1994. He was never convicted.

The fact that so many top communists got off relatively easy is likely one of the greatest shortcomings of an otherwise successful transition from communism to democracy. The communist's conversion to mainstream socialism went far faster than anyone could have imagined provide that there was more than enough amnesia to go around. As a result, the communists turned socialists would often find themselves back in power in the 1990s. Hungary's first postcommunist Prime Minister József Antall acknowledged that what happened in 1989 was not really a revolution and that maybe Hungary should have had one after all. Czech dissident and later President Václav Havel controversially suggested that under totalitarianism everyone was guilty.

Transitional justice efforts, alongside lustration, offer a very mixed bag marked by marginal success in parts of Central Europe and near total failures in the Balkans. In fact, the success or failure of transitional justice does shed some light on the fate of regime change. Debates were heated especially about what should happen to all the officials, especially the secret police, and the files they had amassed. Communist parties were banned but they morphed into socialists anyway and largely re-joined society. At one extreme is Russia, which has consistently avoided a meaningful assessment of the past and genuine nostalgia for the USSR persists. Even now, the Nazi-Soviet Pact of 1939 enjoys wide support and President Putin routinely defended the deal as a necessity. Outside of the Baltic states, the Czech Republic, and Germany, very little was done to deal with the communist past. In the middle of this was Poland and Hungary. In the Balkans, one can say with confidence that politics and blackmail took precedence over meaningful reckonings with the past.

Since East Germany simply disappeared transitional justice efforts were therefore somewhat easier. The GDR's Stasi was a massive network of spies which had over 100,000 employees. It also had between half-a-million and two million collaborators with files on approximately six million citizens—about a third of the population. A good entry point to the study of the Stasi's files would be Timothy Garton Ash's *The File: A Personal History* (1997) where Ash gets the chance to look at his own file that was compiled while he was a younger researcher in East Germany long before anyone dreamed that the Stasi would collapse. Many states grappled with whether or not to open secret service files. For sure, secret services had sought to destroy files in crazy days of 1989 plus agents no doubt tampered with files in other ways. Nonetheless, Germany provided full and unfettered access to the files—some 111 kilometres of shelved documents, 1.8 million images, and over 30,000 audio and video recordings.

As an independent state in 1993, the Czechs went a totally different direction than independent Slovakia. They provided a wide variety of measures that included reparations for those persecuted, the revealing of collaborators and punishment alongside dismissals of senior administration and security officials. They also provided far greater file access to citizens. This meant that citizens could be both rehabilitated and compensated for what happened. Plus, there was some restitution for property nationalized by the communists although this proved to be extremely complicated. The Czechs also gradually allowed access to files and regularly published names of informers. The Slovaks, who headed into a nationalistic and flawed democracy after 1993, had no stake in lustration or transitional justice and largely let things go with very few prosecutions.

In Poland, the process was controversial and still impacts Polish political life. Historians like Jan Gross exposed some of the uglier sides of Poles during German occupation and the nasty role of some Poles in the fate of the Jews largely in a book that examined a pogrom in the town of Jedwabne in 1941 when 300 Jews were murdered by fellow Poles. Later governments led by the Law and Justice Party after 2015 tried to manage the discussion of Polish collaboration and insisted that Poles needed to stop apologizing for the past. What really struck a nerve among Poles was the tendency to say or write "Polish Concentration Camps" as opposed "Death Camps in Poland" as opposed to the correct version referring to German-occupied Poland for example. A 2018 law in Poland made it illegal to accuse the Polish nation of complicity in the Holocaust. But a wider discussion was opened and, as we recall from the introduction, Poland did open the truly magnificent Museum of the History of Polish Jews in 2014. As to the communist period, things were very different than in Czech Republic. Embracing what would become a "forgive and forget" policy, the first post-communist Prime Minister Mazowiecki drew what he called a "thick line" with the past which largely meant transitional justice was delayed. A very restricted lustration and file access came only later in the 1990s but as we shall see in the next chapter, the case was far from closed. Re-opening the communist past proved to be an extremely useful mobilizational tool for Poland's populists.

As we saw in Hungary, Kádár was "retired" and he lived just long enough to see Imre Nagy re-introduced, albeit temporarily into the pantheon of Hungarian heroes after spending more than 30 years in the unmarked grave Kádár had put him in. In 1989, just like elsewhere, the communists set about to destroy as many files as possible or even invent files to discredit people. No big fish went to jail and the communists turned socialists went on to gain immense riches and even regained political power. Hungary thus took a soft approach like Poland. People did not lose public office, there was very limited access to secret files and few people were charged. Odd given the legacy of violence that followed the 1956 revolution. But the case did not close there. Just like in Poland, negotiated transfers of power around roundtables and freedom for the communists was bound to re-surface in ways that would challenge Hungarian democracy. Indeed, with the 2010 election, a real revolution did come 21 years later. For Hungary and Poland's national populists, the wily communists and their secret service allies seized the process and derailed real change. In some countries, retribution was off the table, in other countries, only delayed.

Joining Europe on Europe's Terms

Central Europe was a logical place to start integrating former Eastern Bloc countries into the EU due to the countries' geographical positions and historical ties with countries that were already members. They had also arguably had the easiest transitions to democracy and market capitalism, relative to the rest of the former Eastern Bloc. Hungary, Poland, and Czechoslovakia had created their own new organization called the Visegrád Group in 1991, which signed an association agreement with the European Community that same year. The signing ceremony in Visegrád, Hungary, in 1991 is telling and helps to explain why Central Europe's return to Europe was so successful given there was another Visegrád in Bosnia. There were three extremely capable leaders who successfully prevented nationalism from taking centre stage: Antall, Havel, and Walesa. By 1996, after the split of Czechoslovakia, all four Visegrád countries had also individually applied for membership. The Visegrád Group was an extremely important achievement. As noted, the West was deeply concerned with the potential for the renewal of the interwar scenario for Central Europe which was already playing out in the Balkans. That said, the Central Europeans on their own put paid to that fear because they proved that regional cooperation was real. As important, since the Hungarian minority was another cause for concern, the Hungarians signed a number of basic treaties, under pressure from the EU and NATO, that respected borders and called for minority rights protections. Setting the bar as high as possible, nearly homogenous Hungary adopted extremely progressive minority rights protections in the hopes the states where Hungarians lived would do the same.

The first steps in the process of re-joining Europe were Europe Agreements. These agreements, signed in the early 1990s, were essentially trade agreements and were extremely hard to negotiate and gave everyone a clear understanding of just how difficult this process would be. A precondition for the agreements was that states had to be democratic market economies, with free elections, the rule of law and respect for human rights. Ten countries concluded Europe Agreements—Bulgaria, Czech Republic, Estonia, Hungary, Latvia, Lithuania, Poland, Romania, Slovakia, and Slovenia—later applied for EU membership (between 1994 and 1996) and were admitted in 2004 or 2007 enlargement rounds. The Europe agreements, which in many ways remain the basis of the EU's enlargement process, provided the basis for a slow integration. All the agreements called for the progressive removal of barriers to free trade over a ten-year period, as well as for economic and technical cooperation and financial assistance. Plus, feeling protected by a new rule of law, foreign direct investment rushed in. All domestic legislation also had to be made compatible with EU law. The key criteria for accession would become the Copenhagen Criteria of 1993. Ambiguous and purposely open to interpretation, it laid out the basics: Membership required that the candidate country has achieved stability of institutions guaranteeing democracy, the rule of law, human rights, respect for and protection of minorities, the existence of a functioning market economy as well as the capacity to cope with competitive pressure and market forces within the Union.

Some parts of the criteria were more important than others. For sure, while there was much talk about minority rights, as the Roma can confirm, failures on that front did not block eventual membership. Minority rights in the Copenhagen Criteria recalled the minority rights treaties of the League of Nations in the interwar period that were imposed exclusively on the new states. They did not apply elsewhere and once again, Central Europe got a dose of "do as I say, not as I do".

In 1997, "Agenda 2000" of the European Commission concluded that all but Slovakia met the democratic requirement; all met the second; and all had a long way to go on the third. It recommended that Poland, Hungary, Czech Republic, Estonia, and Slovenia begin accession negotiations. Slovakia, Latvia, Lithuania, Bulgaria, and Romania were excluded but led them to redouble their efforts; all became candidate countries in 2000. It was a massive transformation—GDP's dropped by as much as 30 percent, industrial production almost ceased while the economy was quickly deregulated, the welfare state, a cornerstone of the communist system was almost eliminated, and state assets were privatized. Political and economic reform went hand in hand with creating a whole new set of institutions. To call it a transition does not capture it. The reborn Central Europeans could agree on one slogan keeping in mind Kundera's notion of a kidnapped Europe, they were re-joining Europe, not joining Europe. Even before the Europeans even articulated a way forward to membership, Czechs, Estonians, Hungarians, Latvians, Lithuanians, Poles, and Slovenians were doing everything they could to prove their European bona fides. Only the Slovaks, as noted, opted for a separate path that proved to be merely a dead end. The EU's decision to enlarge made sense. It did help to correct a set of historic wrongs that started in the 1930s, there was a great chance to make money as goods had to be bought and the region was in desperate need of foreign investment and since the region simply had to join as there was no viable plan B, they negotiated as such. The enthusiasm, across all levels, was remarkable. Imagine only that so soon after regaining sovereignty from the USSR, Central Europe was willing to share sovereignty again, this time with the EU. This, more than anything, proved the essential sense of vulnerability, a legacy of the twentieth century, guided policy decisions.

The end of the Cold War did create an enormous opportunity for the then EC which formally became the European Union in 1992 with the Maastricht Treaty. All of Central Europe looked to Brussels for political and economic reasons. It promised the much heralded return to Europe, a transformation to a market economy and the promise of affluence and security. NATO, on the other hand, which had a far lower bar for admission than the EU, offered something even better in a way. It alone could end the deep seated and not unreasonable fear that borders were still negotiable. NATO membership in 1999 for the Czech Republic, Hungary, and Poland was essential and they joined just in time to take part in NATO's first mission: the intervention in Yugoslavia designed to prevent an ongoing humanitarian catastrophe in Kosovo, that started in late March 1999. Slovakia's membership came only in 2004—a delay necessitated by the Mečiar government's legacy.

Integration with the EU was far harder and took longer than anyone expected. For rich and developed states it was easy. In 1995, Austria, Finland, and Sweden joined but they were neither poor nor post-communist. The criteria for them was entirely economic. In the 1980s they had already adopted the EU's acquis, so membership was both a necessity and relatively easy. Their ability to maintain a democracy was not questioned or was their potential for violence against minorities. The enlargement round for Central Europe, the Baltic states and Slovenia was an entirely new ball game—it was economic and political which necessitated an entirely different intervention from Brussels.

Central Europe thus faced very rigid criteria as the EU was genuinely fearful about the impact of such a large enlargement would have on the future of the Union. These states were poor, it would be expensive, people could flood Western Europe with cheap labour. Some argued for a second-tier membership like what perpetually on offer for Turkey. In any case, it was slowness and foot dragging that meant it took nearly 15 years. But, taking the big picture, the enlargement of the EU must be considered as one of the great foreign policy achievements of the twentieth century. Two paths were embraced by what became known as shock therapy or the slow road of, say, Romania, Slovakia, or Bulgaria, where the process was delayed to allow for state capture. Later research proved that the fast road yielded the best results. In terms of political systems, the Czechs, Hungarians, and Poles developed extremely competitive ones quick as well to establish a rule of law that proved attractive to foreign investors.

Conclusion

Let's travel to Bucharest in December 1989 and tell an altogether different story with a totally different ending—not the return to Europe but a return to dark times of the interwar period. Romania, alongside Albania and Bulgaria, had few of the pre-conditions for a successful overthrow of communist power.

Ceaușescu and his family's rule had cut deeper into society, control was more complete, and the people impoverished and cowed. But since Central Europe was having a revolution, Romania had one too, if only for the television cameras. But while 1989 was later contested as a fraud by some Hungarians and Poles, 1989 in Romania (and Bulgaria too) was an undeniable fraud. Speaking to a once terrified people, Ceaușescu's audience turned on him in a second. He visibly panicked and took off later in a helicopter with some loot from his palace. Forced to land by his own air force, he and his wife faced a quick trial, promptly convicted, even more promptly shot and buried in a secret location on Christmas Day. Ceaușescu's second-tier took over and proceeded to thwart Romania's democratization for nearly a decade and got rich at the same time. To prove the point, in June 1990, when the post-communist communists faced demands from students for real change, the government conscripted 10,000 miners to come to Bucharest to beat up the demonstrators. Less reported was the fact that the miners also went on a rampage in the Roma neighbourhoods. Nobody was ever charged. The year 1989 was not always "velvet".

The same was true in Bulgaria where a place coup replaced Todor Zhivkov with largely rule by the security services who also got filthy rich capturing the state. They too delayed democratization for almost a decade. Albania got communists back in power briefly and then communists turned ersatz democrats after and spent the next two decades on a journey largely to nowhere. State capture, politicized transitional justice and polarization defined a never ending transition. Yugoslavia, the one-time hallmark of a new socialism, gave up national communism for nationalism and chose war. The dissidents there were easily co-opted by the new national struggles designed to right grievous historical wrongs. The interwar paradigm was back in the Balkans so Western policy-makers did not get things entirely wrong. In the entire Balkans, communists turned democrats or nationalists provoked massive population flight as the best and brightest saw the writing on the wall and began a now-30-year-long exodus for greener pastures in the EU.

Taking into account revolutionary change in general, Central Europe's story is thus an anomaly. Its entry into the EU in 2004 no doubt took longer than anyone expected. NATO accession proved easier because the bar was considerably lower. The ups and downs of the years that followed and later challenges with the flawed entry of Bulgaria and Romania to the EU in 2007, the financial crisis of 2008, Greece's near collapse and almost exit from the Eurozone, and the migration crisis of 2015 really altered the landscape. Enlargement fatigue, as it is called, set in and the wait for EU membership got longer for the states of the Western Balkans—Albania, Bosnia, Kosovo, North Macedonia, Montenegro, and Serbia. Central Europeans had some luck in 1990 and after. Their non-violent transition proved to be the exception, not the norm as events in Yugoslavia (and not just there but elsewhere in the world.) Even the USSR, which disappeared in 1991, broke apart relatively peacefully as there were nationally motivated conflicts only in Georgia with

Abkhazia and South Ossetia, between Armenia and Azerbaijan over Nagorno-Karabakh and in Moldova within the largely pro-Russian region called Transnistria. Imagine just for a moment a Yugoslav-style disintegration in the USSR. In the end, the Central Europeans had a better elite that did not so easily fall into the trap of nationalism and exclusion. Central Europe had some other advantages. Their populations supported the return to Europe and were willing to pay an extremely high price for a better future. Think only of the price rises that people had to endure. In each country a referendum took place with really incredible support—ranging from 92 percent in Slovakia to a low of 67 percent in Estonia. Czechs, Hungarians and Poles were 77, 77, and 84 percent in favour. The EU was open and willing to take new members and there were no external actors pushing to divide Europe and oppose enlargement. The big question after 2004 was, at least then, seemingly unthinkable but harkened back to some of the misgivings and fears in 1989. What if nationalism was not really dead? What if the EU lacked the leverage to ensure that everything went according to plan?

For Further Study

Books (Fiction and Non-fiction)

Garton Ash, Timothy. *The File: A Personal History*. New York: Random House, 1997.
Garton Ash, Timothy. *The Magic Lantern: The Revolution of '89 Witnessed in Warsaw, Budapest, Berlin, and Prague*. New York: Vintage Books, 1999.
Krapfl, James. *Revolution with a Human Face: Politics, Culture, and Community in Czechoslovakia, 1989–1992*. Ithaca: Cornell University Press, 2013.
Matynia, Elzbieta. *An Uncanny Era: Conversations between Vaclav Havel and Adam Michnik*. New Haven, CT: Yale University Press, 2014.
Mark, James, Bogdan C. Iacob, Tobias Rupprecht, and Ljubica Spaskovska. *1989: A Global History of Eastern Europe*. Cambridge: Cambridge University Press, 2019.
Robin Okey, *The Demise of Communist East Europe: 1989 in Context*. London: Hodder Arnold, 2004.
Ther, Philipp. *Europe since 1989: A History*. Princeton, NJ: Princeton University Press, 2016.

Films

Die Mauer (1990). Directed by Jürgen Böttcher. Germany.
Sweet Emma, Dear Böbe (1992). Directed by István Szabó. Hungary.
Goodbye, Lenin! (2003). Directed by Wolfgang Becker. Germany.
Chuck Norris vs Communism (2015). Directed by Ilinca Calugareanu. Romania.
The Power of the Powerless (2009). Directed by Cory Taylor. USA.
1989 (2014). Directed by Erzsébet Rácz and Anders Østergaard. Denmark.
Remembering Solidarity (2017). BBC. United Kingdom.

CHAPTER 7

A New Central Europe or Past as Prologue?

Between 1989 and 2015, so much changed in Central Europe that it cast doubts on what seemed to be a predictable and stable future. By 2010, a new narrative appeared that seemed to alter the path taken by some countries in Central Europe after 1989. It first appeared in Hungary with the re-election of Viktor Orbán on a stridently nationalist/populist platform, which some likened to a radical right victory. This was followed in Poland by the election of the Law and Justice Party (PiS) to power in 2015. In Germany, the Alliance for Germany, another nationalist but not quite fascist party, started moving up in the polls. There were genuinely radical right parties that did start to do well. In Hungary, Jobbik—Movement for a Better Hungary—could often capture more than 20 percent of the vote. In Austria, the Freedom Party too did well and joined for a brief time as a coalition partner with the mainstream Austrian People's Party between December 2017 and June 2019 until a sordid and laughable attempt in Ibiza to secure Russian campaign help in exchange for lucrative contracts in Austria exposed them as pathetic.

Many analysts started making often facile comparisons to the interwar period, and saw only gloom and the end of the European project. But there were nonetheless things to worry about and it looked as if the region was still vulnerable in the way it had been in the past. Liberal democracy and shared sovereignty under the aegis of the EU, which undoubtedly triumphed in 1989, seemed to be in danger. Populism and nationalism, long viewed as incompatible with democracy, were back and not just in Central Europe. Moreover, the economic story was good but maybe not great. Rapid economic convergence with the West simply did not happen, and while the former communist states definitely got more prosperous, with the Czech Republic being the stand-out, the gap between them and the West remained relatively consistent. Given what was the obvious success of EU (and NATO) enlargement in Central Europe, it seemed out of place to think that some parts of Central Europe would offer a

© The Author(s), under exclusive license to Springer Nature Switzerland AG 2021
R. C. Austin, *A History of Central Europe*,
https://doi.org/10.1007/978-3-030-84543-8_7

new, more nationalist, and sovereigntist view of the future for Europe. The consensus on a European over a national identity and the goals of 1989 was more fragile than many had assumed.

Indeed, the authors Stephen Holmes and Ivan Krastev talked of the end of the period of merely imitating Western Europe's version of capitalism and liberal democracy in their book, *The Light That Failed – A Reckoning*. Anne Applebaum, an extremely astute observer of the region, in her 2020 book *The Twilight of Democracy: The Seductive Lure of Authoritarianism* lamented that so many former friends and colleagues had drifted from the liberal goals of 1989 and found common cause with the illiberal and nationalist forces in ascendance. Krastev and Holmes' notion of imitation has merit as indeed, as we saw in 1990, the states of the region largely copied what they saw in the West because the West had what everyone wanted: prosperity, mobility, and stability. This was not 1917. That would explain, to a degree, the peaceful nature of change in 1989 that was so utterly laudable and seemingly durable. Was there really anything wrong with wanting what the West Europeans had? On the plus side, while obtaining standard of living parity with Western Europe still seems a long way off, the differences are no longer so stark and there is a degree of income equality that is better than much of Western Europe and certainly far better than anything in the United States. Peoples' lives have, by any measure, gotten better. As well, in general, Central Europeans remain extremely favourable towards the EU. There is less enthusiasm for NATO. But the trend is not positive, as enthusiasm for integration is waning.

But what happened between then and now to bring back of some of the demons of the past? Are things that bad? For sure there are seeds of despair in the events that followed 1989. For some, the nature of the peaceful regime change in 1989 fuelled doubts that were exploited by various forces. For certain the European integration process gave them a template they had to follow: work against homophobia, expand minority rights, especially for the Roma, acknowledge and fight domestic abuse, adapt neoliberal policies, establish oversight and regulatory institutions, ensure a free judiciary and privatize assets. Some came to believe that the communists and the liberal elite enablers that shaped 1989 conspired to steal from them by converting communist political power into economic power. Like it or not, the entire EU accession process was undeniably an elite level project that was delivered to the people largely as a *fait accompli* to the people with very little discussion and hardly any space for opposition viewpoints. There were undeniably high levels of corruption and the privatization process enriched often the wrong people throughout the post-communist world. This new narrative has been most obvious in Hungary, Poland, and to a degree Slovakia but far less apparent in the Czech Republic which instead saw a kind of Donald Trump-style plutocratic populism and high levels of corruption.

Some of the other contributory factors are obvious: globalization and its real or imagined impact on national cultures; the benefits of the new era seemed to be unevenly distributed and undeniably the former communists did well out of the process; transitional justice often failed to offer a meaningful reckoning of the past and the really big fish avoided jail; some people, especially in the Balkans, had to live through war plus gangster capitalism that thrived in the grey zones provided by sanctions put in place during the Yugoslav Wars (1992–1995); the 2008–2009 financial crisis and the austerity programmes that followed added to the burdens especially on the poor and emerging middle class, especially in Hungary where hundreds of thousands of citizens were saddled with unpayable debts in foreign currency (over 70 percent of debts were foreign currency denominated); there was a growing generation gap between largely rural and urban areas; there was severe de-population as many of the best and brightest up and left for better opportunities and pay in Western Europe. Hungary and Poland are hardest hit and their future populations projected to decline by 12 percent by 2050. Only the Czech Republic did not experience such a stark decline. Slovakia's population is estimated to decline by almost 9 percent. As a comparison though, by far the worst impact was felt in the Balkans where Bulgaria and Romania saw their populations drop by more than 20 percent and 50 percent of Bosnians live abroad.

Most importantly, in 2015 Europe confronted an unprecedented Refugee Crisis when an estimated one million people—a mix of refugees and migrants but all asylum seekers largely fleeing war in the Middle East and Afghanistan—travelled from Turkey through the Balkans to Central Europe hoping to head to Germany or Scandinavia. Austria, Czech Republic, Hungary, Poland, and Slovakia all stood against allowing migrants or refugees free access to their country. They all refused to take allocated refugees based on quotas from the European Commission and all used the moment to bolster their support with appeals to ever present nativism. In Budapest, after a receiving a second super-majority in Hungary's 2014 national elections, a drifting Prime Minister Viktor Orbán found in the events the very crisis he needed to rejuvenate his rule. In Warsaw too the language from the government also spoke of an imminent threat to European identity, religion, and civilization. Hungary, the first to build a fence along its southern border, resurrected its image as the bulwark against an Islamic invasion. Most people in Hungary, living on a steady diet of government TV news, bought the story. Orbán insisted, not wrongly, that the Schengen border was still a border that Hungary was obligated to defend. The Austrian government, always under pressure from the Freedom Party to restrict immigration, did the same but claimed that they did not technically have a fence.

The August–September 2015 moment was certainly the most important factor in transforming the politics of Europe and elsewhere. Things were made worse by the November 2015 terrorist attacks in Paris and the incidents of sexual harassment in Cologne, Germany on New Year's Eve 2015. Think only of the Brexit vote in June 2016 and the US election that November. Orbán, and the other regional autocrats, were really excited about Trump's victory—not just as a victory for populism but an end to US moralizing and nagging about human rights and rule of law. Brexit in June 2016 and Trump's 2016 election victory were triumphs of nativism and institutional destruction. Add to this there was the growing influence of China and Russia too which offer a potentially new narrative for Central Europe. The Chinese offered substantial investments and hard to turn down loans while Russia focused its influence on throwing doubt on the European project in general, sowing distrust in democracy and heralding itself as the defender of traditional values. Both countries found willing accomplices in the region.

Past as Prologue?

Hungary was the first in the region to chart a new and decidedly anti-democratic path. In fact, while democracy in Czech Republic, Poland, and Slovakia (to say nothing of Austria) still shows signs of resiliency, Hungarian democracy is a fiction. Freedom House, the respected NGO declared in May 2020 that Hungary went from being a semi-consolidated democracy to a hybrid or transitional regime which meant a government meets only some minimal standards for elections of national leaders. Hungary and Fidesz's story is unique. Ousted in a 2002 election, Fidesz spent eight years in opposition. Hungary's socialists governed between 2002 and 2010. Their principal legacy was simple: financial ruin and corruption. Orbán's nationalist Fidesz party easily won a supermajority in the Hungarian parliament in the 2010 vote, referred to as the "revolution at the polls" with just over 50 percent of the popular vote. They received additional stunning victories in 2014 and again in 2018, even though they generally now win less than 50 percent of the vote, setting the stage for permanent rule as the Left opposition self-destructed and by co-opting the policies of the far right in its nativist stance, it also ceased to matter. Jobbik even had to shift from far right to centre right to stay relevant. Hungary no longer has a meaningful opposition outside of the capital and some of other key urban centres.

While some analysts note to some discontinuity between the Fidesz and Orbán of the 1990s with its liberal veneer and the party that came to power in 2010 on closer examination the differences are not so stark. By the mid-1990s Fidesz had already chosen nationalism as its foundation. This was obvious in the period 1998–2002 especially the fetishizing of the Holy Crown discussed earlier, integrating the fate of the Hungarians living in neighbouring countries into domestic policy and opening the Terror House Museum in 2002 which established a distinctly revisionist approach to the period 1944–1990. The museum stands out as an important milestone in the Fidesz programme. Aimed largely at youth in its "in your face" exhibits, it enforces the Hungarian as victim narrative by drawing a single thread through the fascist and communist periods. In opposition for eight years, governed by what many rightly saw as largely former communists plundering the state, Orbán's national populist narrative took shape with his famous quote that the "people cannot be in opposition". It was classic "us"—the real Hungarians—versus "them"—a liberal and cosmopolitan elite who were destroying Hungary. The message worked plus the fact that many voters, then and now, could count on better financial management from Fidesz than their socialist predecessors. Ample transfers from the EU also helped.

When the fate of Central Europe is discussed, Hungary's trajectory, which some argue goes from authoritarianism to freedom in 1989 and all the way back to a new version of what can only be called "goulash authoritarianism" is the most discussed. The Prime Minister called it "Illiberal Democracy" in a speech to party faithful in Romania in 2014 and the term has since stuck. Orbán said a lot then. He attacked the liberal world view, blaming it for the financial collapse of 2008, the miserable fate of ordinary workers and the middle class and the over emphasis on the fate of immigrants to the detriment of citizens. Citing the success of societal organization in China, Russia, India, and Singapore, Orbán, suspecting a new world was on the horizon, felt the tide was turning and that by rejecting illiberalism would finally put Hungary on the right side of history, something that eluded them since 1914. Hungary got an aggressive anti-pluralist government that got so lucky, as events worked in their favour, it could ponder permanent rule. In 2019, Russian President Vladimir Putin declared liberalism "obsolete".

Once in power, Fidesz undertook two quite breath-taking revolutions. Facing an economic crisis almost at the same level as Greece, Hungary needed to gets it fiscal house in order and withdrew Hungary from bailout talks with the IMF. As noted, they forced some bitter pills on largely foreign banks to save hundreds of thousands from bankruptcy. They raised the VAT to 27 percent, settled on a flat tax of 15 percent and saw record increases in tax paying. They lowered the unemployment rate too. They even cut the parliamentary seats from an unwieldy 386 to 199. They also nationalized the sale of tobacco. Even people who could not tolerate the party's often intolerant political messages counted on Fidesz's economic management. Transfer funds from the EU make life better too—they amount to 5 percent of Hungary's GDP. Largely used for infrastructure projects, these funds have the added benefit of being used to line the pockets of Fidesz allies in favour of later party kickbacks.

But it is the political revolution that attracts the most attention and derision. Armed with incredible parliamentary majorities and a weak and fractured opposition, Orbán changed Hungary dramatically. In 2011, Hungary got a new constitution with very little public consultation. Called the "Fundamental Law" this short document, allegedly hastily written on an IPAD, set out an entirely new historical narrative for Hungary. Most tellingly, it called the period from the Nazi occupation in March 1944 until the first free and fair elections in 1990 an "occupation". This, some noted, meant, among other things that Hungary was abandoning any responsibility for the fate of the Jews in 1944. According to the government: No German invasion, no deportations. Not long after that came the strange monument to German occupation which puts in visual form the notion of a helpless Hungary being overrun by nasty Germans. Put in Freedom Square in 2013 under the cover of darkness due to protests, it is an object of interest mostly to tourists. This was part and parcel of Hungary's quest for a useable history which included the glorification of the interwar period under Miklós Horthy as a kind of golden era. Horthy, in the narrative, saved Hungary form the radical left and right and he even tried to save the Jews. Orbán, who surprisingly never drifted towards his own personality cult, hoped to also be Hungary's saviour.

Orbán also reinvented 1956. After all, the socialists, as former communists, could hardly ever be the standard bearers of that moment. The statue of Imre Nagy was moved from near parliament to somewhere less prominent along the Danube, where he now overlooks the former Communist Party headquarters to make room to the resurrected monument to the victims of the Red Terror (1919). The year 1956 is still celebrated, even grander than ever, but the socialist side is out. Emphasis goes to the youngsters who picked up guns to fight emphasizing the struggle for freedom from foreign rule alongside the strength and unity of a reborn Hungarian nation.

On the institutional side, Orbán went after the courts and media with vigour as bastions of the liberal order. In the end, Hungary has ended up with a one-party state. He added loyalists to the constitutional court and lowered the retirement age for judges so there were hundreds of posts to be filled. New media laws, with enormous fines for transgressions, could easily silence anti-government news. Plus, Orbán-friendly business people bought up the media and tuned the message accordingly. Some opposition papers simply closed. The government's significant advertising budget keeps others in line. State television, long the main source for people outside Budapest, is slavishly pro-government and excelled especially at instilling migrant hysteria in 2015 and 2016. For a country with very low levels of knowledge of foreign languages, Orbán's insular message was an easy sell.

A few other features of Orbán's decade plus in power deserve mention. In 2013, he took the bold step of extending citizenship rights to Hungarians living abroad. He was clearly targeting the Hungarians in Romania, Serbia, Slovakia, and Ukraine. The official reason was to simply re-unite the Hungarian nation but others saw it is vote grab for the Fidesz party. Hungarians had already rejected the idea of extending citizenship to Hungarian outside the state in a 2004 referendum sponsored by a nationalist organization. The turn-out was too low to matter as most Hungarians rejected the idea based on the enormous cost of the plan if people started to migrate to Hungary in search of welfare.

Orbán appears to enjoy politics as combat. Out of the migration crisis grew a weird referendum campaign to ramp up fear. New police appeared on the streets in combat gear and carrying big weapons. Preceding the vote, where people were asked if they accepted the EU's resettlement plans, citizens were subjected to a highly charged poster campaign that equated migrants largely with terrorism. Posters went up, in Hungarian, telling migrants they needed to respect Hungarian culture. The target audience was only too obvious. The referendum failed to reach the required turn out for validity but those who did vote were decidedly against migrants being resettled in Hungary. The government continues to demonize the migrants, never using the word refugee fearing it might engender sympathy with the Hungarian refugees of 1956.

One of his strangest battles was against the Hungarian-born billionaire philanthropist George Soros. Soros's Open Society Foundation had already played an outsized role in post-communist Europe and not everyone loved him for it. He was an easy target in a part of the world where anti-Semitism is always there. Orbán simply decided the Soros was the ultimate symbol of everything he opposed—a puppet master controlling Hungary's liberals and, most dangerously, funding the migration campaigns. He first led an unprecedented attack on the Central European University (CEU), a Soros-funded university in downtown Budapest. Using relatively obscure regulations that were impossible for the CEU to adhere too, the CEU's English-language degrees were not accredited. The university was forced to re-locate much of its programming to Vienna. For Orbán, probably the best reason to force the CEU out was because it was the country's best university. The sadder part of the CEU story is the inability of the EU to prevent it even though it was a clear breach of the EU's core values. The United States did nothing either, as President Donald Trump had his own petty issues with Soros.

But Orbán was not finished with Soros. The attack on the CEU, which generated fairly large protests in Budapest, hardly resonated with the people Orbán wanted to mobilize. Nobody outside of Budapest could care about the fate of a relatively small university. The next stage was the Stop Soros campaign where Soros was even more directly linked as the mastermind of the migrant "invasion". Horrible posters showed Soros's face with the line, "Don't let Soros have the last laugh". Most people immediately caught the obvious similarity of these posters to the nasty anti-Semitic posters of the 1930s. The government denied their anti-Semitic intent and trotted out their great ties with Israel as proof of their enlightened attitudes towards Hungary's Jewish community. Other posters portrayed the opposition as merely Soros stooges. His people referred to the EU Commission as the "Soros Orchestra". The Stop Soros campaign included a major crackdown on foreign funded NGOs. The government's obsession with Soros had no bounds and what they expected citizens to believe was incredible. While Hungary was routinely in breach of the EU's "core values", despite the EU invoking the empty threat of Article 7 proceedings, not much happened.

What often garnered less attention in the sea of changes enacted by Fidesz was the remaking of cultural policy since 2010 designed to align Hungarians with more conservative values. In fact, Hungary's was spending more on culture than most other countries and the changes put in place aligned with the other revolutionary changes everywhere. Emphasis was placed on increased funding for key large state institutions like the State Opera or national museums over independent cultural organizations. There is also a new "National Cultural Council" which is comprised of the leaders of these types of institutions which provide centralized leadership over cultural policy and are very much beholden to the government. There is an obvious preference for "symbolic politics" in arts—Hungarian themes, Hungarian spirituality, classic repertoire rather than new, avant-garde works are the order of the day. Government appointees now make up the majority in most cultural decision-making committees. In September 2020, students at Budapest's University of Theatre and Film Arts protested the appointment of a new board of government appointed trustees to run the school. It was not the first university to claim their autonomy was being eroded. The government established also established its own university in Budapest, the National University of Public Service, which seemed to attract all the money.

Even the Academy of Sciences, founded in the nineteenth century by István Széchenyi, ended up under the government's thumb. A July 2018 government decree ordered significant restructuring of the academy's leadership and funding, removing key research institutes from the main academy and establishing a new state research network. The restructuring also put 40 percent of the budget under government control. In addition, the majority of the new board members would be appointed by the Ministry of Innovation and tasked with making funding decisions and selecting directors for research institutes. Hungarian and international researchers immediately expressed serious concern that these new changes would significantly undermine it autonomy, arguing that the government would have the power to control funding for scientific projects and force researchers to support the government's political aims through their findings. Human Rights Watch warned that the move was part of a "broader rule of law backslide" in Hungary and recommended intervention by the EU.

Social policy also underwent major changes designed primarily to prevent Hungary's population decline and the massive flight of working-age population. The constitution or Fundamental Law of 2011 had already come down against same-sex marriages and a new May 2020 law defined gender as "biological sex based on primary sex characteristics and chromosomes". Like in Poland there was a noticeable increase in anti-LGBTQ rhetoric in Hungary—László Kövér, parliamentary speaker, compared adoption of children by homosexual couples with paedophilia and István Boldog, deputy chairman of Fidesz, called for abolition of Budapest Pride, along with the usual pro-Christian, pro-Hungarian themes. Hungary also banned gender studies as a university course and denied proposals for research in the field of gender studies as well.

In keeping with the anti-immigrant hysteria alongside a push for more "Hungarian" babies, the government also brought in a costly new "Family Protection Action Plan"—costs are estimated at 5 percent of Hungary's GDP. In a really strange move, the government nationalized IVF clinics as "strategic" in order to provide free treatment cycles to all women who want them—as long as they are under 40 and not lesbian. Loans offered to young couples up to ten million forint—each time a child is born, payments are deferred—if they have three children within a set timeframe, the loan is written off completely. Couples who take out the loan and get divorced, must pay it back within 120 days. Women who have at least four children are exempt for life from paying income tax but Orbán wants to lower this to three children. The government also added the possibility for grandparents to take a kind of paid maternity leave alongside subsidies for Hungarian families buying seven-seat vehicles. In the end, Orbán hopes the policies can increase the birth rate to 2.1 children per woman by 2030. The birth rate has increased since 2010 from 1.2 births per woman to 1.5 in 2018.

But let us go back to Budapest's Freedom Square, and another monument. On 4 June 2020, Hungary marked 100 years since the Treaty of Trianon and unsurprisingly, Budapest got another monument. Though the ceremony marking the anniversary had to be altered due to COVID-19 restrictions, church bells rang in Budapest, public transit stopped, and Hungarians observed a moment of silence for the treaty that basically ruined the twentieth century for Hungary. But the ceremony was restrained as Orbán no doubt decided that it was not worth rattling the neighbours. Since the ceremony took place during the height of COVID, the pandemic provided the Hungarian government with a graceful way to avoid too much nationalistic drum beating and raising of political tensions. One of the very few silver linings of the global pandemic. The monument itself, named the Monument of National Solidarity, is situated on Alkotmány Street in downtown Budapest, directly facing the Parliament not far from the hodgepodge of monuments on Freedom Square discussed earlier. Designed in a clearly minimalist style, it features a 100-metre long sloping ramp, which descends 4 metres below street level in the shape of a trench. At the end of the ramp, there is a fractured granite block and an eternal flame. Along the walls are the names of all the 13,000 cities, towns, and villages of historic Hungary, according to the final pre-war census of 1910. The project cost five billion forint and joins the list of many other monuments and statues erected since Prime Minister Viktor Orbán has been in power. Some said it was a poor copy of Washington, DC's Vietnam War Memorial.

It was far less controversial than everyone expected. Clearly, Orbán did not want to offend the neighbouring countries too much. Until then, only Romania was on the government's blacklist based on some comments by the Romanian president opposing even limited autonomy for the Hungarian community there. Plus, in May 2020, Romania declared 4 June a public holiday to celebrate their victory in 1920. The Hungarians have their provocations too—the flag of the Szeklers, the Hungarians living in Romania's Transylvania—flies on the Hungarian parliament alongside the Hungarian flag where the EU flag should be. Critics of the monument claim that it is the usual revisionism from the Fidesz government in that it ignores the multicultural nature of historic Hungary, which included Slovaks, Romanians, Croatians, Roma, and Serbs among others and their undeniably bad experience under the Dual Monarchy. They also say the monument—and the entire subject of Trianon—has been exploited by Orbán in order to increase nationalist sentiments and garner the support of Hungarian minorities abroad. In any case, Orbán surely sees himself as the saviour of the nation—he saved Hungary from financial ruin, then the migrant invasion, then from George Soros and the CEU, and finally by invoking emergency powers, he saved them from COVID-19, even though Hungary had the highest death rate in all of Europe and second in the world. At least that is the story people were told. Orbán used the pandemic to grab emergency powers which were best put to work in ensuring that nobody criticized the government's response to the pandemic while rushing through legislation totally unrelated to the pandemic.

In Poland, the PiS came first to power in 2005 promising a new narrative of Poland's past, especially as it related to the Second World War, renewed anti-communism and a stronger link to the Catholic Church. In 2010, en route to a memorial for the massacre at Katyn Forest during the Second World War, the plane crashed in bad weather killing the Polish President, Lech Kaczyński, his wife and nearly 100 more senior officials and the crew. Kaczyński's twin brother, Jarosław, stepped in as the new PiS leader. They secured the presidency in May 2015 and a parliamentary majority in 2015. With less than 40 percent of the popular vote, they defeated the Civic Platform, now the main opposition party. If the new Hungarian Constitution noted that the twentieth century had "led to a state of moral decay" and called "for spiritual and intellectual renewal". The PiS slogan was similar: "Poland in Ruins". It was a classic national populist campaign: hating the Poles that malign Poland or remind Poles of misdeeds during the Second World War. A new historical narrative was on offer that whitewashed some of the less pleasant aspects of the past.

The focus went on "gender ideology" as a threat to the Polish nation. They also injected even more polarization into Poland and they have proven to be incredibly successful at dividing Poland into two very hostile camps. Like Fidesz, they used the 1989 moment as a "fraud" or "sell-out" to the communists to advance their ideas. In fact, the PiS questioned large parts of the Poland's post-communist transition. The 2019 general elections gave them another majority but again, nothing like the Fidesz victories in terms of seats. Unlike in Hungary, Poland still has a potent opposition and a vibrant civil society. Plus, the PiS did not have the majority in parliament to bring in a new constitution like Orbán did. The Constitutional Tribunal was first to change then came a new media law that put state media in the government's hands. This was followed by sweeping changes to the National Council for the Judiciary, the Supreme Court along with general courts that put them in the hands of the governing party and a clear attack on judicial independence. The government argued that prior to 2015 the courts were corrupt and inefficient and that judges were beholden to that favoured liberal interests that were out of step with the new Poland. PiS attacked other independent institutions too and brought in major changes to education especially. They tried to re-model Poland so took a page from Orbán's playbook and went after the institutions they deemed as essentially enemies. The EU and the United States condemned the moves but nothing stopped them. The EU even started Article 7 for possible breaches in EU standards. But invoking Article 7 requires unanimity from member states and Hungary offered to stick by the Poles and save them from the "bureaucrats" in Brussels.

Not surprisingly, Poland has some of the strictest laws on abortion within the European Union and an intense internal debate on the issue that intensified during the COVID-19 pandemic. In April 2020, the Polish government, without warning, revived discussion on controversial legislation stemming from a citizen's bill put forth by anti-abortion activists in 2017. Under the country's constitution, Polish citizens can submit new legislation to parliament, provided they gather at least 100,000 signatures in support. The bill in question, titled the "Stop Abortion" project, arrived in the lower house with 830,000 signatures and would ban abortion in cases where the foetus is malformed. These cases account for the majority of abortions in Poland. The bill was never passed and had remained inactive in parliamentary commission until 2020.

Under Poland's laws, which are strongly influenced by the Catholic Church, abortion is only allowed when the foetus is malformed, the health or life of the mother is endangered, or in cases of rape or incest. According to official numbers, just over 1000 abortions were performed in Poland in 2018, but according to the Federation for Women and Family Planning (Federa), as many as 150,000 women accessed abortions through other means. Many are able to order medical abortion pills early in their pregnancies, and some travel abroad to access abortion services, often to Germany or the United Kingdom. Critics of Poland's laws point out that even in situations deemed acceptable for legal abortion, women still face challenges, as doctors can refuse to provide services based on personal beliefs and may not refer patients to an appropriate healthcare provider. Citizens who help women obtain abortions can face a three-year jail term.

COVID-19 drastically reduced women's access to safe abortions; abortion was not deemed an essential service, international travel was largely banned, and lockdowns limited women's privacy and autonomy at home. When Poland's borders closed, the support group Abortion Without Borders experienced a huge increase in calls from Polish women terrified by the difficulties accessing abortion services. The government's April 2020 vote to increase abortion restrictions occurred when public protest was impossible due to lockdown measures. Nevertheless, Polish women protested by posting pictures online and by queuing outside grocery stores, standing two metres apart and holding posters. In 2016, Polish protests made international headlines, as thousands of pro-choice activists took to the streets, causing the government to back down from implementing a complete abortion ban. The April 2020 vote concluded with similar uncertainty; the bill was sent back to parliamentary commission for further work.

On 10 June 2020, like in Hungary, a new "Family Charter" was launched designed to address population decline. It defended and expanding financial support for parents and seniors, stated that marriage must remain between man and woman and did not allow for consent for the adoption of children by homosexual couples. It further proclaimed to defend children from LGBTQ "ideology" and prohibited "the propagation of LGBT ideology" in public spaces. Not surprisingly, Poland ranked lowest of European nations for LGBTQ acceptance and LGBTQ discrimination has grown in the past year—spurred by PiS party and legal advice group Ordo Iuris (also focused on tightening Polish abortion laws). By early 2020, around 100 municipalities in Poland have adopted resolutions against "LGBT propaganda"—some local councils declare their municipalities to be "free of gender ideology and LGBT". In the 2020 Presidential election, which was won narrowly by the PiS candidate Andrzej Duda against the progressive Warsaw mayor Rafał Trzaskowski. Duda's campaign relied heavily on a conservative Catholic message which played well in the countryside, especially in the east of the country. He even deemed LGBTQ ideology as more dangerous than communism.

Alongside this came aggressive pro-natal policies. The Family 500+ Program, in existence since 2016, states the programme's goals are to increase number of births, reduce poverty, and invest in families. It provides a monthly allowance of 500 zloty to families—initially this was for families with more than one child, since 1 July 2019, it has been expanded to every child under 18 regardless of family size or income. The programme cost 31 billion zlotys in 2019—projected to cost 41 billion in 2020. There is also a Large Family Card (programme on government website)—for families of at least three children, discounts on various goods and services like rail, culture, sport activities. So far, births have only decreased.

In terms of employment, the government also stated that 2020 would "be a good year for Polish employees". A series of employment initiatives, including a significant increase in the national minimum wage, where part of an aggressive package to raise living standards. Prior to the fall 2019 election, Law and Justice promised voters that, if re-elected, it would increase the minimum wage by a whopping 78 percent over the next four years. The party had already brought changes for Polish employees as part of their goal to "improve living conditions for ordinary Poles". In 2017, the government introduced a new minimum hourly wage act, specifically targeting civil law employment contracts. Until that year, some of the Polish workforce was employed through these unregulated work contracts, which paid low wages with no guaranteed minimum wage that did not provide sick leave, maternity leave, or severance pay. The 2017 law enforced the hourly minimum wage and raised it raised from 13.00 PLN to 17.00 PLN. It also provided wage protection for senior employees. Some argued that the changes were grounded in securing votes instead of stimulating the economy. Others question whether the wage increases will improve the living conditions of ordinary citizens in a country where 98 percent of citizens earn less than the average wage in Germany. In response to the minimum wage increase, some Polish business owners are replacing employees with automated machines or robots to cut costs, and a recent study showed that a quarter of Polish companies planned to put recruitment on hold from January 2020—with just under a fifth making staff cuts.

But something extraordinary was happening. Many Poles are returning home after living abroad. As noted, after Poland's EU accession in 2004, large numbers of young Poles left in search of better opportunities. By 2018, 2.5

million Poles were working abroad, mostly in the United Kingdom. Brexit was a catalyst for many Poles to consider returning to their homeland; in 2018, the number of Poles living abroad dropped by 85,000, according to government statistics. This is something that other countries can only dream about. Polish expats cited the Brexit uncertainty, personal or familial ties, and improved work opportunities in Poland as reasons for their return (large companies including JPMorgan and Google have recently set up headquarters in Poland). The COVID-19 pandemic also encouraged many Poles to go home. By early April 2020, more than 55,000 had returned to Poland on repatriation flights operated by the national carrier LOT.

In keeping with a new narrative for Poland's past, in February 2018, the government passed a bill that made it a criminal offence to refer to Polish guilt in the Holocaust. Under the law, which was proposed by PiS, anyone who accused Poland of complicity with the Nazi regime could face up to three years in prison. The legislation sparked an international outcry and, in particular, was strongly condemned by the United States and Israel. Reports emerged of diplomatic tensions between Washington and Warsaw, and even of U.S. threats to suspend security cooperation with Poland (these reports were dismissed as false by both American and Polish officials). Some Israeli officials compared the law to Holocaust denial, and Israeli Prime Minister Netanyahu responded by stating, "One cannot change history, and the Holocaust cannot be denied."

But in June 2018, Polish Prime Minister Mateusz Morawiecki suddenly intervened and removed the portion of the law that would charge those accused with a criminal offence. Instead, people accusing Poland of Nazi complicity would be charged with a civil offence and could face a fine instead of jail time. Morawiecki stated that he hoped these changes would improve Poland's relations with Israel, and added, "Those who say that Poland may be responsible for the crimes of World War II deserve jail terms ... but we operate in an international context, and we take that into account." Critics of the bill argued that it was intended to fuel nationalistic sentiments and that it threatened free speech and academic discourse. Though the law referred only to accusations against Poland as a country—and not against individuals who may have been complicit in Nazi crimes—and stated that it supported artistic and historical research, many still believed that wording left room for varying legal interpretations and could silence important historical debates.

Czechs, as in the interwar period, again appeared to be the exception to the region's democratic backsliding. Contesting 1989 is hardly part of the picture and, moreover, Czechs seem more willing to defend the gains of 1989 and liberal democracy more generally. However, Czech democracy faced challenges too. The internal political situation was quite stable. Since the late 1990s, power had been essentially contested between two main parties—Miloš Zeman's left-wing Social Democrats and Václav Klaus's right-wing liberal Civic Democrats. Both Klaus and Zeman had been key figures 1989. But the otherwise successful transition where people did see massive improvements in their standard of living, was marred by increasing corruption and apathy. But on the plus side, Czechs seemed to better understand that the threats to their democracy were real and that the gains of 1989 were to be defended. Thankfully, the Czechs, alone of the post-communist states in Central Europe, get where they are and who they are. They spend less time assessing the east-versus-west orientation that occurs in Hungary, Poland, and Slovakia. According to polls, they have a solid sense of identity, and their place in the world, connected to Western Europe, especially Germany and their membership in the EU and NATO. For the most part, they have avoided the far-right politics of Germany, Hungary and Poland. They do not exhibit the higher levels of anti-Semitism present in Hungary, Poland or Slovakia nor the far higher tendency to believe in conspiracy theories that characterizes Hungarians, Poles and Slovaks.

Czech politics got different with the arrival of the Slovak businessman Andrej Babiš in 2011 when he created a political movement called ANO (*Akce nespokojených občanů*, or Action of Dissatisfied Citizens). He later transformed it into a political party the following year. Strangely, given what would happen later, his essential message was anti-corruption and that since he was so rich, he could not be corrupted. His CV was odd but not untypical of the former communists who made it big. Plus, he was accused of being an informant for the secret police. He was not the ideologue Kaczyński or Orbán—he lacked their bitterness too. He likely entered politics to protect his business interests. His party did well in 2013 with just under 20 percent of the vote and formed a coalition with the Social Democrats. Babiš was finance minister. In 2017, Babiš' ANO won big—more than 30 percent of the vote. Czechs even got their first far-right party in parliament too—the Freedom and Direct Democracy Party led by Tomio Okamura, a Czech-Japanese national and former popcorn salesman. Babiš was Prime Minister in a highly unstable environment. In a real first for post-1989 politics, Babiš had to count on support of the Czech communist party to stay in power. Most Czechs were not happy. Many worried that Babiš was set to take the Czech Republic down the same path as Hungary and Poland. If Czechs now had their Trump, in President Miloš Zeman they had their Boris Yeltsin who made gaffe after gaffe with his often racist remarks. His clearly pro-Russian positions were another setback. The difference between them and Václav Havel could not have been more obvious. The government readily joined the anti-migrant coalition. Zeman, like Orbán, said that Islamic culture was incompatible with Europe's and if allowed into the Czech Republic, warned of the arrival of Sharia Law, women in burqas, and public beheadings. In the wake of Brexit, Zeman joined Václav Klaus in supporting a referendum on EU membership.

As well, Babiš was no ordinary businessman. He had built a huge agricultural and media empire. His presence was everywhere especially in the less than beautiful yellow fields of canola flowers in Moravia and elsewhere. It was alleged that one of his companies took EU funds that the firm was not eligible for. An EU and Czech anti-fraud investigative team concluded in January 2018 that the firm had provided false information. The case is ongoing. There were other issues too which served to totally rejuvenate Czech civil society along the lines of what Václav Havel had laid out in his seminal *The Power of the Powerless*. Out of the Babiš premiership came the "Million Moments for Democracy" which led a series of massive demonstrations. Even the famous Czech NHL goalie and Olympic gold medallist Dominik Hašek joined in and spoke of the need for defending 1989 and lamenting the shame of having Babiš as Prime Minister. What really enraged everyone was the attempt by Babiš, with the support of Zeman, to interfere in the judiciary to ensure a better verdict and more compliant courts. This was exactly what had occurred in Hungary and Poland and Czechs were well aware where threats to judicial independence led.

In June 2019, the Czechs experienced their biggest demonstration since 1989 with 250,000 people protesting. The movement capitalized even more on the November 2019 30th anniversary of the collapse of Czech communism. Not surprisingly, the movement invoked Masaryk's humanism, the success of the interwar Czechoslovak government in staving off fascism and intolerance and the execution of Milada Horáková in 1950. It grew and grew with countless petitions and demonstrations. But Babiš stayed in power. Zeman, ever the folksy town drunk, dismissed the protestors as just the Prague coffee house crowd. The numbers involved put paid to that lie. In the end, Czechs had shown their elite that the path chosen by Hungary and Poland was not for them.

Slovakia has proven to be a similar success after facing far greater threats to democracy then the Czechs. After the ousting of Mečiar in 1998, Slovakia's democracy seemed solid but there were always figures and parties, just like in Hungary and Poland, which advocated for populism, nationalism and authoritarianism. Slovakia had its Slovak National Party with its extreme nationalist stance combined with anti-Roma and anti-Hungarian policies. There was also the neo-fascist People's Party—Our Slovakia which linked its ideology (and uniforms) to the Nazi puppet state of Jozef Tiso. But on the other hand, its commitment to all things Europe and thus the most integrated state set them apart from other Visegrád states—Slovakia even joined the Eurozone in 2009. Until now, Slovaks, unlike the Hungarians and the Poles, have not questioned the central tenets of their EU membership as they understand that the Europe of nations, as envisioned by Kaczyński and Orbán, would be harmful to Slovak interests. They had no Kaczyński, Orbán or Babiš. Just a normal democracy or so it seemed. In 2006, the Slovak political scene became dominated by the SMER-SD (Direction—Social Democracy) of Robert Fico, a leftist party with a strong populist orientation. It slid easily into the type of crony capitalism that prevailed during the Mečiar years. In 2016, the electoral landscape changed as the Ordinary People and Independent Personalities Party (OL'aNO) appeared and the neo-fascists got seats in the parliament with 8 percent of the vote, a far cry from the 20 plus percent the neo-fascists were accustomed to getting in Hungary. The migrant crisis of 2015, just like in Poland, emboldened ethnocentric ideas that are never far from the surface in Slovakia. Hardly anyone supported the resettlement of refugees in the country and the political elite capitalized on this.

However, things changed really dramatically in February 2018 when a young investigative journalist, Ján Kuciak and his fiancé, Martina Kušnírová, were brutally murdered in their home east of Bratislava. Before his murder, Kuciak had been investigating the corrupt links between Slovak oligarchs and leaders of the SMER-SD governing coalition. The murders were an enormous blow for Slovakia and all the assumptions about the state of the country were overturned. Massive protests, focused on the main shortcoming in Slovak democracy—corruption—were the biggest since 1989. Taking a page from the Hungarian playbook, the government tried to link with the protests with George Soros, the go-to demon for embattled leaders, and other foreign interests in order to discredit them. They failed and the government collapsed as Prime Minister Robert Fico, who had dominated Slovak politics for 12 years, and his Interior Minister Robert Kaliňák resigned in March. The Slovaks proved again that they could defend their democracy vigorously as the protest movement, which became known as "For a Decent Slovakia", was largely led by youth. Unlike in Hungary, where public pressure on the government has been minimal, Slovaks did prove that they could make a difference. Keep in mind that the only time when Hungarians came out in enough numbers to force change since Orbán came to power was in 2014 when the government tried (and failed) to impose an onerous tax on internet usage.

The murders led to a surprisingly serious investigation with real charges which helped restore some faith in Slovak democracy and particularly the justice system. Two men were sentenced in the murder in early 2020 and the businessman who had ordered the killings, Marian Kočner, was later acquitted in September 2020 due to lack of evidence while another defendant was sentenced to 25 years for his role in the murders but a re-trial was later ordered. Prosecutors alleged Kočner had developed a web of people who he had paid to keep an eye on more than 20 journalists. Plus, the accusations added, he had bribed any number of people in the police and courts. To some, Kuciak's investigative work got too close and risked destroying his business empire. It was also alleged that he paid the assassins 70,000 euros to kill two people, including Kuciak. In addition to lengthy prison sentences, the murders provoked a substantial number of arrests of 13 judges for obstructing justice in the Kuciak case. The fact that the case went so far is an important milestone as elsewhere in the region, where rule of law for everyone is often a fraud, there would have been few repercussions especially in the Balkans where oligarchs and mafia enjoy the full protection of the state and verdicts are often for sale. What happened in Slovakia went a long way to restore trust in state institutions.

In subsequent elections, in a near repeat of 1998, in the 2019 presidential election and 2020 parliamentary elections new people came to power and the former governing party lost big and so did the extreme nationalists. The 2019 presidential election saw a stunning victory by the anti-corruption lawyer, environmental activist, pro-EU, liberal and Slovakia's first female president Zuzana

Čaputová. She promised a whole different approach while acknowledging that too many people have been left behind. Čaputová's victory heralded to some that national populism and illiberalism had suffered a blow. The 2020 elections brought another democratic coalition on a strong anti-corruption platform with the Ordinary People party appointing the new Prime Minister, Igor Matovič in a four-party coalition. The neo-fascists also upped their vote a bit too. But Slovaks roundly supported Matovič's party because of its commitment to ending corruption as they were totally sickened by what the Kuciak case had revealed in their sordid political life.

Germany, long the key country for Central Europe, did not suffer the same fate as say Hungary or Poland. Until the Alliance for Germany (AfD in German) showed up and shifted to the far right, Germany largely avoided radical right parties and strong Euro-sceptic forces. Germany has the National Democratic Party that is essentially neo-Nazi but the party has never won any seats in parliament. However, the migration crisis, Chancellor Angela Merkel's acceptance of so many immigrants with the phrase "We will manage" (*Wir schaffen das*) when she permitted refugees to exit Hungary and travel through Austria to Germany, her suspension of the Dublin regulation, which essentially meant that asylum claims must be made at the first point of entry into the EU, changed the political landscape of Germany. This meant that hundreds of thousands of asylum seekers found their new homes in Germany.

The AfD was founded in 2013 as a group of intellectuals opposed to the Euro but morphed into an anti-immigrant, anti-Islam party that offered a new narrative for Germany's past that survived and thrived largely because of the Refugee Crisis of 2015. It morphed into radical right populist—nativist—xenophobic, racist, and nationalist. It found its main constituency in the old East Germany where population decline was most felt despite the substantial money transferred from West to East—in the form of a solidarity tax now being phased out—since unification. The AfD did best in places where more people had left. They also capitalized on the descendants of those Germans expelled after the Second World War who felt ignored by the mainstream parties. The AfD did extremely well in the 2017 German election with over 12 percent and becoming the third largest party. But its future is not necessarily bright. The immigrants who arrived in 2015 have not proven to be a catastrophe and immigration is no longer front and centre the way it was 3–5 years ago. Attention shifted to the COVID-19 pandemic where the governing parties largely won plaudits for the handling of the crisis.

External Players

While Russian influence in the region is at best overstated, the Russian leadership certainly seeks to restore its dominant position in Central Europe after the shock of EU and NATO enlargement through a divide and rule approach largely through the internet. But the region is divided on Russia and finding supporters has proven harder in some places than others. Plus, Russia, when compared to the EU, does not really have that much to offer beyond cheap energy and a simplified and nostalgic narrative about an unknown past. Unlike the EU, Russia is hardly an infrastructure builder. The messages focus on the dangers of Islam, the threat of LGBTQ rights and the demise of the nation state under the aegis of the EU. NATO, according to the information campaign, is merely designed to subject Central Europe to an American-led world order.

But it was the anti-migration narrative that got the most attention. While leaders in Czech Republic, Hungary and Slovakia talked about lifting the sanctions imposed on Russia because of the 2014 occupation of Crimea, nobody broke ranks with the EU. Only Hungary has developed significant ties with Russia and indeed Orbán has met Putin on more occasions than any other European politician other than Angela Merkel, the Chancellor of Germany (2005–2021). A key project was the construction of a new nuclear power plant in central Hungary awarded to Rosatom, a Russian state company, without a tender. The Russians provided the financing too. Prague and Bratislava walked away from power plants constructed by the Russians. But nobody can avoid Russian energy supplies—the Czech Republic is the best off—only 66 percent share of all gas imports come from Russia. Hungary and Poland sit at 81 percent and 83 percent and Slovakia is tops the list with 93 percent dependency. Germany gets about 40 percent of its natural gas from Russia. One can understand Orbán when he says that good relations with Russia are a necessity. For Russia, the gains are obvious—they gain influence in the EU and NATO.

Russian tactics are well known. They use the media especially, but also academia too. Hungary is the most susceptible to Russian influence for a number of reasons. As noted, the government often pursues anti-Western policies and highlights its "Eastern opening" and the Eastern roots of the Hungarians. Hungary's media milieu is also the least pluralistic in the region and state media often use dubious Russian sources like RT and Sputnik as sources.

Aside from Russia's meddling, many also fretted about China's growing influence in Central Europe but this also proved to be overstated. The People's Republic of China had two big initiatives they hoped would expand their influence in Central Europe. There was the 17+1, a Chinese-instigated multilateral platform that was developed with the hope of deepening China's relationship with the region. The 17+1 consists of Albania, Bosnia and Herzegovina, Bulgaria, Croatia, the Czech Republic, Estonia, Greece, Hungary, Latvia, Lithuania, Macedonia, Montenegro, Poland, Romania, Serbia, Slovakia, and Slovenia. It is teamed up with the Belt and Road Initiative (BRI) that through massive infrastructure projects seeks to better connect the Eurasian continent. Despite all the doom and gloom about deepening Chinese influence and the potentially harmful effects of that, the 17+1 platform is not a huge success at anything more than getting people to talk about China. This is evidenced by limited trade interdependency and low levels of Chinese investment. Only Hungary has seen big investments especially in a somewhat dubious rail link between Belgrade and Budapest that was the result of a highly secretive deal. As noted earlier, Hungary signed on to a massive Chinese university campus as well, but popular opposition shelved the idea. In a direct rebuttal to Orbán's approval of the campus, showing once again the significance of street names in Hungary, the liberal Budapest mayor abruptly changed several street names to show support for Hong Kong and Tibet. China puts its money in Western Europe, which has the companies and research and development tools they seek. Central Europe is key to the German automobile supply chain but they are merely a workshop. Moreover, China had no real soft power in Europe as few look to the Chinese governance model with anything more than disdain. The situation is different in the Balkans where Chinese loans and money diplomacy have met been met with open coffers especially in Serbia and Montenegro.

But things changed in unforeseen ways with the global pandemic of 2020 and not just for China. In June of that year, Czech's declared the COVID-19 virus eliminated and celebrated with 500-metre-long table stretched across the Charles Bridge in Prague for dinner, drinks, and photos. The event was described as a "symbolic farewell" to the COVID-19 pandemic. Indeed, if one looked at Central Europe in the summer of 2020, it seemed as if the region had gotten things right. At the time, the Czech Republic had registered fewer than 12,000 COVID-19 infections and 350 deaths, a much smaller number than many of its European counterparts. Austria, Hungary, Germany, Poland, and Slovakia were in similar optimistic positions, and articles began to appear in the international media recognizing Central Europe's successful handling of the pandemic's spring wave. Austrian Chancellor Sebastian Kurz even invited the Czech Republic to a meeting of seven nations, which included New Zealand and Denmark, to share and discuss best practices for handling the virus. Not everyone was convinced. Not long after the Czechs' COVID farewell dinner, infections began to surge throughout Central Europe, and, by October, the Czech Republic was recording the highest virus transmission rate in Europe. By February 2021, the Czech Republic (population ten million) has registered 1,134,957 cases of COVID-19 and 18,913 deaths. Hungary, Slovakia, and Poland follow closely behind in per capita infections and fatalities.

Central European countries made headlines many times throughout 2020; for their handling and mishandling of the pandemic, for their interference in the EU budget and COVID-19 recovery package negotiations, for their leaders' often questionable attempts to consolidate power—and for their citizens' attempts to resist and protest. Earlier than many Western European nations, they implemented strict lockdowns and enforced mask-wearing and other measures aimed to protect their fragile healthcare systems. Whereas some decisions were lauded as prudent, others sparked international criticism. On 30 March, the Hungarian parliament passed a set of emergency laws making it a criminal offence—punishable by up to five years in prison—to spread misinformation about the pandemic, and, most notably, giving Prime Minister Viktor Orbán the power to rule by decree for an unspecified time period. While some EU members condemned Orbán's actions, and the European Parliament organized a debate regarding the situation, as usual, Hungary faced no formal consequences, and, within three days of adopting the measures, the Hungarian parliament urgently passed another law ending legal gender recognition for transgender citizens—seemingly a strange priority in the midst of the emerging global pandemic.

Nevertheless, Hungary and its Central European neighbours appeared to have success. Searching for an explanation, some analysts pointed to the early lockdowns, as well a multitude of other possible factors, including lower population density in the region, childhood TB vaccines specific and a general lower life expectancy of its population (meaning fewer old people left alive for COVID to kill). Hungary's Prime Minister was especially nervous as he was not accustomed to dealing with a crisis that he did not invent. As the months went on, however, the situation changed drastically and the statistics started telling a totally different story. Pandemic safety measures relaxed over the summer, and public messaging became muddled and confused, as leaders contradicted their own advice in the most blatant of ways. Low trust in public institutions made things even worse. In fact, the pandemic really laid bare how little faith people have in their leaderships who generally asked people to do things they would never do. Moreover, outside of Austria, the health care systems were simply unable to cope and the lack of investment in health care was obvious to everyone.

The second and third waves of COVID hit harder and deadlier for most nations worldwide, but Central Europe did especially poorly. Previous policy weakness made clear just how bad things were: dilapidated healthcare infrastructure, such as test-and-trace systems, low hospital bed capacities, and shortages of doctors and nurses, intensified the crisis. This lack of personnel and resources is partly due to the westward emigration of many of the countries' most skilled citizens within the past decades. Poland, for instance, had only 238 doctors per 100,000 inhabitants in 2020 (the lowest ratio in the EU), and Hungary's underfunded healthcare system had made international headlines prior to the pandemic, as Viktor Orbán poured government money into the wrong places.

These examples of problematic and inconsistent leadership exacerbated already existing distrust in government, as well as widespread misinformation. In an October 2020 survey, 54 percent of Slovaks reported that they did not know what to believe when it came to COVID-19, and recent reports from the region point to high rates of vaccine hesitancy. In early February 2021, nearly 50 percent of Czechs expressed an unwillingness to get vaccinated due to safety fears and disinformation, and a November 2020 poll revealed that fewer than 15 percent of Hungarians were willing to receive a COVID vaccine. This marked a drastic change in public sentiment, as Hungary previously had one of the highest measles, mumps, and rubella (MMR) vaccination coverage rates in the EU. A poll from 2018 reported that 91 percent of Hungarians believed vaccines were "generally safe". In February 2021, Slovakia briefly became the nation with the most COVID-19 deaths per population size in the world, as the so-called UK variant of the virus became the dominant strain in the country. Cases were also again on the rise in the Czech Republic, and political chaos in the Czech government continued confusion surrounding emergency regulations. A survey in early February 2021 found that 47 percent of Czechs did not stay home when they had virus symptoms, 45 percent believed virus risks were exaggerated, and 76 percent of Czechs did not trust government messaging regarding the pandemic. When the European Union planned to begin vaccinations across the bloc on 27 December 2020, Hungary once again went rogue and began vaccinations one day early. Hungary also broke with the EU and purchased vaccines from China and Russia, despite polls from the Hungarian population that showed much higher trust in Western vaccines. The Hungarian government could not resist attacking the EU for its slow delivery of vaccines, basically accusing Brussels of killing Hungarians and thus forcing them to buy from China and Russia to save Hungarian lives.

But COVID's story in the region tells a bigger story. While Europe in general had some of the highest death rates in the world, post-communist Europe was particularly bad with the Czech Republic, Hungary, and Slovakia in the top ten highest death rates in the world—Poland was 16th. It highlighted the shortcomings of the 30 plus years of transition, the total failure to invest in health services and the general distrust of government that prevailed. To some extent as well, COVID strengthened the anti-democratic tendencies in some countries due to the massive amount of power that drifted to the executive branch of government, the amount of money spent on advertising COVID information that landed with government-friendly media certainly amplified governments' ability to control not just the COVID-19 message and the impact of prolonged public lockdowns on civic engagement. Hungary went the furthest when prison sentences of up to five years were introduced for spreading false information about the pandemic. The Czech Republic changed health ministers four times in the first 14 months of the pandemic—one clashed with Prime Minister Babiš on face masks—Babiš was opposed, one violated his own government's COVID-19 measures when he was caught in what should have been a closed restaurant, another failed to disclose property and income. More so than any other country in the region, the Czech Republic confronted a leadership vacuum. For the most part, the Visegrád governments failed utterly in the management of the pandemic and largely sowed confusion and distrust.

Despite the fear and chaos of the pandemic, Central European civil society found ways to make their voices heard, especially in Poland, which was encouraging. In late October 2020, when the Polish Constitutional Court ruled that abortions in the case of foetal abnormalities (which accounted for 98 percent of all legal abortions in Poland, already one of the most restrictive countries in the EU) were illegal, massive protests broke out across the country on a scale not seen since the Solidarity movement of the 1980s. The protests lasted days, culminating in a demonstration in Warsaw that drew upwards of 100,000 people. On a smaller scale, students at the Budapest University of Theatre and Film

Arts held a weeks-long blockade outside their institution, protesting against the appointment of a government-selected university board, which they claimed would dangerously limit academic freedom and autonomy. In October 2020, over 5000 protesters marched in Budapest in support of the students. These actions brought back memories of public support for the Central European University although those protests still did not prevent the government from essentially shutting down the university and forcing it to move to Vienna. Along with the de-recognition of transgender rights in early April 2020, the Hungarian parliament passed another devastating law for LGBTQ citizens in December, banning adoption for same-sex couples and infuriating many Hungarians.

In the second half of 2020, Hungary and Poland continued to make headlines on the international stage, obstructing the 25 other EU nations as the bloc attempted to pass a historic 1.82-trillion-euro budget deal. The deal also included a 750-billion-euro stimulus package aimed to help member states recover from the pandemic. With the existing budget set to expire later in the year, EU leaders met in July 2020 for their first in-person gathering since the pandemic began. For five contentious days, they debated elements of the budget text, eventually deciding that all states would jointly borrow funds on an unprecedented scale. Despite reservations by the "Frugal Four" (Austria, Denmark, the Netherlands, and Sweden), the EU eventually agreed to move forward with the budget, and European Council President Charles Michel announced just before 6 am on 21 July, "We did it! Europe is strong. Europe is united!"

But he might have spoken too early. Written into the budget was a clause stipulating that recovery funds could be linked to member states' adherence to the rule of law, and that EU authorities could withhold funds if there was a "generalized deficiency" regarding the rule of law in any EU nation, such as threats to their independent judiciary. This clause required only a qualified majority to pass at the July talks, but it would require full consensus by all member states in order for the new budget to be made legal and officially passed through the European Parliament by the end of the year. As technical negotiations began in the autumn, Hungary and Poland took issue with the "rule of law mechanism", as it became known in the political jargon, and made clear that they were willing to veto the entire budget deal if this clause was not amended. In late September, Polish Prime Minister Mateusz Morawiecki warned that there would be "no Polish consent" that might allow the EU "to threaten us with a finger only because someone likes our government less", and Orbán took issue with the "vague" definition of rule of law, stating in November, "Such difficult to define concepts create opportunities for political abuses and violate the requirement of legal certainty." Orbán also suggested that the rule of law mechanism had been included to punish him for his stance on migrants, and, in early December, he further stoked the fire by blaming a familiar enemy and conspiracy theory target, writing: "Europe must not succumb to the [philanthropist George] Soros network."

As we have seen, the EU has struggled with how to handle Poland's and especially Hungary's democratic backsliding as both states slipped precipitously in all indicators. Democracy watchdog Freedom House downgraded its ranking on Hungary from "Free" to "Partly Free" and called it a "transitional/hybrid regime". Poland was deemed a "semi-consolidated democracy" with particular concern noted over attacks on LGBTQ communities and illiberalism. Previous attempts to reign in both countries have failed, and many EU lawmakers saw the new 2021–2027 budget as a chance to finally change things by threatening to withhold much-needed cash. Critics had long accused leaders of larger powers, such as Germany's Angela Merkel, of failure to act in dealing with Orbán and Morawiecki. Some pointed to Germany's extensive business dealings with Hungary especially in the auto industry and its complicated history with Poland dating back to the Second World War as reasons that might explain Merkel's hesitancy. In addition, the EU's consensus based structure limits its ability to implement sanctions, as Article 7 of the EU Treaty requires unanimous consent from all member states and would thus always allow Hungary and Poland to veto any punitive measures.

In 2020, Germany, holding the rotating presidency of the Council of the EU, was faced with brokering a compromise between Poland and Hungary and the rest of the bloc regarding the budget and stimulus package. As negotiations persisted throughout the autumn, Germany toned down the budget text, narrowing the definition of the rule of law by tying it more directly to the spending of EU funds and removing the threat of an EU investigation if corruption were suspected. When Poland and Hungary still vetoed the deal in November, EU leaders were forced to further amend the text so as not to risk sabotaging the entire package. The final version, presented in early December, stipulated that, should any nation wish to challenge the legality of the rule of law mechanism at the EU Court of Justice, then the European Council would refrain from implementing the mechanism until after the Court had made its decision. The new text also specified that the rule of law mechanism only applied to the 2021–2027 budget, therefore exempting any previous actions by member states from scrutiny. Finally, the clause included language stressing that the Council would "strive to formulate a common position" if a country facing sanctions wished to have its case discussed further.

These amendments seemed to please Hungary and Poland, and, on 10 December, the budget and recovery plan were finally approved by all nations, with all sides claiming victory. As predicted, Orbán and Morawiecki vowed to take the rule of law issue to the Court of Justice, with Orbán announcing, "Congratulations to Mateusz [Morawiecki] … and congratulations to myself!" Morawiecki also warned other EU nations that the rule of law mechanism could be abused: "Today we fear that we might be attacked in an unjustified way, but of course in the future any country … might also be attacked." Angela Merkel, who faced criticism for bowing to pressure from Orbán and Morawiecki, admitted, "I know that there are deep wounds sometimes between member states", and French President Emmanuel Macron tweeted, "We said it: we don't sacrifice either the recovery or the rule of law. Commitment kept! The recovery plan advances. Europe needs it!" Belgian Prime Minister Alexander De Croo took a more neutral approach, saying, "I do not think that it is a victory of one over the other. This is just a good way going forward." We must wait and see whether the compromises to Hungary and Poland went too far as the rule of law debacle will move to the European Court of Justice.

Conclusion

Despite the doom and gloom that the media churned out in the wake of the Refugee Crisis, later the COVID-19 pandemic and the perceived democratic backsliding in Hungary and Poland, things were not maybe as bad as they seemed. For sure any notion of Weimar syndromes was overstated and some of the post-war institutional architecture proved more durable than expected. After all, even the bad guys in Central Europe want seats in the European parliament, if only for the perks and terrific salaries that the European Union provides. Sure, Euro-scepticism exists but by and large, Central Europeans—Austrians, Czechs, Germans, Hungarians, Poles, and Slovaks—remain committed to the European project. As noted, when Kaczyński or Orbán rails against Europe, it largely an attack on Brussels—comprised almost exclusively of unelected officials. Too much of their cash comes from the EU as an institution to make it their lightning rod.

As much as Central Europe has a shared history, its future may suggest something different. At present, there is no such thing as a unified Central European identity. Austrians, Czechs, Germans, Hungarians, Poles, and Slovaks had widely differing responses to surveys and the messages are very mixed. Germans are overwhelming supportive of the EU while Austrians are more ambivalent. Despite recent democratic backsliding in the region, attitudes towards Europe and NATO remain quite positive. In the Czech Republic and Hungary, support for the EU resembles a U-curve, as the youngest and oldest generations overwhelmingly wish to remain in Europe. With the exception of Poland, where support for EU membership is strangely highest among the oldest generation (65+), younger Central Europeans appear more satisfied with the EU than their elders. The highest support for NATO is found among all Poles of all generations, whereas only 38 percent of Slovaks aged 65+ would vote to remain in NATO.

In general, young people are still the most Western-oriented, with the exception of those in Poland—another anomaly. Support for the West is highest among Hungarians aged 18–24, which could represent their dissatisfaction with Hungary's current regime and explain why the population declines so rapidly. Belief in conspiracy theories is widespread and more common in older respondents. Slovakia is by far the most conspiracy-prone of all Central European countries. It is the only country where the majority of respondents (52 percent) believe that world events are shaped by secret societies seeking to establish a totalitarian world order and that Jews have too much power and secretly control many governments and institutions worldwide. Over 25 percent of respondents in Poland and Hungary also demonstrate anti-Semitic beliefs, whereas Czech Republic stands out as the only country where most respondents of all ages disagreed with anti-Semitic conspiracies. Looking back on the developments of 1989, young people in Slovakia and Czech Republic generally view the fall of Communism more positively than their older generations. The majority of Poles across all generations view it positively, whereas Hungary stands out as the only country where young people are unsure of their feelings; over 40 percent of Hungarians aged 18 to 24 do not know whether the fall of Communism in 1989 was a positive development.

That said, given that Czechs, Poles, and Slovaks have shown a willingness to push back against some of the nastier attacks on democracy, the story is largely about Hungary where the attack on liberal democracy started as an attack on pluralism but then became simply an attack on democracy. That then begs the question is how dangerous is the governance model of Budapest to the rest of Europe? Orbán once opined that in 1989 Hungarians thought Europe was their future but that 30 years later it was the Hungarians embodying Europe's future. History suggests otherwise—Hungary will not determine the fate of the rest of Europe. However, where Hungary's model is most worrying is in the Balkans where EU hopefuls predominate. Orbán has proven very popular there and one can see the implementation of Orbán-esque policies towards the judiciary, the media and culture.

The key lesson for the EU, and this is at least acknowledged in the Balkan accession process, is that rule of law is the key. In Hungary and Poland, attacks on courts were integral to these government's agenda. But the other challenge is that the EU does not have that much leverage on member states. The accession process, as we saw, imposed all kinds of conditions on potential member states that they willingly adopted for the sake of "re-joining Europe". The hubris of 1989 meant the withering away of the nation state was destiny. After membership, the drift from some of the EU's core values—respect for human dignity and human rights, freedom, democracy, equality and the rule of law—at first unthinkable, was maybe impossible to reverse. The EU's toolbox could not deal with something that so few expected. Worse still, the Central Europeans could not be lectured to or told to shut up as they were in 2003 by then French President Jacques Chirac when some of them broke ranks with the EU and sided with the United States in the Iraq war. By 2019, Poland and Hungary were in trouble again. Reports were written and tabled in the European Parliament, threats were made, but nothing substantial happened. Orbán, now the longest serving leader in the EU, has lots of allies and huge influence despite Hungary's small size. Hard to imagine that the EU allowed a university to be closed under really dubious circumstances in one of its member states. There were other major transgressions too and not just in Central Europe. But the malignant forces that aligned in the 1920s and 1930s to ruin the world were not the same this time around.

For Further Study

Books (Fiction and Non-fiction)

Applebaum, Anne. *Twilight of Democracy: The Seductive Lure of Authoritarianism.* New York: Penguin Random House, 2020.

Kovács, János Mátyás and Balázs Trencsényi, ed. *Brave New Hungary: Mapping the "System of National Cooperation."* Lanham, MD: Lexington Books, 2019.

Krastev, Ivan. *After Europe.* Philadelphia: University of Pennsylvania Press, 2017.

Krastev, Ivan and Stephen Holmes, *The Light that Failed – A Reckoning.* London: Allen Lane, 2019.

Porter, Anna. *The Ghosts of Europe: Journeys Through Central Europe's Troubled Past and Uncertain Future.* Toronto: Douglas & McIntyre, 2010.

Films

The Érpatak Model (2015). Directed by Benny Brunner. Netherlands.

Fire at Sea (2016). Directed by Gianfranco Rosi. Italy.

Spectres are Haunting Europe (2016). Directed by Maria Kourkouta and Niki Giannari. France and Greece.

Peasant Common Sense (2017). Directed by Vít Janeček and Zuzana Piussi. Czech Republic.

The State Capture (2019). Directed by Zuzana Piussi. Slovakia and Czech Republic.

The Driven Ones (2020). Directed by Stephan Wagner. Germany.

Progress in the Valley of the People Who Don't Know (2019). Directed by Florian Kunert. Germany.

Inside Europe: Ten Years of Turmoil. BBC Two. United Kingdom.

Additional Reading

Survey Books on Central Europe

Berend, Ivan T. *History Derailed: Central and Eastern Europe in the Long Nineteenth Century*. Berkeley: University of California Press, 2003.

Bideleux, Robert and Ian Jeffries. *A History of Eastern Europe: Crisis and Change*. London: Routledge, 1998.

Connelly, John. *From Peoples into Nations: A History of Eastern Europe*. Princeton, NJ: Princeton University Press, 2020.

Crampton, R.J. *Eastern Europe in the Twentieth Century – And After*. London: Routledge, 1997.

Johnson, Lonnie. *Central Europe: Enemies, Neighbors, Friends*. Third Edition. New York: Oxford University Press, 2010.

Magocsi, Paul Robert. *Historical Atlas of Central Europe*. Toronto: University of Toronto Press, 2018.

Mazower, Mark. *Dark Continent: Europe's Twentieth Century*. New York: Vintage Books, 2000.

Morys, Matthias, Editor. *The Economic History of Central, East and Southeastern Europe: 1800 to the Present*. Milton: Taylor and Francis, 2020.

Okey, Robin. *Eastern Europe 1740–1985: Feudalism to Communism*. London: Routledge, 1991.

Wandycz, Piotr S. *The Price of Freedom: A History of East Central Europe from the Middle Ages to the Present*. London: Routledge, 2001.

Winder, Simon. *Germania*. New York: Farrar, Straus and Giroux, 2010.

Central Europe: Country-Specific Surveys

Austria

Beller, Steven. *A Concise History of Austria*. Cambridge: Cambridge University Press, 2006.

Jelavich, Barbara. *Modern Austria: Empire and Republic, 1815–1986*. Cambridge: Cambridge University Press, 1987.
Steininger, Rolf, Günter Bischof, Michael Gehler, ed. *Austria in the Twentieth Century*. New Brunswick, NJ: Transaction Publishers, 2002.

Czechoslovakia

Skalnik Leff, Carol. *The Czech and Slovak Republics: Nation versus State*. Boulder, CO: Westview Press, 1997.
Innes, Abby. *Czechoslovakia: The Short Goodbye*. New Haven, CT: Yale University Press, 2001.

Czech Republic

Fawn, Rick. *The Czech Republic: A Nation of Velvet*. Amsterdam: Harwood Academic, 2000.
Mahoney, William M. *The History of the Czech Republic and Slovakia*. Santa Barbara, CA: Greenwood, 2011.
Stolarik, M. Mark, ed. *The Czech and Slovak Republics: Twenty Years of Independence, 1993–2013*. Budapest: Central European University Press, 2016.

Germany

Alter, Peter. *The German Question and Europe: A History*. London: Oxford University Press, 2000.
Fulbrook, Mary. *A Concise History of Germany*. Cambridge: Cambridge University Press, 2004.
Orlow, Dietrich. *A History of Modern Germany: 1871 to Present*. Upper Saddle River, NJ: Pearson Prentice Hall, 2008.

Hungary

Lendvai, Paul. *Hungary: Between Democracy and Authoritarianism*. London: Hurst & Co., 2012.
Kontler, László. *A History of Hungary: Millennium in Central Europe*. New York: Palgrave Macmillan, 2002.
Molnár, Miklós. *A Concise History of Hungary*. Cambridge: Cambridge University Press, 2001

Poland

Prazmowska, Anita J. *A History of Poland*. New York: Palgrave Macmillan, 2011.
Porter-Szűcs, Brian. *Poland in the Modern World: Beyond Martyrdom*. Chichester: Wiley-Blackwell, 2014.
Lukowski, Jerzy and Hubert Zawadzki. *A Concise History of Poland*. Cambridge University Press, 2001.

Slovakia

Henderson, Karen. *Slovakia: The Escape from Invisibility.* London: Routledge, 2002.
Kirschbaum, Stanislav J. *A History of Slovakia: The Struggle for Survival.* New York: Palgrave Macmillan, 2005.
Teich, Mikuláš, Dušan Kováč, and Martin D. Brown, ed. *Slovakia in History.* Cambridge: Cambridge University Press, 2011.

Index

A
Adamec, Ladislav, 132, 133
Adenauer, Konrad, 96
Albania, 24, 28, 34, 40, 41, 43, 78, 79, 88, 96–98, 103, 119, 120, 127, 128, 139, 143, 144, 164
Andrássy, Gyula, 18, 21
Andropov, Yuri, 120
Anschluss, 28, 41, 48, 81, 104
Antall, József, 129, 139, 141
Anti-semitism
　in Austria, 20, 47
　in Czechoslovakia, 33, 42
　in Germany, 48
　in Hungary, 19, 160
　in Poland, 33, 160
Auschwitz-Birkenau, 59, 60
Austria, v, vi, 2, 5, 7, 9, 10, 13, 15–20, 22–25, 28, 30–32, 34, 35, 37–41, 43, 45, 47–49, 63, 67, 72, 77, 79, 81, 82, 87, 89, 99, 103–105, 108, 121, 127, 131, 132, 135, 143, 147, 149, 150, 163, 165, 166, 168
　Austro-fascism, 28, 39
Austria-Hungary, 17–24, 29

B
Babiš, Andrej, 160, 161, 167
Battle of White Mountain, 8
Beneš, Edvard, 32, 49, 86, 94–97

Berlin, 2–4, 10, 16, 17, 45, 56, 61, 63, 65, 66, 68, 69, 72, 75, 80, 82, 83
　Wall, 127, 131, 132
Biľak, Vasil, 111
Bolshevik Revolution, 24
Bolshevism, 30, 37, 38, 57
Brezhnev Doctrine, 119, 120, 127
Brezhnev, Leonid, 110, 111, 119
Budapest
　liberation of, 51, 75
　monuments, 2, 155
Bulgaria, 28, 34, 43, 78, 79, 103, 120, 123, 125, 128, 139, 141–144, 149

C
Čaputová, Zuzana, 162–163
Ceaușescu, Nicolae, 98, 120, 121, 124, 125, 139, 144
Charter 77, vii, 114, 118, 123, 131
Chernenko, Constantine, 120
China, viii, 110, 136, 150, 151, 164, 165, 167
Churchill, Winston, 4, 42, 77–82
Civic Forum, 114, 132, 134
Clémenceau, Georges, 24
Communism
　censorship under communism, 109, 110, 112, 137
　censorship under Habsburg Empire, 15

Communism (*cont.*)
  economy under, 91, 142
  opposition to, 33, 95, 115, 138, 150
  purges, 101
  takeovers, vii, 88–96, 102
Congress of Vienna, 10, 12
COVID-19, 155–157, 159, 163, 165–167, 170
Czechoslovakia
  under Communism... takeovers, vii, 94–96
  German expulsions... Beneš Decrees, 70, 94
  Hyphen War, 133
  Lidice, 76
  lustration, 133
  monuments, 4
  1989 revolution, 96
  Protectorate of Bohemia and Moravia, 43
  relations with Jewish population, 32
  Sudeten Germans, 32, 37, 42, 86
  Sudetenland, annexation, 42
  Theresienstadt, 49
  Velvet Divorce, 134

D
Displaced persons camps, 87, 88
Dmowski, Roman, 33
Dollfuss, Engelbert, 39, 40
Dual Monarchy, 18, 155
Dubček, Alexander, 109–112, 121, 133

E
Eichmann, Adolf, 51, 83
Einsatzgruppen, 50, 58, 59, 82
Elizabeth (Sisi) of Austria, 18
European Union
  accession to, 123, 136, 138, 148, 158, 171
  enlargement, 141–145, 147, 163

F
Ferdinand, Franz, 1, 14, 23
Fico, Robert, 161, 162
Fidesz, v, 130, 150–156

Forman, Miloš, 110
Frank, Hans, 52, 83
Franz Joseph I, 14, 15, 17, 18, 20, 21, 25, 29
French Revolution, 9–11

G
German Democratic Republic, 96, 103
  1989 revolution, 131, 136
  Leipzig demonstrations, 127
Germany
  and Czechoslovakia, 38–40, 49, 79
  fascism, 38, 96, 147
  First World War, 2, 36, 38, 55
  and Hungary, vi, 24, 31, 39, 43, 49–51, 79, 149, 160, 163, 165, 169
  Locarno Treaties, 34, 37
  and Poland, vi, 30, 33, 42, 45, 46, 52, 71, 79, 81, 92, 93, 103, 149, 160, 165
  relations with Jewish population, 51
  reparations, 27, 34, 48, 80, 81
  re-unification, 2, 136, 137
  Second World War, 10, 23, 45–47, 163
  unification, 11, 17–22, 28, 136
  See also German Democratic Republic
Glasnost, 122
Gömbös, Gyula, 36
Gomułka, Władysław, 92, 93, 106, 115, 116
Gorbachev, Mikhail, vii, 47, 83, 110, 120–122, 124, 127–129, 137
Göring, Hermann, 83
Gottwald, Klement, 94, 95, 98, 102, 109
Greece, 11, 34, 35, 43, 78, 103, 104, 144, 151, 164
  population exchange with Turkey, 35

H
Habsburgs
  commemoration, 1
  1848 revolutions, 7
  memory of, 18
Havel, Václav, 86, 110, 114, 124, 128, 132, 133, 135, 139, 141, 160, 161

Helsinki Accords, 114, 118
Henlein, Konrad, 38
Heydrich, Reinhard, 48, 76, 83
Hitler, Adolf, 2, 10, 20, 21, 25, 28, 30, 32, 33, 36–43, 46–48, 50–52, 54–58, 62–64, 66, 68, 70, 72, 79, 81, 83, 98, 105
Holocaust
   Final Solution, 56
   in Germany, 56–58
   ghettos, 58
   in Hungary, 3
   Jewish question, 41, 57
   in Poland, 56, 58, 140
   returning home after, 85
Holy Roman Empire, 10
Honecker, Erich, 120, 121, 131, 136, 139
Horáková, Milada, 102, 161
   trial of, 102
Horthy, Miklós, 3, 29, 30, 35, 36, 41, 42, 50, 51, 75, 91, 98, 152
Hoxha, Enver, 88, 98, 120, 121
Hungary
   under Communism... takeovers, vii, 89
   Arrow Cross, 36, 50, 51, 91
   communist takeovers in... salami tactics, 91
   1848 revolutions, 7, 11–13
   Goulash Communism, 107, 109, 137
   illiberalism in, 151
   monuments, 2–4, 151, 155
   nationalism, 2, 7, 14, 22, 36, 161
   and neighbouring states, 31, 108, 124, 150
   1989 revolution, 107, 123, 130, 131
   1956 revolution, vii, 91, 106–109, 130, 141
   relations with Jewish population, 3, 50, 51
   relations with Roma, 31, 155
   Trianon, 31, 33, 42, 43, 129
Hus, Jan, 7, 36
Husák, Gustáv, 112, 120, 121, 133

I
Iliescu, Ion, 128
Illiberalism, 151, 163, 169

J
Jaruzelski, Wojciech, 118, 120, 129, 137
Jobbik, 147, 150
Joseph II, 1, 20, 23

K
Kaczyński, Jarosław, 156
Kaczyński, Lech, 156, 160, 161, 170
Kádár, János, 101, 105–111, 120, 121, 124, 128–131, 140
Károlyi, Mihály, 26, 28–30
Katyn massacre, 83
Khrushchev, Nikita, 104–106, 110, 111, 115, 119
Klaus, Václav, 134, 135, 159, 160
Kohl, Helmut, 69, 128, 136
Kossuth, Lajos, 13–16, 21
Kováč, Michal, 135
Kubišová, Marta, 132
Kuciak, Ján, 162, 163
Kun, Béla, 29, 31, 35, 91
Kundera, Milan, 5, 77, 110, 142
Kušnírová, Martina, 162

L
Law and Justice Party, 33, 76, 77, 140, 147
League of Nations, 25, 33, 34, 38, 78, 142
Lebensraum, 46
Lenin, Vladimir, 24, 25, 29, 37, 117
LGBTQ rights
   in Germany, 64
   in Hungary, 157, 168
   in Poland, 154, 157
Lueger, Karl, 20
Lustration, 133, 138–141

M
Maria Theresa, 1, 9, 23
Marshall Plan, 48, 88, 95, 102, 104
Masaryk, Jan, 95, 96
Masaryk, Tomáš Garrigue, 24, 32, 36, 38, 95, 96, 102, 161
Matovič, Igor, 163
Mazowiecki, Tadeusz, 137, 140
Mečiar, Vladimír, 134–136, 143, 161

Merkel, Angela, 163, 164, 169
Mikołajczyk, Stanisław, 92, 93
Million Moments for Democracy, 161
Milošević, Slobodan, 125, 128, 135
Molotov-Ribbentrop Agreement, 46, 47
Monuments
   in Czechoslovakia, 4
   in Germany, 151
   in Hungary, 2–4, 151, 155
   in Poland, 2, 77
Morawiecki, Mateusz, 159, 168, 169
Munich Conference, 45
Mussolini, Benito, 21, 28, 36, 38–41

N

Nagy, Imre, 3, 105–107, 110, 112, 121, 127, 130, 140, 152
   reburial of, 107, 127, 130
Napoleon, 9–11, 13, 20
National awakenings, 6, 10, 11, 32
Nationalism
   in Czechoslovakia, 43
   in Germany, 147
   in Hungary, 2, 7, 14, 22, 36, 161
   in Poland, 2, 33, 43, 161
   in Slovakia, 42, 129, 161
National Socialists (Nazis), 37–41, 53–55, 58–60, 62, 64, 66, 70, 71, 76, 82, 85, 104
Nazi-Soviet pact, 40, 46, 78, 84, 90, 127, 139
Normalization, 38, 109–115, 127, 131
North Atlantic Treaty Organization (NATO), vii, 31, 103, 105, 119, 135, 136, 141, 143, 144, 147, 148, 160, 163, 164, 170
Nosek, Václav, 95
Novotný, Antonín, 109, 110
Nuremberg trials, 72, 82–84

O

Okamura, Tomio, 160
Operation Barbarossa, 52, 55–56
Opletal, Jan, 132
Orbán, Viktor, 7, 29, 130, 131, 147, 149–153, 155, 156, 160–162, 164–166, 168–171
Ostpolitik, 129
Ottoman Empire, 6–8, 11, 25, 35

P

Paderewski, Ignacy, 24
Palacký, František, 15, 16, 18
Paris Peace Conference
   Treaty of Sèvres, 35
   Treaty of St. Germain, 28–33
Perestroika, 122
Petőfi, Sándor, 7, 13, 14, 106
Piłsudski, Józef, 33, 37, 98
Poland
   collaboration with Germans, 59, 93
   under Communism...
      takeovers, 92, 93
   corridor, 33, 37
   Danzig (*Gdańsk*), 33
   German expulsions, 81, 86
   Nazi invasion of, 46, 47, 52
   1989 revolution, 128, 137
   partitions of, 9, 54
   relations with Jewish population, 33
Polish Peasants' Party, 92, 93
Pope John Paul II, 116
Popiełuszko, Jerzy, 118
Porajmos, 61
   See also Roma
Potsdam Conference, 71, 80, 82
Prague
   monuments, 4, 75
   Prague spring... socialism with a human face, 96, 103, 106, 108–111, 120, 131, 133, 134
Princip, Gavrilo, 23, 25
Public Against Violence, 132, 134

R

Rajk, László, 3, 91, 101, 105–107, 130
Rákosi, Mátyás, 90, 91, 98, 101, 105–107, 130
Reagan, Ronald, vii, 2, 75, 124
Red Army
   in Czechoslovakia, 95
   in Germany, 51, 66–68
   in Hungary, 51, 69, 107
   in Poland, 70
Refugee Crisis (2015), v, 149, 163, 170
Roma
   in Czech Republic, 4, 5
   discrimination against, 135, 161
   in Hungary, 31, 155
   Porajmos, 61

Romania, 28, 30, 31, 34–36, 43, 78, 79, 89, 98, 103, 107, 120, 122, 124, 125, 127, 128, 139, 141–144, 149, 151, 152, 155, 164
 and Hungary, 30, 31, 34, 36, 43, 78, 89, 98, 103, 107, 124, 141, 152, 155
Russia, vi, viii, 5, 9–11, 22, 24, 25, 29, 33, 57, 75–77, 79, 87, 91, 120, 129, 135, 136, 139, 150, 151, 163, 164, 167
 See also Soviet Union

S
Schuschnigg, Kurt, 40, 41
Show trials
 in Czechoslovakia, 102
 in Hungary, 101, 107
Šik, Ota, 109, 110
Slánský, Rudolf, 102
 trial of, 102
Slovakia
 Hlinka Slovak Peoples Party... Hlinka guard, 37, 42, 49
 National Uprising, 49
 split from Czechs, 134
Solidarność (Solidarity), 33, 114, 117, 118, 124, 128, 131, 137, 138, 163, 167
 Gdańsk Agreement, 117
Soros, George, 153, 155, 162, 168
Soviet Union
 influence on communist countries, 120
 invasion of Czechoslovakia, 111
 invasion of Hungary, 50
 invasion of Poland, 52
Stalin, Joseph, vii, 20, 21, 29, 37, 38, 45, 54, 55, 65, 71, 75, 77–82, 87–90, 92, 94, 96–98, 101–106, 109, 115, 121, 130
Štefánik, Milan, 32
Szálasi, Ferenc, 36, 51, 91
Széchenyi, István, 12–14, 18, 20, 21, 154
Sztójay, Döme, 51, 91

T
Teleki, Pál, 30, 50
Tiso, Jozef, 161
Tito, Josip Broz, 88, 98, 101–103, 106, 107, 120
Transylvania, 7, 14, 30, 50, 155
Trotsky, Leon, 24, 25, 27, 29
Turkey, 35, 143, 149
 population exchange with Greece, 35

V
Vaculík, Ludvík, 110, 111, 114
Versailles Treaty, 27, 28
Vienna, vii, 1, 7, 8, 10, 13, 14, 16–28, 41, 42, 50, 65, 69, 75, 82, 85, 91, 110, 153, 168
Vienna Awards, 42, 50
Visegrád Group, 141
von Bismarck, Otto, 16–18
von Metternich, Klemens, 10, 13, 15
von Ribbentrop, Joachim, 41, 46, 83

W
Waldheim, Kurt, 104, 105
Walentynowicz, Anna, 117
Wałęsa, Lech, 117, 137, 138
Warsaw Uprising, 54
Wilson, Woodrow, vi, 24, 27, 30, 33, 34, 40
Workers' Defence Committee, 116

Y
Yalta Conference, 45, 71, 77–81, 85, 120
Yugoslavia, 28, 31, 34, 35, 43, 50, 78, 79, 82, 88, 89, 91, 96–98, 102–104, 106, 108, 125, 128, 129, 135, 143, 144
 wars, 82, 98, 128, 135

Z
Zeman, Miloš, 159–161
Zhivkov, Todor, 120, 121, 139, 144

The manufacturer's authorised representative in the EU is Springer Nature Customer Service Centre GmbH, Europaplatz 3, 69115 Heidelberg, Germany. If you have any concerns regarding our products, please contact ProductSafety@springernature.com

Printed and bound by CPI Group (UK) Ltd, Croydon, CR0 4YY

25/03/2026

02078225-0010